Reasons For Belief

John M. Oakes, Ph.D.

Reasons For Belief

A Handbook of Christian Evidence

Illumination Publishers International
www.ipibooks.com

ipi

Reasons For Belief
A Handbook of Christian Evidence

Copyright © 2005 by John M. Oakes

ISBN: 978-0-9767583-3-4

All rights reserved. No part of this book may be duplicated, copied, translated, reproduced or stored mechanically or electronically without specific, written permission of John M. Oakes and Illumination Publishers International.

Printed in the United States of America
11 10 09   2 3 4 5

Cover Graphics by William To
Front Cover Photos – First Century Tomb courtesy Julie Geissler,
Sennacherib Prism © Copyright The British Museum,
Babylonian Chronicles © Copyright The British Museum,
David Stela courtesy of Israeli Muesum,
Hebrew Text courtesy of Israeli Museum
Back Cover Photos –
Cyrus Cylinder © Copyright The British Museum,
Gospel of John Fragment courtesy of John Rylands Library,
Background Hebrew Text of Psalms

Previous ISBN 0-9653469-7-8.
Formerly published by Great Comission Inc., in 2001.

All scripture quotations unless otherwise indicated, are taken from the NEW INTERNATIONAL VERSION. Copyright ©1973, 1978, 1984 by the International Bible Society. Used by permission of Zondervan Publishing House. All rights reserved.

The "NIV" and "New International Version" trademarks are registered in the United States Patent Trademark Office by the International Bible Society. Use of either trademark requires the permission of the International Bible Society.

Published by
Illumination Publishers International
6010 Pinecreek Ridge Court
Spring, Texas 77379
www.ipibooks.com

ipi

Dedication

*To
Jan
Benjamin
Elizabeth and
Kathryn*

Acknowledgements

It is useless to attempt to reason a man out of what he was never reasoned into.

Jonathan Swift

I would like to thank a number of friends who have helped me to complete this project. I am grateful to those who helped edit the manuscript, including Brian Craig, Amy Morgan, Rex Geissler, Douglas Jacoby and of course, my mother, Ruth Oakes. William To deserves credit for enthusiastic attention to the cover art.

Also helpful have been those who provided encouragement and support over the years to my pursuit of these topics. Gary Bishop and Gregg Marutzky got me going, John Clayton provided inspiration with his example, Douglas Jacoby called me higher spiritually and intellectually, Mike Taliaferro provided enthusiasm for the task and Foster Stanback spurred me on (and provided financial support). Thank you.

Above all, I am thankful to my wife Jan, who has put up with late nights, priorities reshuffled and mental energy redirected without complaining—in fact with great support and love.

Contents

Foreword.. 9

Introduction... 10

Chapter 1 - Who Does This Man Think He Is?.............. 11

Chapter 2 - Why Should I Believe In Jesus?.............. 31

Chapter 3 - The Ultimate Miracle........................ 55

Chapter 4 - We Should Have Known It Was Coming.......... 82

Chapter 5 - Visions of the Future...................... 112

Chapter 6 - A Remarkable Collection.................... 143

Chapter 7 - Let the Stones Speak....................... 170

Chapter 8 - Science and the Bible: Mortal Enemies?..... 210

Chapter 9 - The Bible: The Greatest Book Ever Written.. 236

Appendix A
Translations of the Bible............................. 250

Appendix B
The Nature of Faith................................... 252

Foreword

John Oakes has done us a great service with his new book, *Reasons for Belief*. When I read the manuscript in South Africa, I thoroughly enjoyed it. Every page is packed with detail and information. John has a knack for taking complicated issues, and crystalizing the truth from all the confusion. This book will help all those who believe in Jesus, but have a whispering voice in the background somewhere telling them that science has proven their faith to be outdated. This book will move those who are not Christians to see just how rational the Christian faith really is. I know that the reader will return to these pages again and again, finding answers, information, and inspiration.

This is a topic I love. I often speak on Christian evidences. In my travels as a minister, I have had the opportunity to speak on six continents in almost fifty nations. Everywhere I go, faces light up when evidences for our faith are presented. Campus students love to get factual answers to some of the attacks against Christianity they hear on campus. Parents love to get factual answers to some of the questions their kids are asking. Those who are just beginning to study the Bible, as well as non-Christians, love to get practical evidence that will help them to give their lives in faith to Jesus. Whether it is in Africa, Asia, or America, this is an important topic and John has placed before us a thorough explanation. We are all joyfully indebted to him.

I know that this book will encourage many disciples. I also know that many skeptics will get their questions answered so that they can move on to become disciples of Jesus. My encouragement to you: Don't just enjoy the book. Rather, master the material. Share it with others. Let the confidence that it instills impact your campus, neighborhood, and work place. Let us all recapture the confidence and excitement of those early disciples from the first century.

Mike Taliaferro
San Antonio, Texas
2005

Introduction

> *Always be prepared to give an
> answer to everyone who asks you to
> give the reason for the hope that you have.*
> — *1 Peter 3:15*

Almost twenty years ago, three graduate student friends, Gary Bishop, Mark Hermsmeyer, Paul Keyser, and I set about to make a list of basic areas of evidence that support Christianity. In about five minutes we came up with a list that is essentially the outline of this book. Since that time, I have spent countless hours researching these issues and have had the opportunity to speak on them in many situations. After reading dozens of books on Christian apologetics, it became clear that there is no book available that deals with all these subjects in a concise yet comprehensive way. Few if any books cover all these topics. Some are too simple to be a useful reference tool. Others only delve into one or two areas of evidence, sometimes with such technical detail as to make them inaccessible to most readers, while at the same time skipping other very important areas of evidence.

Therefore, upon the encouragement of friends, I set out to write this book. It is not my intent to provide an exhaustive treatment of each subject, as each could justify an entire book in itself. I have attempted to provide sufficient background to deal with most of the common issues that come to mind for those who ask good, hard questions. I have attempted to provide additional references for those who would like to develop a particular topic more thoroughly.

In gathering material, I have taken great pains to use only that evidence which will hold up well to criticism. It is my experience that many authors in apologetics tend to throw in anything that appears to support their point, whether or not the evidence will actually hold up to the scrutiny of those who have carefully researched these subjects. In areas that are more subjective, particularly in the final chapter, I have tried to point out that I am expressing my own opinion.

Many who ask questions regarding Christian faith do so as a smoke screen to hide more fundamental issues of the heart. It is hoped that those who read this book are engaged in a sincere search for truth. If this work is of some help to those who with humility and sincerity of heart seek for the truth, then to God be the glory.

John Oakes
San Diego, California
2005

Chapter One
Who Does This Man Think He Is?

> *"Is this not Jesus, the son of Joseph, whose father and mother we know? How can he now say 'I came down from heaven.'"*
>
> —*Anonymous onlookers after Jesus claimed to be the bread of life.*

We will begin with a scenario. Imagine for a moment that you are having an informal conversation with a close friend. Your friend's name is Jim. In the course of the conversation, Jim tells you that he has the ability to raise people from the dead. How would you respond to this claim? Assuming that up until now you have thought of your friend Jim as a fairly normal person, how would this shocking claim affect the way you think about him?

Perhaps your first response to a situation like this would be to chuckle, with the assumption that your friend Jim would soon lighten the tense atmosphere by joining in the laughter. Very funny, Jim. But imagine instead that he gives you an offended look and says to you, "Look, I am serious, I have the ability to raise people from the dead. You don't believe me? Let me tell you about Mariana and William." Imagine your friend continues by relating a story with specifics about two different people he had raised from the dead. Jim describes in detail how the two had died and the manner in which he had resurrected them. He even mentions a few witnesses you can contact if you want to verify the claim.

What are you thinking about your friend now? Different possible explanations of Jim's sudden bizarre behavior begin to race through your mind. Has he gone off the deep end? Is he trying to practice his poker face by seeing how big a lie he can get people to believe? He seems so sincere that for just an instant, the possibility that he may really have raised someone from the dead pops into your head. Of course, you reject this idea almost instantaneously because to accept the premise that your friend raised someone from the dead would imply that it is actually you who is going crazy.

What would you do next? You would perhaps play along for just a little while, pretending you are at least open to believing your friend is telling the truth. You might begin plying Jim with a number of leading questions. You might ask him where he got this ability, or where the people he raised from the dead are right now. Alternatively, you might say, "Come on Jim, quit the game, you are starting to scare me," in order to see if he will lose nerve and admit it is all a joke.

If neither of these tactics works, you might change the subject for now, but later on begin to do some investigating on your own. If you were a true friend, you would be extremely concerned about your friend. If word of his behavior were to get out, Jim's reputation as a normal, reasonable guy might be permanently damaged.

Now imagine going to one of the witnesses Jim has told you about. You discretely tell this person the story about what Jim has said to you. Imagine for a moment how you would feel if this witness responded by telling you that he or she has absolutely no idea what you were talking about. Now your investigation is heading toward a conclusion. You will go back to Jim and directly confront him with what is obviously a lie. His response to the confrontation will tell you whether he is lying or whether he has lost his mind.

But what if the witness confirms Jim's claim? What if all the witnesses were to confirm the claim that Jim really did raise two people from the dead? Would you be inclined to believe Jim was telling the truth? The explanation that Jim is insane is starting to appear a bit shaky. Your brain is racing. What scenario can explain what is happening here? *OK, I am a rational person—there is a rational explanation for this whole thing.* You decide that for some bizarre reason, Jim has decided to play a very detailed practical joke on you and some of your friends. He has gone so far as to set up an elaborate scheme, including setting up "witnesses" to confirm his story. When you think about the fact that Jim is one of the greatest practical jokesters you know, the story begins to fit together.

Still, you cannot let it go unexamined. You confront one of the supposed witnesses with your scenario, and finally he cracks a smile. You both start a good laugh. The mystery is solved.

But what if this tactic does not work? What if one by one, each of the witnesses was to confirm that everything said was true, even when confronted with your claim that this was all a setup?

The story could continue in this vein for a while, but one point is clear: If someone you know well were to claim he had the power to raise people from the dead, you would find it all but impossible to accept the claim, no matter how seriously it was made. You would assume that your friend was either a blatant liar or that he was crazy: that the elevator was not stopping at all the floors, as they say.

But there was once a man who claimed, not just to his friends but also openly to the public, that he could raise people from the dead. That man was Jesus Christ. John 11 records a situation in which one of Jesus' best friends had died. In fact, Jesus' friend Lazarus had been dead and in a tomb for four days when Jesus came to Bethany. Let us examine this remarkable account of Jesus and his friend Lazarus.

From what is described in John chapter 11, along with the other references in the New Testament to Lazarus and his sisters Mary and Martha, one can infer that Jesus was a very close friend of this family. It would appear that Jesus had a habit of staying with Lazarus and his sisters when he came up to Jerusalem.

> Now a man named Lazarus was sick. He was from Bethany, the village of Mary and her sister Martha. This Mary, whose brother Lazarus now lay sick, was the same one who poured perfume on the Lord and wiped his feet with her hair. So the sisters sent word to Jesus, "Lord, the one you love is sick" (John 11:1-3).

When Jesus heard this plea for help, his response was remarkable. "Yet when he heard that Lazarus was sick, he stayed where he was two more days" (v. 6). Surely Jesus was well aware that Mary and Martha considered this a dire emergency. Why did Jesus wait for two days before responding? Was he too busy to respond to the pleas of a dying friend? Possibly Jesus delayed coming to Bethany, perhaps at least partly because he knew what he would do with Lazarus. Two days later he said to his apostles, "Lazarus is dead, and for your sake, I am glad I was not there, so that you may believe. But let us go to him" (v. 14,15).

When Jesus arrived at Bethany, he explained to Lazarus' sister Martha as she grieved over her brother's death, "I am the resurrection and the life. He who believes in me will live, even though he dies; and whoever lives and believes in me will never die. Do you believe this?" (John 11:25,26) This is the first of the claims of Jesus Christ that we will look at in this chapter.

JESUS: LORD, LIAR OR LUNATIC?

The theme of this section is *Jesus: Lord, Liar, or Lunatic*? We will be asking a simple question in this chapter: What is the most reasonable explanation for the claims of Jesus? During his time on earth, Jesus made some astounding claims about himself. How is one to deal with these claims? Putting aside emotion, what is a reasonable explanation for what Jesus claimed about himself? Did Jesus really make these claims? Given the context of the audience to whom Jesus made the claims, what was he really saying about himself? How did the people of his day respond to Jesus' claims? What are some of the ways people today respond to Jesus? Why are modern-day responses to Jesus radically different from those of people who actually heard them firsthand?

Besides considering carefully what is the most reasonable explanation of Jesus' claims about himself, these claims will be compared to those of other well-known religious leaders. Finally, we will consider what would be a reasonable response for a modern person to have in light of his or her understanding of the claims of Jesus.

This argument is not exactly brand new.[1] In fact, those who seek to defend faith in Jesus Christ have often returned to the Lord, Liar or Lunatic argument because it is so compelling. Besides, all three words start with an L, which makes it roll off the tongue quite nicely.

Let us return to the story in question. Jesus has just made one of the most amazing (or outrageous) claims ever made by a human being. Jesus has claimed not just that he has the power to raise people from the dead; he has gone much further than that! Jesus has made the claim that he is the resurrection and the life. Jesus claimed that he was the actual source of resurrection for all humanity. He did not just claim to be a channel for some power greater than himself to raise someone from the dead. Jesus claimed, "He who believes in me will live, even though he dies; and whoever lives and believes in me will never die" (John 11:25-26).

Martha's response to Jesus' claim is very interesting. Essentially, she said, "Yes, Jesus, I know you are the resurrection and the life. I know you offer eternal life, but that is not what I was asking. I was asking whether you would resurrect my brother Lazarus physically from the dead right now." What amazing boldness! What nerve! Martha must have been very close to Jesus to make this request of him.

In response to Martha's request, Jesus went to the tomb. Mary, the sister of Martha, was weeping and crying out loud that Jesus could have healed him, if only he had come in time. Apparently Mary's faith was not as strong as Martha's. In one of the most compelling scenes in the gospels, Jesus responded to the emotion of Mary by weeping openly.

Lazarus had been dead and placed in the tomb for four days already. In a warm climate such as that in Palestine, a body will begin to decompose in just a few hours. No wonder that Martha responded to Jesus' command to remove the stone at the front of Lazarus' tomb by saying, "But Lord, ...by this time there is a bad odor, for he has been there four days" (John 11:39).

---

1. For example, Josh McDowell presented this argument in his book *Evidence That Demands a Verdict* (Thomas Nelson, 1999), originally published in 1972. This argument was originated by C. S. Lewis in his well-known book, *Mere Christianity* (Harper, San Francisco, 2001), originally published in 1943. In a more recent treament, Douglas Jacoby adds a fourth "L". Jesus is Legend, Liar, Lunatic or Lord. Douglas Jacoby, *True & Reasonable* (Illumination Publishers, Spring, Texas, 2004).

> When he had said this, Jesus called in a loud voice, "Lazarus, come out!" The dead man came out, his hands and feet wrapped with strips of linen, and a cloth around his face. Jesus said to them, "Take off the grave clothes and let him go" (John 11:43,44).

What a dramatic scene! Imagine the emotions of those in the crowd who witnessed this sensational event. After struggling with the grave clothes for a few moments, Lazarus, stiff but very much alive, came out of the tomb, dragging the strips of cloth behind him. How would you have felt if you had witnessed this amazing event?

> Therefore many of the Jews who had come to visit Mary, and had seen what Jesus did, put their faith in him (John 11:45).

I would think so! Jesus had a way of making an earth-shattering claim and following it up with an action that proved the truth of what he was claiming. Remember that Jesus claimed not just to be able to resurrect people physically from the dead—he claimed to *be* the resurrection and the life for all mankind. Immediately after making this astounding claim, Jesus backed it up in the most dramatic fashion possible. He raised a man from the dead whose body was already at the point of producing the putrid odor of decomposition.

Let us now return and apply the illustration that began this chapter to this situation. Assume for a moment that you were a contemporary to these events, but not an actual eyewitness. Imagine someone told you about Jesus and Lazarus. What would be a reasonable response to this outrageous claim? And how could you explain the fact that such a large number of people actually believed the claim without further investigation? Remember your response to your friend Jim. The absolute last conceivable explanation of the claim would be that it was actually true, yet you could see a great number of people believing that Jesus could raise people from the dead.

There is some parallel here, but there is also a very big difference between Jim and Jesus. The reason a number of people could believe his claim to be the resurrection and the life is that Jesus' life and ministry backed up his claims. The fact that Jesus' life and ministry backed up his claims will be a recurrent theme in this chapter.

It is worth noting that not all the witnesses to this awesome event were convinced about Jesus. They were convinced that Jesus had raised Lazarus who had been dead for four days. How could they deny that? However, they were not convinced that it was a good thing.

But some of them went to the Pharisees and told them what Jesus had done. Then the chief Priests and the Pharisees called a meeting of the Sanhedrin. "What are we accomplishing?" they asked. "Here is this man performing many miraculous signs. If we let him go on like this, everyone will believe in him, and then the Romans will come and take away both our place and our nation."

Then one of them, named Caiaphas, who was high priest that year, spoke up, "You know nothing at all! You do not realize that it is better for you that one man die for the people than that the whole nation perish" (John 11:46-50).

Some of the witnesses believed that Jesus had the power to raise people from physical death. They saw the event happen right before their eyes, so it was difficult to deny the fact. However, it would appear that they did not believe his claim that he was *the* resurrection and the life. Otherwise they would not have tried to murder him.

The point of considering the response of both those who believed and those who definitely did not believe is this: If Jesus was a liar—if he was making false and outrageous claims—then the most reasonable response would be to oppose him with all the energy one possessed. If Jesus were a liar, then he would have been an extremely dangerous person. In fact, that was how the Sanhedrin[2] viewed Jesus. To them, he was a very dangerous threat to their position. If Jesus was crazy, then the most reasonable response would have been, first, to totally reject his message, and second, to lock him away before he got himself or someone else hurt. On the other hand, if Jesus' claims were true, the only reasonable response would be to worship him as Lord.

Given the character and the life of Jesus (more on that later), the Sanhedrin knew he was not insane, but being unwilling to accept that he was who he claimed to be, they assumed he was a liar, a pretender. As mentioned above, a reasonable response for one who believed Jesus was a liar was to oppose him vigorously. That is certainly what they did. The statement of Caiaphas is ironic. He wanted Jesus to be murdered in order to save the Jewish people. A short time later, Jesus was indeed killed so that the Jewish people would not perish. In fact, Jesus died so that all men "shall not perish, but have everlasting life"(John 3:16).

In this, the first of the claims of Jesus that we will look at, one finds Jesus claiming to be the resurrection and the life. He backed up his claim by raising Lazarus from the dead in the most dramatic

---

2. The Sanhedrin was a council of Jewish religious leaders. They were a ruling body of the Hebrew aristocracy. The Romans allowed the Sanhedrin authority in Judea over religious matters.

fashion. In the event, as described by John, one can find two responses: the response of putting faith in Jesus and the response of wanting to kill him. As we look at some of the other claims of Jesus about himself, this pattern will become familiar.

Jesus made a great number of claims about himself. It is not the purpose of this chapter to catalog them. The New Testament book that contains the greatest number of the claims Jesus made about himself is the gospel of John. We will therefore look at a few of the claims of Jesus as recorded in this concise biography.

THE BREAD OF LIFE

One of the claims of Jesus that was least understood by his hearers is found in John 6:35. To a large crowd, Jesus boldly declared, "I am the bread of life." What was Jesus claiming? Was he claiming to be edible food? Not likely. Was he claiming to be able to provide physical food for those who believed in him, or perhaps for everyone, regardless of whether or not they believed in him? Is there some spiritual, rather than physical implication of this claim? The context of this statement of Jesus will answer the question, but first let us consider an incident that had occurred just the day before.

> Some time after this, Jesus crossed to the far shore of the Sea of Galilee (that is the Sea of Tiberias), and a great crowd of people followed him because they saw the miraculous signs he had performed on the sick. Then Jesus went up on the hillside and sat down with his disciples. The Jewish Passover Feast was near.... Jesus said, "Have the people sit down." There was plenty of grass in that place, and the men sat down, about five thousand of them. Jesus then took the loaves, gave thanks, and distributed to those who were seated as much as they wanted. He did the same with the fish. When they had all had enough to eat, he said to his disciples, "Gather the pieces that are left over. Let nothing be wasted." So they gathered them and filled twelve baskets with the pieces of the five barley loaves left over by those who had eaten (John 6:1-4, 10-13).

One can assume that a large proportion of the crowd that heard Jesus claim to be the bread of life had also participated in the meal of bread and fish the day before.[3] It is certainly not a coincidence that the

---

3. This can be seen in John 6:22,25 where John states that the crowd which had stayed on the opposite shore with Jesus was the same who met him on the other side of the lake, near Capernaum.

claim followed the miracle. Jesus had a habit of backing up his claims about himself by performing a miracle that related to the claim.

There is one question that will be raised by the skeptic at this point. "How do we really know that Jesus did this supposed miracle?" Or for that matter, one might ask how one can be sure he really made the claim to be the bread of life. This is absolutely a legitimate question. The same question could have been asked in regard to the miracle of raising Lazarus from the dead or the claim that preceded it. This is a reasonable inquiry, but the author would beg the patience of the reader. This very important issue will be dealt with carefully in chapter two—the chapter on miracles.

But let us return to the lake in order to consider the claim in its context,

> So they asked him, "What miraculous sign then will you give that we may see it and believe you? What will you do? Our forefathers ate the manna in the desert; as it is written: 'He gave them bread from heaven to eat.'"
>
> Jesus said to them, "I tell you the truth, it is not Moses who has given you the bread from heaven, but it is my Father who gives you the true bread from heaven. For the bread of God is he who comes down from heaven and gives life to the world."
>
> "Sir," they said, "from now on give us this bread."
> Then Jesus declared, "I am the bread of life. He who comes to me will never go hungry, and he who believes in me will never be thirsty. But as I told you, you have seen me and still you do not believe. All that the Father gives me will come to me, and whoever comes to me I will never drive away. For I have come down from heaven not to do my will but to do the will of him who sent me. And this is the will of him who sent me, that I shall lose none of all that he has given me, but shall raise them up at the last day. For my Father's will is that everyone who looks to the Son and believes in him shall have eternal life, and I will raise him up at the last day" (John 6:30-40).

Jesus was certainly not claiming here to be physical food, or to provide physical food to eat. He was claiming to be spiritual food which, when eaten, would lead to eternal life. Jesus claimed that through a relationship with him, people could go to heaven. What an awesome claim! The situation is quite similar to that in John 11 in which Jesus performed a miracle (raising Lazarus) to confirm a spiritual claim (to *be* the resurrection and the life). In this case, Jesus performed the miracle of creating bread to confirm the claim that he was the bread of life.

It is interesting to note that Jesus' claim to be the bread of life caused them to think about the relationship between Jesus and Moses. They asked Jesus by what authority he could call upon them to follow him. They reminded him that Moses had given them bread (manna) in the wilderness in order to allow them to continue following him through the desert. Jesus turned their argument around on them by pointing out that Moses did not actually give them bread. It was God who had given them the manna. It came from heaven. The manna that came from heaven helped Moses accomplish the mission God had given him. Presumably, he gathered some of the manna himself in order to eat it. Jesus was very different. Just the day before, he had given them bread, not from heaven, but from his own hand.

Jesus went on to say that he was the spiritual bread that came down from heaven to give true life to the world. "I am the bread of life." Coming from a human being, this claim is so outrageous that it is hard to know how to respond to it. Imagine your friend Jim saying, "I am the bread of life that came down from heaven." As if claiming to resurrect people wasn't enough, now he has definitely lost it. This claim, if true, is even more unreasonable.

What was the response of the crowd to this claim? They began to grumble.

> At this, the Jews began to grumble about him because he said, "I am the bread of life that came down from heaven." They said, "Is this not Jesus, the son of Joseph, whose father and mother we know? How can he now say, 'I came down from heaven'?" (John 6:41,42).

This seems like a somewhat muted response, but given that Jesus had only recently given them actual physical bread to eat, it might explain a relatively tame reaction, compared to some of the others we will see in this chapter. The comment, "Is this not Jesus, the son of Joseph,..." seems to imply that they were unsure how to react to him. They had not yet decided whether he was Lord, Liar or Lunatic. What about you?

CLAIMS OF OTHER SPIRITUAL LEADERS

We will get back to a few more of the claims of Jesus, but first let us consider what the claims of some other well-known religious leaders or teachers have been throughout the ages. These claims, and the evidence for the validity of these claims, will reveal more clearly the uniqueness of what Jesus said about himself.

There are many candidates for a list of well-known religious leaders and their claims about themselves. Space will not allow us to consider the claims of such men as Baha'u'lla (founder of the Baha'i faith), Nanak (original guru of the Sikh faith), Lao Tzu (author of the *Tao Te Ching*, and principle figure of Taoism), Mahavira (greatest teacher of the Jain religion, and a contemporary of Gautama Buddha), or more modern figures such as Mary Baker Eddy (creator of the Christian Science movement), Ellen G. White (principle prophet of Seventh Day Adventism) or Sung Myung Moon (originator of the Unification Church, also known somewhat perjoratively as "the Moonies"), and the list could go on. We will consider below just a few of the most well-known leaders of world religions. They will be discussed in chronological order.

First, consider Moses. He certainly was a religious leader. What did Moses claim about himself? The Bible refers to Moses as the most humble man on earth,[4] so not surprisingly, it is difficult to find him making open claims for himself. However, from what is recorded about his life, one could conclude that he claimed to be a spokesperson for God. He claimed to have seen some manifestation of God, both in the burning bush and on Mount Sinai. On both occasions he claimed that God spoke to him directly. God did work a number of miracles through Moses, or at least through the rod that God had given him. One can assume that at least part of the reason God worked miracles through Moses was to confirm Moses' claim to speak for him. Moses definitely did not claim to be the resurrection and the life or to be the bread that came down from heaven, nor, for that matter, did he make any of the other claims of Jesus that we are considering in this chapter.

It would be helpful to compare the claims of a Hindu religious leader to those of Jesus. Hindu scripture includes epics about Krishna coming to earth. But these epics are clearly mythical. As a result there is no single historical figure from the Hindu religion that could be considered its founder.

Next, consider the claims of the Buddha. Gautama Buddha was a historical figure who lived from 567 to 487 BC. He was the founder of what is known today as Buddhism. What did Buddha claim for himself? He claimed to be a good teacher with a worthy approach on how to live. Among other things, he proposed an eight-fold path or philosophy for life. Long after he lived, some claimed that he had worked miracles, but there is no record of the Buddha himself, or of any contemporary ever claiming that he performed miracles. Buddha made no great claims about himself and he made no claims remotely like those of Christ.

---

4. Numbers 12:3

What about Confucius? Like Buddha, Confucius is an historical figure. It is interesting to note that Buddha, Confucius and Mahavira were all contemporaries. Confucius lived from 551 to 478 BC. He espoused a philosophy which evolved into the religion that is now known as Confucianism. Along with Buddhism, it is a dominant religion in China today. However, Confucius made no major claims for himself. Somewhat similar to Buddha, he simply taught a way of life that he felt was wise. He emphasized tradition and family worship. One could claim that he was more of a philosopher than the founder of a religion. There is no comparison between the claims of Confucius and Christ.

Next, consider the claims of Muhammad. Muhammad certainly was an historical figure. He lived from AD 570 to 632, having founded the religion that is now known as Islam. In some sense, Muhammad made similar claims to those of Moses. He claimed to be a prophet of God. He claimed to have seen some angels, and to have received the collection of writings now known as the Qur'an by direct revelation of God. Muhammad did not claim to be a miracle worker. He did not claim to have the power to raise people from the dead. He certainly did not claim deity for himself.

Let us consider as our final example a religious leader closer to our own time. Looking at the claims of a more recent religious figure could help us to better understand how the claims of Jesus Christ might have emotionally impacted his contemporaries. The life of Joseph Smith may help to put the claims of Jesus into a more modern perspective. Smith was the founder of the Mormon Church (the largest branch of the Joseph Smith movement uses the name, *The Church of Jesus Christ of Latter Day Saints*). Because Joseph Smith lived in the early nineteenth century, it is easy to discover what Smith claimed about himself.

Joseph Smith made claims about himself that were somewhat similar to those of Muhammad. Smith claimed to be a prophet. He claimed to receive direct revelation from God. He claimed that an angel gave him a number of golden tablets, which were covered with some sort of ancient language used in Egypt, and to be given the power to "translate" this language into English.[5] The supposed translation of the writing on the tablets is known as *The Book of Mormon*. Although speaking in tongues was especially popular in the early Mormon movement, Joseph Smith never claimed to work the kind of public miracles such as one can find in the New Testament. He did not claim to be the Messiah, to be without sin, or to be deity *per se*. Given some of the flaws in Smith's

---

5. Joseph Smith and the Mormon Church claimed that these tablets were taken back to heaven by an angel, so one would be wise to be skeptical of whether they ever existed at all, let alone their authenticity.

character,[6] his claims are made dubious to say the least, but in any case, his claims about himself do not even approach those of Jesus Christ.

It is a very popular modern idea to equate figures such as Moses, Muhammad, Jesus Christ, Buddha and others as all being religious leaders of more or less equal status. Given the claims of the religious leaders as listed above, and assuming that the claims of others not mentioned in detail are similar, a question comes to mind. If one considers the nature of the claims of Jesus as compared to the others, is this a reasonable comparison to make? Is it reasonable to say that Hinduism, Islam, Buddhism, Christianity, and any of a number of other religions are all just different ways to the same end? It would appear that the evidence speaks for itself.

OTHER CLAIMS OF JESUS

Back now to considering a few of the major claims of Jesus as recorded in the book of John.

> You diligently study the Scriptures because you think that by them you possess eternal life. These are the Scriptures that testify about me, yet you refuse to come to me to have life (John 5:39,40).

There are actually two claims here. First, Jesus claimed that those who come to him would have life. This is similar enough to the claim to be the bread of life to justify moving to the other claim contained in this passage. In the passage quoted above, Jesus claimed that the Old Testament prophesied to the Jews specific details about his own life. A similar quote from Luke might make the implication of this claim clearer:

> He said to them, "This is what I told you while I was still with you: Everything must be fulfilled that is written about me in the Law of Moses, the Prophets and the Psalms (Luke 24:44).

Given that the Law, the Prophets and the Psalms were the three divisions of the Hebrew Old Testament, Jesus was claiming that all the prophecies of the Messiah in the entire Old Testament were written about him. He also claimed that he fulfilled all the Messianic prophecies during his lifetime. Taking John 5:39,40 and Luke 24:44 together,

---

6. As one of a number of examples, Smith was arrested and convicted in Bainbridge, New York of deceiving people as a diviner and treasure-hunter.

Jesus claimed that the fact of his fulfilling all the prophecies about the coming savior should have provided strong evidence to support his claim to be the Messiah—strong enough proof that only those who stubbornly refuse to believe would conclude anything differently. The entire fourth chapter in this book will be devoted to investigating this claim of Jesus. In it we will look at a number of specific prophecies about the Messiah that Jesus fufilled.

Here one has another example of a claim of Jesus that he backed up by what he did. Jesus claimed to be the Messiah, and he backed it up by fulfilling all the prophecies of the Messiah. What was the response of the hearers to this claim? To those who were not ready to accept the clear evidence because they were not ready to come into the light, the response was to refuse to believe. Many, however, responded by believing in Jesus. In fact, if one studies the sermons recorded in the book of Acts, one will discover that the prophecies about the Messiah were always or nearly always a part of the gospel sermons in the early church.

Has anyone else ever made a claim similar to this? Sun Myung Moon claims that certain specific prophecies point toward him. Joseph Smith claimed that some Old Testament prophecies were fulfilled by his movement. Others have claimed to be the Messiah, either directly or indirectly, but none was so bold as to claim to be the fulfillment of all the Messianic prophecies. Considering that the Old Testament predicted that the Messiah would be born in Bethlehem (Micah 5:2-5), this one prophecy alone would rule out virtually every possible claimant to be the culmination of all the prophecies about the Savior. Dozens of other examples could be mentioned. By the way, was your friend Jim born in Bethlehem?

WITHOUT SIN

The next claim of Jesus that we will investigate is found in John 8:46. Brace yourself for this astounding claim:

> When he (Satan) lies, he speaks his native language, for he is a liar and the father of lies. Yet because I tell you the truth, you do not believe me! Can any of you prove me guilty of sin? If I am telling the truth, why don't you believe me? (John 8:44-46)

What nerve! Jesus was openly claiming that he was without sin! Has anyone ever made this claim? Even a deranged person would know enough not to try this one. Jesus declared before a large crowd, some of who had known him since he was a youth, that he had never sinned.

The response of the crowd is very telling in this case. One can assume that there was a bit of silence after Jesus asked this unbelievably bold question. Probably his hearers ran back their own mental tapes. Obviously Jesus has sinned at least once. Let's see... what about the time he overturned the tables in the Temple? Despite the height of emotion, he was in control the whole time. I will have to admit that that was truly righteous anger. What about the time he disobeyed his mother when she asked him to come home and stop preaching? Didn't Jesus break the command to obey your parents? Well, I guess not, as we must obey God, rather than men.

Next, the crowd may have considered what the response would be if they made a similar claim about themselves. Imagine if one of us were to ask the question "Can any of you prove me guilty of sin?" in front of people who have been close friends for years. The first response would be hearty laughter. For those of you who are married, imagine if you said to your spouse: "Can you prove me guilty of sin?" For those who are not married, imagine asking a question like that of your parents or your siblings. Ha, Ha! Good joke!

Surely the crowd struggled to think of an example of an actual sin Jesus committed. Even the believers were probably taken aback by this astonishing question and claim of Jesus. But what was the response? Did anyone come up with a single example of an actual sin? No! Not even one. For lack of being able to think of even one sin, their answer was, "Aren't we right in saying that you are a Samaritan and demon-possessed?" (John 8:48). What were they left with? Jesus is either a liar (Samaritan is a close enough equivalent for this crowd) or a lunatic (demon possessed). These are the only other possibilities if Jesus' claim is not true.

But that still leaves the original claim unanswered. They could accuse him of being a liar or a lunatic, but not of being a sinner. Jesus never sinned. This bold and emphatic truth rings across the ages. Jesus was without sin.

I AM GOD

Surely, the reader is already convinced that Jesus made some bold claims—claims that no sane person has ever made in the history of mankind. Jesus is about to take it just one step higher. The claims in John 8:49-59 and John 10:27-30 are similar enough that they will be taken together. We will start with John 8:49-58:

> "I am not possessed by a demon," said Jesus, "but I honor my Father and you dishonor me. I am not seeking glory

for myself; but there is one who seeks it, and he is the judge. I tell you the truth, if a man keeps my word, he will never see death."

At this the Jews exclaimed, "Now we know that you are demon-possessed! Abraham died and so did the prophets, yet you say that if a man keeps your word, he will never taste death. Are you greater than our father Abraham? He died, and so did the prophets. Who do you think you are?"

That was a good question, but to continue:

Jesus replied, "If I glorify myself, my glory means nothing. My Father, whom you claim as your God, is the one who glorifies me. Though you do not know him, I know him. If I said I did not, I would be a liar like you, but I do know him and keep his word. Your father Abraham rejoiced at the thought of seeing my day; he saw it and was glad."

"You are not yet fifty years old," the Jews said to him, "and you have seen Abraham!"

"I tell you the truth," Jesus answered, "before Abraham was born, I am!"

The claim we will focus on here is primarily contained in the last verse quoted, but before that, another very interesting claim of Jesus is found in this section. Jesus said to the Jews that if they would keep (obey) his word, they would never taste death. Jesus was not talking about the death of the physical body. Jesus claimed that by obeying him, people would not taste the second death.[7]

After Jesus told the people that he was the source of eternal life, they repeated the charge that he was demon-possessed, which would appear to be the closest New Testament equivalent to being insane. They sarcastically asked Jesus, "Who do you think you are; are you claiming to be better than Abraham?" To paraphrase Jesus' answer: "Yes, I am much greater than Abraham. He foresaw my coming, and was fired up." The crowd was almost beyond words at this statement. "What, you have seen Abraham?"

Jesus' response to the people is one of the most profound statements ever made.

"Before Abraham was born, I am."

---

7. The second death is a biblical term for hell (Revelation 20:14).

Does the translation quoted here have it right? Wouldn't it more appropriately be translated as the following?

"Before Abraham was born, I AM."

In Exodus chapter three, when Moses asked God who he should tell the Israelite people had sent him to them, God replied to him: "This is what you are to say to the Israelites: 'I AM has sent me to you'"[8] (Exodus 3:14). In John 8:58, Jesus was telling the people, I am the almighty God! He could have said, "before Abraham was born, I *was*," but he did not. This was no accident. Jesus said to the people, "I am God."

Some people have said that Jesus never claimed to be God, or to be deity (to use the theological term). They do this despite such passages as John 8:58. If the gospel of John is an accurate account, then Jesus definitely claimed deity for himself.

How can one be sure Jesus is claiming to be God? Look at the response of the crowd.

> At this they picked up stones to stone him, but Jesus hid himself, slipping away from the temple grounds (John 8:59).

To the Bible student familiar with Exodus chapter three, the implications are clear. They were also clear to the crowd. Their immediate reaction was not to accuse him of lying or being crazy. Their immediate reaction was to pick up stones to kill him. This was blasphemy of the highest order. Jesus claimed to be God!

For the unconvinced, let us continue to the next passage. In John chapter ten, one finds Jesus in Jerusalem in wintertime. The suspense of the people was palpable. They asked him to commit one way or another as to whether he was going to publicly claim to be the Messiah. In response, Jesus gave them more than they bargained for.

> "My sheep listen to my voice; I know them, and they follow me. I give them eternal life, and they shall never perish; no one can snatch them out of my hand. My Father, who has given them to me, is greater than all; no one can snatch them out of my Father's hand. I and the Father are one" (John 10: 27-30).

When Jesus said he and the Father were one, he was claiming to be God. This is not to be compared, for example, to a member of a close-

---

8. In the English translations of Exodus, I AM is capitalized because it represents the Hebrew Tetragrammaton, JHVH, the holy name of God.

knit group saying, "we are one." Jesus was openly claiming equality with the Father in heaven. In case there is any mistake about this claim, consider the response of the Jews to Jesus' statement:

> Again, the Jews picked up stones to stone him, but Jesus said to them, "I have shown you many great miracles from the Father. For which of these do you stone me?"
> "We are not stoning you for any of these," replied the Jews, "but for blasphemy, because you, a mere man, claim to be God" (John 10:31-33).

As the Jews said, Jesus claimed to be God. Did Jesus deny that was what he was claiming? Did he say something like "Hold on, folks, you have me all wrong. I am not claiming to be God, I am just claiming to be really close with him"? The answer is no. Rather than deny their accusation that he was claiming to be God, he confirmed it by referring to the many miracles he had worked to prove his authority to make these claims.

Who else in history has claimed to be God? Jesus did not claim to be *a* god, he claimed to be *the* God. Even pathological liars are not so foolish as to try this one. Yes, some people with major psychological issues in their lives have claimed to be God, but of course no one takes them seriously because they are unstable and unable to verify the claim.

Imagine if your friend Jim claimed to be God. You would no longer be thinking of him as a liar. The idea that he was playing some sort of trick on you, like with the resurrection claim, would not even enter your head. If you concluded that Jim was serious, then only one possibility would remain. Jim has gone mad! It is not that the elevator does not stop at all the floors; the elevator is not stopping at any floors at all.

Yet the fact remains that a man once made this claim openly before people who knew him well, and many of those who knew him accepted the claim and followed him. Those not prepared to accept the claim went for the only other reasonable option. They picked up stones to stone him. What is a reasonable response to a person who makes such a claim? Who is this man?

THE ONLY WAY

As we continue to consider what would be a reasonable response to the claims of Jesus, let us look at just one more of the great number of claims Jesus made. It is found in John 14:6,7:

"I am the way and the truth and the life. No one comes to the Father except through me. If you really knew me, you would know my Father as well. From now on, you do know him and have seen him."

There is a sense in which this claim of Jesus is not as dramatic as some of the others mentioned above. Jesus declared to the Jews and indirectly to us that he is the only way to come to God to have a relationship with him. Yet, this claim is perhaps the most controversial of all in the modern religious context. As mentioned previously, it is a very common view today that Jesus was a good person and that he provides a valid way to come to understand truth, but that he is just "one of many paths to the same thing." This view cannot be reconciled with the claim Jesus made here in John 14:6.

Many have proclaimed to be *a* way to God, but has anyone else ever claimed to be *the* only way to God? Yes, some deranged people have made such claims, but no one besides Jesus Christ has made this claim publicly and been taken seriously.

It is in a sense unfortunate, at least for this study, that Jesus made this claim before his disciples only, as it would have been helpful to consider the reaction of those unable to accept this claim of Jesus. It is not hard to imagine what the response of the crowd might have been. One can assume that none in the crowd would have responded by concluding that Jesus was a nice teacher with a good philosophy. It is easy to imagine a response such as "demon-possessed" or "a deceiver of the people," or "let us stone him," but it is difficult to even imagine someone going away after hearing this with a lukewarm response.

A REASONABLE RESPONSE

This brings the question to its conclusion. What is a reasonable response to the claims of Jesus? Jesus claimed to be the only way to God, to be the culmination of all Old Testament prophecy, to be the bread of life, to be the one who will raise the dead. He claimed to be God in the flesh.

From a logical point of view, the possible reasonable responses seem clear. One can accept that Jesus was who he said he was. If one accepts that Jesus' claims are valid, then a reasonable response would be something similar to the response of many of those who heard the first gospel sermon preached: "Brothers, what shall we do?" (Acts 2:37).

If one cannot accept the claims of Jesus, what would be a reasonable response? Throwing stones at him would not make sense in a modern setting. A more reasonable response for one who cannot accept Jesus' claims in our world would be to actively oppose Christian teaching. If Jesus was a liar, then he certainly was not a "good teacher." If Jesus is not *the* way, then he most certainly is not *a* way to get to God.

The only reasonable response to the claims of Jesus are to either accept him as Lord of one's life, with all the implications involved, or to strongly reject his teaching as a fraud at best and dangerous at worst.

Why, then, is this the response of so few people in the modern world? The great majority either ignore Jesus, or accept him as merely a good teacher. Some even admit that he is Lord, at least in theory, but do not actually make him Lord of their own life. Relatively few have one of the responses described above. Why is that?

One possible answer is that the responses listed above are the "logical" responses, but people are not logical. We like to think we are logical, but in the final analysis, we are emotional rather than logical beings. When our intellect comes into conflict with our emotions and our deep desires, the intellect loses nearly all the time. The heart rules the person, even if that person does not acknowledge that they have a "heart."

Another possible answer is that many have not truly been confronted with the claims of Jesus. This could easily be the case with a person who does not claim to be a Christian, or one who has never read the Bible. It might even be the case for some who have gone to a church. Even some churchgoers have never been truly confronted with the Jesus of the New Testament.

It would appear to be the mission of those who accept the claims of Jesus to get his claims before as many people as possible, so that this illogical response can be changed to a more reasonable one.

Perhaps the reader is still somewhat on the fence about these questions. They are encouraged to continue reading and to consider some of the evidence still to be presented that will dramatically support the claims of Jesus to be Lord.

JESUS' CLAIMS ABOUT HIMSELF IN THE BOOK OF JOHN

Claim of Jesus	Scripture	Hearer's Response
Fufilled all the Old Testament prophecies of the Messiah	John 5:39	Refused to come to him
I am the bread of life	John 6:35	Grumbled
A life without sin	John 8:46	Jesus is demon-possessed (crazy)
I AM God	John 8:58	Attempted to stone him
I and the Father are one	John 10:30	Attempted to stone him
I am the resurrection and the life	John 11:25	Plotted to murder him
I am the only way to God	John 14:6	No negative response (Jesus talking to his disciples)

For Today

1. Can you think of or have you ever heard of a logical alternative to the "Lord, Liar or Lunatic" explanation for the claims of Jesus? For those willing to do some research, consider Douglas Jacoby's book *True & Reasonable* (Illumination Publishers Intl., Spring, Texas, www.ipibooks.com).

2. Find three additional claims of Jesus in the book of John beyond those listed in this chapter. Consider how they might overlap with or perhaps compliment those used as examples here.

Chapter Two
Why Should I Believe in Jesus?

> *Jesus did many other miraculous signs in the presence of his disciples, which are not recorded in this book. But these are written that you may believe that Jesus is the Christ, the Son of God, and that by believing you may have life in his name.*
>
> *John 20:30,31*

What evidence did Jesus point to in order to support the claims he made about himself? The answer is that Jesus backed up his claims about himself by pointing to the miracles he worked.

> "Don't you believe that I am in the Father, and that the Father is in me? The words I say to you are not just my own. Rather it is the Father, living in me, who is doing his work. Believe me when I say that I am in the Father and the Father is in me; or at least believe on the evidence of the miracles themselves" (John 14:11).

The apostles were clear that the miracles Jesus worked were the bedrock evidence to support what he claimed about himself:

> Jesus did many other miraculous signs in the presence of his disciples, which are not recorded in this book. But these are written that you may believe that Jesus is the Christ, the Son of God, and that by believing, you may have life in his name (John 20:30,31).

However, this argument may not by itself convince the skeptic. First of all, we are not eyewitnesses. Even the Bible acknowledges that it is harder for one who is not an eyewitness to the events to be convinced: "Blessed are those who have not seen and yet have believed" (John 20:29). It is fair and reasonable for the skeptic to ask several questions. How do I know Jesus really did these things? How reliable are the eyewitnesses? What is a miracle, anyway? How does one distinguish a true miracle-worker from a charlatan? The two thousand years that separate us from the events certainly make these questions very reasonable to ask.

On a personal note, although there were other factors and events in my life that played a role, it was reading the book of John that cemented my faith in Jesus from the very beginning. The writer of John fully intended to use the miracles recorded in the book to convince skeptics. I am one skeptic who counts himself among those who have been convinced by the events that are recorded in John. Nevertheless, the questions posed above are quite legitimate. These and other questions will be considered in this section.

WHAT IS A MIRACLE?

The first order of business is to carefully define the term miracle as it will be used in this discussion. Someone might claim that the definition of the word miracle is obvious, and he might have a point. However, the word is used in a variety of ways in different contexts. A careful definition is required. This will not be *the* definition of the word miracle, but a useful one for this discussion.

To put it simply, a miracle is an event that clearly defies one or more of the laws of nature. It is an event that has no "natural" explanation. It is, by definition, *super*natural. Let us be careful here. By this definition, an event that cannot be explained by any *known* natural process is not necessarily a miracle.

As an example of a situation that could not be explained by any *known* natural law, consider the following scenario. If one were to take a time machine back four hundred years with a battery, a light bulb and a couple of pieces of wire in hand, one could perform a "miracle," which would be to light a light bulb. This event would not violate what physicists know as Ohm's law. However, the existence of electrical current was not known four hundred years ago. This demonstration might be called a miracle by an observer in the year 1600, but by our working definition, it would not be a miracle.

The skeptic might argue at this point that using this definition, there is no way to say for certain that any event is truly a miracle. Maybe there is some unknown natural law out there that can explain all the events recorded in the Bible. In fact, some supposed Bible believers with humanizing tendencies have attempted to explain away many of the miracles in the Bible by proposing some sort of natural explanation. Some examples will be listed on the following pages.

Nevertheless, as we will see, there are events recorded in the Bible that no one would debate are miracles by the definition used here.

What about some modern definitions of the word miracle? For example, American baseball's "Miracle Mets" of 1969. Perhaps many of the readers are too young to know what that refers to, but what about the more recent example when Reggie Miller (apologies to the non-sports persons among us, but he is a future basketball Hall of Fame guard for the Indiana Pacers) scored eleven points in the last twelve seconds of a basketball game to pull off a miracle victory? Was this a miracle? And what about the stupendous fall of the Iron Curtain in 1989?

Obviously, the fall of the Iron Curtain is not a miracle by the definition used in this chapter. There is a clear distinction between miracle and the miraculous signs performed by Jesus. When Reggie Miller scored a trio of three point baskets and a couple of free throws in twelve seconds, it was a *very surprising and unusual* event. Very surprising events are often called miracles in the common vernacular. There is nothing wrong grammatically or otherwise with calling Reggie Miller's efforts a miracle, but anyone can see that that effort was not a violation of natural law or of the possible scenarios of a basketball game.

There are a number of events recorded in the Bible that almost certainly were miracles, but would not pass the test of being a miracle according to the definition we will use. For example, there are a number of plagues recorded in the book of Exodus that were initiated by Moses in order to convince the Pharaoh to let the Hebrew slaves leave Egypt. One of these was the plague of locusts (Exodus 10:1-20).

Devastating swarms of locusts are a natural phenomenon in Africa. Although the timing of the locusts appears too perfect to be a coincidence, there is a possible "natural" explanation for the plague of locusts that is recorded in Exodus. It is the personal opinion of this author that this was not a natural event. However, by the more conservative definition we will use, it is not.

Other examples could be cited, such as the huge flocks of quail in the middle of the desert (Exodus 16:13, Numbers 11:31) provided to feed the wandering nation of Israel. In Numbers, the writer even provides the explanation that a wind drove the quail into the desert, providing a sort of pseudo-natural explanation. Nevertheless, the context provided by both Exodus and Numbers clearly implies that this was an event caused by God. However, by our conservative definition, it is not a "miracle."

In order to establish the point that there still remain a significant number of events recorded in the Bible that, if true, would definitely be miracles even by the most conservative of definitions, consider the following examples. When the River Nile turned to blood (Exodus 7:

14-23), that would definitely be a miracle. When the Red Sea parted, leaving behind dry ground, assuming that this is a faithful record of an actual event, that would certainly be a miracle. There is no conceivable natural explanation of this sort of thing. When a person who had already been dead for four days—whose body already smelled strongly of decay—was raised to life, would certainly be a miracle. When Jesus created out of nothing enough bread and fish to feed five thousand men, plus the women and children present, this would without question be a miracle. This, of course, assumes that the event described in all four gospels is an accurate record of an actual event. The issue of whether the miracles recorded in the Bible, especially in the New Testament, are records of actual events will be a significant aspect of this chapter. Many other works performed by Jesus could be added to this list of miracles. They will be mentioned in due course.

LET'S SEE IF YOU CAN DO IT

In order to illustrate the definition of a miracle, I have occasionally pulled a trick on my friends in the context of a small group Bible study. I have put a glass of water on a table in front of the group and then asked for a volunteer. I then have asked the volunteer to close his or her eyes, to concentrate their thoughts very carefully, and to turn the water into wine. The group has occasionally offered the option of turning the water into grape juice or another concoction. It is not difficult to guess the outcome of these attempts. Despite all the concerted efforts of the person who was put on the spot, the attempts never proved successful.

This is a humorous situation. Why is that? It is humorous because everyone in the room knows that it is clearly impossible to turn water into wine. Even the person who shuts his eyes and concentrates deeply does it with just a bit of a grin, knowing that this is really just a joke. Some have claimed the ability to work modern-day miracles, often in a religious context. It is not the purpose here to judge one way or another whether such claims of miraculous events are genuine or not. However, it is safe to say that no modern-day miracle worker would be willing to put his or her claims to miraculous powers on the line publicly in an attempt to turn water into wine.

This illustration provides some context to the definition of miracle we will use. It would certainly be a miracle to turn water into wine. Water from a well contains only hydrogen and oxygen atoms (with a very small concentration of such ions as sodium, magnesium, calcium, chloride and sulfate). Wine contains a great variety of organic compounds, which include the elements carbon, nitrogen, phosphorus and so forth. None of these elements are present in tap water in any significant amount. There is no natural law that would allow one kind of atom to be converted into another kind of atom, never mind having those atoms be arranged into the correct molecules required to produce wine. Probably the reader did not need this scientific explanation to be convinced that it would be a violation of natural law to turn water into wine. The most hardened skeptic would be willing to admit that if someone were able to pull off the feat of turning water into wine, it would be a miracle.

As will be seen, many of the miracles that New Testament writers record Jesus performing are of the sort that, if they did happen, they would be a miracle by even the most stringent conceivable definition.

HOW DO WE KNOW THESE EVENTS ACTUALLY HAPPENED?

The example of turning water into wine was chosen for a reason. This was perhaps not the "greatest" miracle Jesus performed (assuming it is possible to rate miracles on a scale). However, it was the first of his recorded public miracles. This example is so important that the biblical record is presented here in full:

> On the third day a wedding took place at Cana in Galilee. Jesus' mother was there, and Jesus and his disciples had also been invited to the wedding. When the wine was gone, Jesus' mother said to him, "they have no more wine." "Dear woman, why do you involve me?" Jesus replied, "My time has not yet come." His mother said to the servants, "Do whatever he tells you." Nearby stood six stone water jars, the kind used by the Jews for ceremonial washing, each holding from twenty to thirty gallons. Jesus said to the servants, "Fill the jars with water"; so they filled them to the brim. Then he told them, "Now draw some out and take it to the master of the banquet." They did so, and the master of the banquet tasted the water that had been turned into wine. He did not realize where it had come from, though the servants who had drawn the water knew. Then he called the bridegroom aside and said, "Everyone brings out the choice wine first and then the cheaper wine after the guests have had too much to drink; but you have saved the best till now." This, *the first of his miraculous signs*, Jesus performed in Cana of Galilee. He thus revealed his glory, and his disciples put their faith in him (John 2:1-11).

The wine even tasted very good. If this event is a faithful record of an actual event, then Jesus was a miracle worker. If he really turned water into wine, then his claims about himself would be dramatically validated. In that case, it would be clear that the New Testament records the life of what is unquestionably the greatest man who ever lived.

However, the skeptic must be allowed his or her day in court. How do we really know that what is recorded in John chapter two is a faithful record of an actual event? How can one be sure this story wasn't just fabricated to justify calling people to believe in this person Jesus? This is a very fair question. Indeed, it is intellectually dishonest to avoid answering it. Besides, to run and hide in the face of this perfectly reasonable question would be to shut the door to faith for those who are skeptical but open-minded. The apostle Paul and other great teachers in the early history of the Christian church did not avoid tough intellectual questions.[1] In fact, Peter gave a strong admonition to the disciples to "always be prepared to give an answer to everyone who asks you to give the reason for the hope that you have." "Everyone" would include those who are difficult to convince.

There are a number of very good reasons to believe that the New Testament provides a faithful record of the life of Jesus Christ, and more specifically of the miracles he worked. Let us consider some of these.

How do we know the miracles of Jesus recorded in the four gospels really happened? The question of the reliability of the writers of the Bible, and especially of the New Testament, will be a very important issue throughout this book, so the topic will be addressed carefully.

First, Jesus did many of his miracles openly before the public. This point will be brought out a number of times in this chapter, using specific examples. Jesus did not just perform miracles in front of followers who were predisposed to accept that he was a miracle-worker. In the case of the water-to-wine example, no one except perhaps his mother expected him to be able to perform a miracle. Sometimes, Jesus performed miracles in a very private setting, so as not to draw attention to himself, but at other times, as we will see, he performed the most convincing miracles right in front of his harshest critics.

There were many thousands of eyewitnesses to the miracles Jesus performed, yet where is the historical record of his contemporaries who stepped forward and claimed that his miracles were a hoax? There is no such record. In fact, as we will see, both Roman and Jewish

---

[1]. For example, consider Paul's address to some of the intellects of his day in Athens (Acts 17:16-34).

contemporary records report miracle working without accepting the implications, but also without refuting the actual events.

In an attempt to refute the claims that the Bible faithfully records miraculous events, Bible skeptics have asserted that the Bible was not written until well into the second century AD. If this claim were true, it would allow several generations for the eyewitnesses to die and memories of actual events to fade, and perhaps allow for the writers of the New Testament to create myths about a miracle-worker who never existed.

Unfortunately for those who used to make such a radical claim, it has been thoroughly refuted, so that even the greatest enemies of Christianity who are intellectually honest no longer make such charges. The evidence for the date of writing of the New Testament will be reserved for chapter six, but it will suffice for now to state that it can be shown beyond a reasonable doubt that most or all of the New Testament was written while a great number of the eye witnesses to the events were still alive and able to refute any outrageous claims.

In fact, within just a few weeks of the death of Jesus Christ, on the day of Pentecost, Peter was able to declare openly before a huge crowd in Jerusalem, the city where Jesus performed many of his miracles:

> "Men of Israel, listen to this: Jesus of Nazareth was a man accredited by God to you by miracles, wonders and signs, which God did among you through him, *as you yourselves know*" (Acts 2:22).

It was common knowledge throughout Palestine that Jesus was performing all kinds of incredible miracles. Where are the people who stood up in the crowd on the day of Pentecost and declared that Peter was giving false testimony about the miracles of Jesus? They would have been either laughed at or perhaps treated much worse by a crowd who were well aware of the kinds of miracles Jesus had been doing throughout Judea and Galilee for the previous two to three years. It is commonly accepted that Jesus' miracles were a factor in his execution.

Feel free not to take Peter's word for it if you like. Historical records exist that prove that even the enemies of Jesus were well aware of the kinds of undeniable miracles Jesus worked during his ministry.

As an example of a non-Christian author who referred to the miracles of Jesus, consider Flavius Josephus. Josephus was a Pharisee, as well as a commander of the Jewish forces whose rebellion ultimately resulted in the destruction of Jerusalem in 70 AD. Interestingly, by the time of the destruction of Jerusalem, Josephus had switched sides, and was with the Roman army that sacked and destroyed Jerusalem.

Josephus wrote about Jewish history for a largely Roman audience. In his history of the Jews,[2] one can find the passage:

> Now there was about this time Jesus, a wise man, if it be lawful to call him a man, for he was a doer of wonderful works, a teacher of such men as receive the truth with pleasure. He drew over to him both many of the Jews, and many of the Gentiles.

Josephus reports that Jesus was a "doer of wonderful works," an obvious reference to his miracles. Josephus was born in AD 37 or 38. He published his *Antiquities* in AD 93 or 94. As a Pharisee, he surely knew many who were eyewitnesses to some of the events that are recorded in the gospels.

Josephus had an ambivalent attitude toward Christians. It is at least as interesting to look at some of the writings of the Jewish leaders who were vehemently opposed both to Jesus Christ and to the movement that he began.

For example, a very interesting passage can be found in the *Talmud*. The *Talmud* is a set of rabbinical teachings and commentaries to the Old Testament produced in the first and second century AD. In one section of the *Talmud*, known as the *Baraila*, one can find the following comment about the person Jesus:

> On the eve of the Passover they hanged Yeshu and the herald went before him for forty days saying (Yeshu) is going forth to be stoned in that he hath practiced sorcery and beguiled and led astray Israel. (Babylonia Sanhedrin 43a)

The author continues on to relate how Jesus was ultimately hanged (crucified). What is interesting is that in this passage it is stated that Jesus practiced sorcery. In other words, the Jewish leaders were not able to refute the well-established fact that Jesus worked many wonders; they simply accused him of doing them by the power of the devil. This is almost the identical charge to that recorded in the book of Matthew.

> They brought him a demon-possessed man who was blind and mute, and Jesus healed him, so that he could both talk and see. All the people were astonished and said, "Could this be the Son of David?"
> But when the Pharisees heard this, they said, "It is only by Beelzebub, the prince of demons, that this fellow drives out demons" (Matthew 12:22,23).

---

2. Flavius Josephus, *Antiquities*, xviii.3.3. The reader should note that some scholars question whether this passage was in the original work of Josephus.

It is interesting that in both the gospel of Matthew (see Luke 11:14-20 as well) and in writings of Jewish teachers such as that quoted above, a fourth explanation besides Lord, Liar or Lunatic is presented. The Jews accused Jesus of being a servant of the Devil. It was so hard to make the insanity charge stick, that the leaders of the Jews took an interesting tactic. They admitted that Jesus worked miracles, which would on the surface appear to validate his claims. However, they claimed that Jesus worked his signs by the power of demons. It is interesting to notice that Celsus, the Greek philosopher and enemy of Christianity, made similar charges concerning the miracles of Jesus. Celsus was a second century philosopher who was particularly critical of the Christians. Like the Pharisees, he did not deny that Jesus worked miracles. Rather, he claimed that Jesus worked his signs and wonders through sorcery.[3] Jesus easily dealt with the accusation in the case in question. He answered the Pharisees by asking them how the devil could drive out the devil.

> "If Satan drives out Satan, he is divided against himself. How then can his kingdom stand? And if I drive out demons by Beelzebub, by whom do your people drive them out? So then, they will be your judges. But if I drive out demons by the Spirit of God, then the kingdom of God has come upon you" (Matthew 12:26-28).

The Pharisees had no answer to this question because there was none. From the facts of Jesus' life, there was simply no way to support the charge that he was a servant of the devil. The crowds could never be won over by this argument, so the Pharisees abandoned it.

There are other reasons to accept as fact the miracles that Jesus worked. Before going into the last argument for the reliability of the New Testament accounts of the miracles of Jesus, consider the following outline of evidence to support belief in these miracles.

1. A great number of the miracles were done publicly, often in front of the greatest skeptics and harshest critics of Jesus.

2. There were thousands of eyewitnesses, both believers and unbelievers, from various backgrounds to these events.

3. The apostles openly proclaimed that Jesus worked a great variety of miracles during the lifetime of those who could have refuted the claims. This is a matter of historical record. (This fact is a notable

---

3. Origen, *Contra Cesium*, 1:38 and 2:48.

exception to the claims the believers in other great religious leaders have made.)

4. Both Roman and Jewish histories report at least the general fact that Jesus worked "wonders."

5. Because the wonders and signs of Jesus were common knowledge, the Pharisees and Rabbis in the time period in question tended to claim Jesus did his signs by the power of demons, rather than refute that the miracles occurred.

6. Those who recorded the miracles most carefully and thoroughly (the gospel writers) have every appearance of being absolutely reliable. All but Luke were eyewitnesses of the events they recorded.

RELIABLE WITNESSES

If the gospel writers, Matthew, Mark, Luke and John, are reliable reporters of actual events, then obviously Jesus worked miracles. The first five points listed above powerfully attest to the fact that Jesus worked miracles. The gospel records contain the actual accounts of many specific miracles that are essential to the discussion at hand. Therefore the reliability of these writers is a very important issue. A discussion of the reliability of the authors of the gospels is essential to other chapters in this book as well, particularly the one on the resurrection, so this matter will be considered carefully.

What kind of people were the apostles? Two of the gospel writers, Mark and Luke, were not even apostles, so what about them? How do we even know that the people named at the top of these books are the actual writers? We will delay answering the last of these three questions until chapter six.

The four gospel accounts have every appearance of being an accurate record. When the accounts themselves overlap, they are quite similar but not exactly the same. If they were all prepared from a single but falsified account, copied by each author, they would be essentially identical. If the accounts were separate records of a number of liars, they would differ on very important specifics (similar to a number of false witnesses in a court). The fact is that the gospel accounts are very similar. The differences they contain represent the varied perspectives of different eyewitnesses as recorded by themselves or by those close to them. These slight (but non-contradictory) differences actually supports the claim that they are genuine accounts.

Besides, the gospels certainly record a number of mistakes and sins of the apostles themselves,[4] producing a strong appearance of genuineness. One finds Peter and the other apostles making blunders and committing outright sins. However, there is no evidence of the character of the apostles (or Luke or Mark for that matter) being dishonest in any way. The critics of the New Testament cannot produce a single example of a false witness or even of a bad character in any of the important witnesses. As with Jesus himself, the accusers could claim bad intent or deceit, but could produce no specific evidence to support the claim.

What is the external evidence of the character of the witnesses of these events? History reports that the apostle James was martyred.[5] Church tradition records, with varying reliability, that all the apostles besides John were martyred as well. According to tradition, they tried to kill the apostle John too, but failed. It is very telling to note that not a single one of the significant eyewitnesses recanted, even at the point of death. None said "Look, we were only making this up to get supporters for our movement," or anything even remotely resembling this sort of thing. Is it possible to believe that every one of the apostles along with dozens of other eyewitnesses would willingly die for a lie? This defies everything we know about human nature.

There are a number of examples of extreme persecutions of the Christian church throughout the ages. In general, some remained faithful, but some recanted at the point of the sword. However, in the case of the New Testament eyewitnesses, not a single one recanted: not one! If they were aware that the whole thing was premised on a pack of lies, it is absolutely inconceivable that not a single one would recant. The words of Paul concerning the death of Jesus ring true here:

> Very rarely will anyone die for a righteous man, though for a good man someone might possibly dare to die. But God demonstrates his own love for us in this: While we were still sinners, Christ died for us (Romans 5:6-8).

This statement about Christ's death would hold equally well for the first century martyrs who were very well aware of whether the miracles really happened. Would anyone die for what they know to be a lie? Perhaps someone would, but certainly not one hundred percent of the people involved. This argument seems impossible to deny, so the skeptics ignore it.

---

4. For example John 12:4-6, Luke 18:15,16, and Mark 9:33-35
5. Josephus mentions this event in an account that parallels the New Testament. Josephus, *Antiquities*, xx.9.1, though a number of critics doubt the veracity of this entry.

Let those who can, mount an argument against the reasoning previously outlined. Much more will be said in this work regarding the reliability of the Bible as a whole. We will now move on to consider the actual miracles that Jesus did. We will also ask questions about why he worked these miracles, as well as what is implied about Jesus by the miracles he performed.

WHY MIRACLES?

It may seem obvious why Jesus worked miracles, but upon closer inspection this becomes an interesting question. Jesus worked miracles for different reasons in different situations, although I think there is one overriding purpose.

That one overriding purpose of the miracles was to validate his message. In this context, John 20:30,31 and John 10:37,38 have already been mentioned. A related statement can be found in Hebrews:

> This salvation, which was first announced by the Lord, was confirmed to us by those who heard him. God also testified to it by signs, wonders and various miracles and gifts of the Holy Spirit distributed according to his will (Hebrews 2:3,4).

The author of Hebrews appears to be applying this concept to the entire New Testament, but it certainly applies specifically to the miracles of Jesus.

Two good examples of Jesus confirming his message by a miracle that correlated with the message have already been given in the previous chapter. When Jesus said he was the bread of life, he had just recently produced enough bread to feed several thousand people, along with some fish. Apparently, Jesus created bread "out of thin air." Another example we have looked at of Jesus confirming a claim with a miracle is in the case of Jesus claiming to be the resurrection and the life, followed by his raising Lazarus from the dead.

Let us consider another of Jesus' miracles that he used as direct evidence to support one of his most controversial teachings. It is found in Mark chapter two. In this situation, some people brought a paralyzed man to Jesus. When they could not get into the room where he was teaching the people, they lowered the paralytic through a hole they dug in the roof.

> When Jesus saw their faith, he said to the paralytic, "Son, your sins are forgiven."

> Now, some of the teachers of the law were sitting there, thinking to themselves, "Why does this fellow talk like that? He's blaspheming! Who can forgive sins but God alone?"
> Immediately Jesus knew in his spirit that this was what they were thinking in their hearts, and he said to them, "Why are you thinking these things? Which is easier, to say to the paralytic, 'Your sins are forgiven,' or to say, 'Get up, take your mat and walk'? But that you may know that the Son of Man has authority on earth to forgive sins...." He said to the paralytic, "I tell you, get up, take your mat and go home."
> He got up, took his mat, and walked out in full view of them all. This amazed everyone and they praised God, saying, "We have never seen anything like this!" (Mark 2:5-12).

It is easy to see why they were amazed. Imagine what your response would have been to this riveting event. Jesus proved he had authority to forgive sins by healing a man who was apparently hopelessly paralyzed. This was no short-term slight improvement. This was a complete and permanent change.[6] Several other examples could be given of Jesus working a miracle to provide validation for a specific claim he made about himself.

Another reason Jesus mentioned for working some of his miracles was as a direct response to a person's faith. This might have been a secondary reason, but on a number of occasions Jesus specifically stated that he worked a miracle at least in part out of a response to a person's great faith. In fact, the miracle mentioned above is a case in point. Another example of this is found in Matthew 9:18-26.

> While he was saying this, a ruler came and knelt before him and said, "My daughter has just died. But come and put your hand on her, and she will live." Jesus got up and went with him, and so did his disciples.
> Just then a woman who had been subject to bleeding for twelve years came up behind him and touched the edge of his cloak. She said to herself, "If I only touch his cloak, I will be healed."
> Jesus turned and saw her. Take heart, Daughter," he said, "Your faith has healed you." And the woman was healed from that moment.

---

6. There are a couple of other claims and at least one miracle in this event not yet highlighted. Jesus is claiming to be *the* Son of Man. He is claiming to be able to forgive sins. He also shows the miraculous ability to know the thoughts of a person's heart.

> When Jesus entered the ruler's house and saw the flute players and the noisy crowd, he said, "Go away. The girl is not dead but asleep." But they laughed at him. After the crowd had been put outside, he went in and took the girl by the hand, and she got up. News of this spread through all that region.

Because of the simple faith of the woman with the bleeding problem, Jesus healed her. The resurrection of the ruler's daughter is another example of a miracle that Jesus might not have worked if not for the faith of the requestor. Many examples could be mentioned in which Jesus performed a miracle in response to a person's faith.

A third reason Jesus worked some of his wonders was to meet the crying need of a suffering person. Jesus had compassion, not just for the spiritual suffering of lost people, but also for those in physical or emotional distress. At times this provoked Jesus to intervene in a situation to bring relief. These miracles were occasionally not done in a public manner, as they were not intended to prove anything or even to serve as a public reward for faith.

As an example, one could mention Mark 7:32-35, in which Jesus healed a deaf and mute person, for no obvious reason other than the fact that the man was in need of help. Another example would be the widow from Nain whose only son had died. This event would be an extreme tragedy in any setting, but for a widow in Israel to lose an only son was a particularly devastating blow.

> When the Lord saw her, his heart went out to her and he said, "Don't cry." Then he went up and touched the coffin, and those carrying it stood still. He said, "Young man, I say to you get up!" The dead man sat up and began to talk, and Jesus gave him back to his mother (Luke 7:13-15).

What compassion! What love! What power—to raise someone from the dead! Remember the evidence listed above to support the claim that the miracles recounted in the gospels are accurate records of actual events (more evidence will be presented in chapter six as well). This event really happened. Jesus was a worker of wonders.

Perhaps enough examples of miracles performed by Jesus have already been given to solidify this point, but let us consider a few of the other signs that the gospel writers recorded. Specifically, let us consider what the miracles that Jesus worked say about what kind of person he was.

One of the well known miracles of Jesus occurred on the Sea of Galilee (In fact, either the sea itself, or the region immediately around it, was the scene of the majority of the recorded miracles Jesus worked.). However, this miracle brought things to another level for the apostles. When Jesus calmed a storm by simply speaking, thus changing the environment around them as far as they could see, it must have had a dramatic effect on their view of who Jesus was. One can find the account in Luke 8:22-25 (also see Mark 4:35).

> One day Jesus said to his disciples, "Let's go over to the other side of the lake." So they got into a boat and set out. As they sailed, he fell asleep. A squall came down on the lake, so that the boat was being swamped, and they were in great danger. The disciples went and woke him, saying, "Master, we're going to drown!" He got up and rebuked the wind and the raging waters; the storm subsided, and all was calm. "Where is your faith?" he asked his disciples. In fear and amazement they asked one another, "Who is this? He commands even the winds and the water, and they obey him."

This was an impressive event. It certainly made an impact on the apostles who were with Jesus. They had already seen Jesus work a number of miracles on individual people. However, when Jesus calmed a storm in a way which changed the entire physical environment around them as far as they could see, it must have affected their view of him from that time forward.

At first glance it might seem surprising that those who had already witnessed Jesus turning water into wine and healing hundreds of people, along with a number of other wonders, would be so amazed when Jesus calmed the storm. Remember, though, that this was a demonstration of power on a massive scale. It revealed Jesus' power in a new, awesome and perhaps even ominous way. In a few short moments it hit these men that this Jesus was in control of the entire world.

This is what Jesus calming the storm demonstrated. He proved that he had (and still has, of course) ultimate power over the physical world: to bring rain or prevent it, to control the wind and the climate. Bottom line, they now realized that Jesus held in his hand the power to determine whether they could successfully put food on the table. The apostles were already well aware that Jesus was a man of great power, but this one event must have hit them like a freight train (excuse the anachronistic simile). Bear in mind that control over the natural world was the ultimate focus of all the ancient pagan religions. The apostles suddenly realized that Jesus held the key to all the power that every religious person had ever sought to tap by their worship. What a revelation!

The next miracle we will consider is found in Mark chapter eight.

> He told the crowd to sit down on the ground. When he had taken the seven loaves and given thanks, he broke them and gave them to his disciples to set before the people, and they did so. They had a few small fish as well; he gave thanks for them also and told the disciples to distribute them. The people ate and were satisfied. Afterward the disciples picked up seven basketfuls of broken pieces that were left over. About four thousand men were present. And having sent them away, he got into the boat with his disciples and went to the region of Dalmanutha (Mark 8:6-10).

Of course, this miracle is similar to the feeding of the five thousand that we already considered. Because Mark records both the feeding of the five thousand (Mark 6:30-44), and of the four thousand, and because the details of the accounts differ greatly, one must assume that Jesus performed a similar miracle a second time.

What does this miraculous event tell us about Jesus? For one thing, in this miracle, Jesus showed thousands of people that he could create something out of nothing. He proved that he was *a* creator, if not *the* Creator. Jesus made fish out of nothing, and it was already cooked and ready to eat. The bread had the appearance of having had yeast added to the dough so that it would rise. Jesus got around the whole process of kneading, punching dough and so forth. He made bread, ready to eat, out of absolutely nothing. Before thousands of witnesses, Jesus provided dramatic evidence that what is claimed about him in Colossians 1:16 is true—"For by him all things were created: things in heaven and on earth."

This is not the only miracle Jesus performed which showed that he could take care of people's most basic needs. Consider Matthew 17:24-27:

> After Jesus and his disciples arrived in Capernaum, the collectors of the two-drachma tax came to Peter and asked, "Doesn't your teacher pay the temple tax?"
> "Yes, he does," he replied.
> When Peter came into the house, Jesus was the first to speak. "What do you think, Simon?" he asked. "From whom do the kings of the earth collect duty and taxes—from their own sons or from others?"

"From others," Peter replied.

Then the sons are exempt," Jesus said to him. "But so that we may not offend them, go to the lake and throw out your line. Take the first fish you catch; open its mouth and you will find a four-drachma coin. Take it and give it to them for my tax and yours."

Presumably, when Peter went out to fish, he did indeed find the four drachmas in the first fish he caught. Otherwise, Matthew, an eyewitness to the event, certainly would not have recorded this story.

In this case, Jesus either created a gold coin out of nothing inside the fish, or he was somehow miraculously aware that a fish had swallowed a gold coin. He then caused Peter to catch that particular fish. Apparently, the coin even had the proper Roman markings on it. Jesus proved himself capable of taking care of Peter's need to pay taxes!

What things do people worry about? They worry about food and shelter, they worry about money, and they worry about their health. We have already seen Jesus prove he had control over the first two, but what about the third major concern of all people? Did Jesus have power to affect people's health?

The answer is a resounding yes! Almost certainly, healings were the most common of Jesus' miracles. The healings Jesus performed were in general not of the debatable variety. Most of us have been exposed to healings, either in person, or through television or radio, or through secondhand accounts. Perhaps some of these events are true miracles. However, in most cases, the miraculous nature of many modern-day "healings" is dubious. Many involve improvement of sight or lessening of a limp or reduction of a fever. The point is not to settle the issue here, but to point out that a number of the healings Jesus performed were undeniably miracles.

Jesus healed a man born blind (John 9:1-41). He healed a man who had not walked for thirty-eight years, and the man jumped up and began walking (John 5:1-15). He simultaneously healed ten men who had leprosy, and they were completely cured (Luke 17:11-19). These were not debatable miracles. Some of Jesus' healings are summarized in Matthew 11:4-6:

> Jesus replied, "Go back and report to John what you hear and see. The blind receive sight, the lame walk, those who have leprosy are cured, the deaf hear, the dead are raised, and the good news is preached to the poor. Blessed is the man who does not fall away on account of me."

The testimony of the gospel writers is that Jesus healed several thousand people with various kinds of disease and disability. He did so in public settings where his enemies could see the healings so that any attempt at faking so great a number of miracles would have been nearly impossible.

Through his miracles, Jesus proved that he had control over the principal things people worry about such as money, food, shelter and health. Besides this, through his miracles he proved that he had control over the spiritual world as well. Jesus was able to rebuke and drive out demons. We will consider just one example of this sort of miracle.

In Mark 5:1-20 and Luke 8:26-39, one can find accounts of a man who was, to use more modern terminology, absolutely insane. "The man lived in the tombs, and no one could bind him any more, not even with a chain. For he had often been chained hand and foot, but he tore the chains apart and broke the irons on his feet. No one was strong enough to subdue him. Night and day among the tombs and in the hills he would cry out and cut himself with stones." This was clearly a desperate situation. This man was totally out of control. In order to heal him, Jesus rebuked the demons that had overtaken him and forced them into a herd of pigs. The pigs rushed into the lake and drowned.

Our "modern" sentiment makes us hesitate to identify the problem of this man as demon-possession. However, given that Jesus was able to heal a person who was clearly in an absolutely hopeless situation, who are we to deny his diagnosis of the situation? How is one to explain the pigs suddenly diving into the lake? Simply denying the existence of forces of evil does not make them cease to exist. Through this and other miracles, Jesus proved he controls the spiritual realm.

Through another sort of miracle, Jesus proved that he also had power to access the world of the mind. Dozens of examples could be mentioned, but consider the situation when Jesus met Nathanael for the first time (John 1:44-51). When Nathanael first heard about Jesus he was very skeptical. However, when Jesus actually met Nathanael, he was able to tell him where he had been and what he had been thinking about. Any doubt that this was a miracle is removed by Nathanael's response to Jesus knowing his thoughts: "Rabbi, you are the Son of God; you are the King of Israel."

Through his miracles, Jesus proved that his disciples could afford to put their complete trust in him. He had control over money, food, shelter, health and the spiritual world. He even had access to the world of their minds. This list of phenomena Jesus could control leaves one major human concern. In addition to all these miraculous acts, Jesus proved that he had power over the ultimate human fear: death. The resurrection of Lazarus from the dead has already been described in detail. Jesus also raised a young girl who had died (Luke 8:49-56).

Through his miracles the words of Jesus in John 16:33 take on new meaning, "...in me you may have peace. In this world you will have trouble. But take heart! I have overcome the world."

Others have claimed to work miracles, but where are the examples of people being raised from the dead in open view, before both believers and nonbelievers? Jesus was the greatest worker of miracles in history, without a doubt.

There is one last miracle to consider, which is unquestionably the greatest of all the miracles of Jesus. This will be the subject of chapter three.

THE MIRACLES JESUS DID NOT DO

Before moving on to the greatest miracle of all, please consider one more thought-provoking question. Are there any kinds of miracles Jesus might very well have worked, but that he did not do (or at least that are not recorded in the gospels)? If so, what do the miracles that Jesus did *not* do say about him?

The answer is yes, there are some notable types of miracles that Jesus could conceivably have performed, but which there is no record of him doing. For instance, there are no examples of Jesus working a miracle to force someone to do something against their will. Jesus would not even heal people who did not want to be healed (John 5:6). Jesus never compelled anyone to obey him in any way. It is certainly conceivable that the one who could know our every thought could also control our thoughts, but there is no record of Jesus doing anything like this.

If the gospel record is to be believed, Jesus did not perform miracles in an attempt to manipulate people into following him. If anything, he often underplayed the miraculous nature of what he had done. Jesus worked miracles in response to the faith of individuals, to meet needs, or to support his claims about himself, but there is no record of him attempting to whip up a crowd by working wonders.

The historical record of the miracles of Jesus appears to exclude manipulation and violating the "free will" of individuals as a motive. It is obvious what this implies about the man. Jesus scrupulously avoided the use of emotion or spectacle to force people to believe in him.

There is another kind of miracle of which there is no record either in or out of the Bible. Jesus never performed a miracle to benefit his own comfort. As far as the record shows, Jesus never made food for himself when he was hungry, although he certainly could have done so. Jesus got tired. As best we can tell, he never miraculously gave himself a boost of energy to get through a tough time.

The greatest example of this idea is found when Jesus was on the cross. On the night he was arrested, when his friends asked whether they should prevent his arrest by force, Jesus replied, "Do you think I cannot call on my Father, and he will at once put at my disposal more than twelve legions of angels? But how then would the Scriptures be fulfilled that say it must happen in this way?" (Matthew 26:53,54).

The miracles recorded in the gospels leave no doubt that Jesus could have saved himself from the incredible pain and suffering caused by scourging and crucifixion. The same one who could calm a storm or make bread and fish out of nothing certainly could have performed a miracle either to prevent the crucifixion in the first place, or to come down from the cross and end the torture. However, he did not, despite being taunted to do so by his persecutors. The miracles that Jesus did not do say a lot about the man.

REASONS FOR UNBELIEF

At this point, the readers could perhaps be broken into three categories. There are those who began this book already believing in the inspiration of the Bible, in the validity of the claims of Jesus, and in his ability to work miracles. Perhaps their faith has been deepened through what they have read so far.

Another definable group could be described as follows. They began reading the book either as unbelievers, or as ones who were a bit skeptical, but not really sure about what they believed. However, through what has been presented they are either now convinced that Jesus is who he said he was, or at the very least have had their unbelief shaken. They find these ideas interesting, and want to read on to continue to have their thinking challenged.

A third group might be described as Bible skeptics both before and after reading these chapters. They definitely remain unconvinced that Jesus even made the claims recorded in the Bible, and discount the recorded miracles of Jesus as either hoaxes or as false records. They are willing to read on, but primarily to satisfy their own curiosity about how the other side thinks.

For people in category number one or two, the arguments presented so far may seem very reasonable. These people may ask how others could remain skeptical in spite of what seem to be convincing arguments. I would suggest a few possible reasons that some are so difficult to convince. Why do some people at least appear to refuse to believe? (Admittedly, this is a somewhat prejudiced way to put the question.)

One reason for disbelief is emotional. We humans like to think of ourselves as rational. We like to think that we use common sense based on the preponderance of the evidence, to arrive at what we believe to be true. The plain truth is that this is very often not the case.

Many of our assumptions and beliefs are based on emotion. There are many obvious examples that may be listed. For example, it is certainly true that those who have been abused by family members find it difficult to trust people. This is especially true when the negative experiences have happened to young people. They find it extremely difficult to trust people in general, even when there is no actual evidence at all to cause a lack of trust in one particular individual. This lack of trust is not because they have studied out the statistics and reached the conclusion that there is a high probability that they will be abused by anyone they choose to put their trust in. The root of their insecurity is emotional, not rational.

Many who are unable to accept the evidence in support of Christianity have an emotional basis for their unbelief as well. Perhaps they have had a bad experience with a hypocritical religious person. It is difficult to grow up in modern society without having some experiences like this. Perhaps as teens they watched a seemingly defenseless religious person mercilessly persecuted by their peers. Events such as these can have a powerful and even permanent effect on our subconscious mind. Just as in the case of the person who was abused by someone close to him or her when they grew up, this kind of experience may very easily cause one to become completely immune to rational argument. It can become literally impossible to convince a person of the validity of an argument by use of evidence if the reason they do not accept the argument is emotional.

Another reason that some are unable to come to belief despite convincing evidence is intellectual pride. It is a fact of human nature that it is difficult for people to admit that they have been wrong. Presumably few people would argue with this claim. The longer and more loudly one has defended oneself, the harder it becomes to back down and admit being wrong. Sometimes throwing evidence in the face of someone who has taken a strong stand has the exact opposite effect of what was intended. It can actually harden a person's position rather than soften it.

Again, we like to think of ourselves as rational beings, but when our pride is at stake, we can appear to be very foolish in the way we deal with the truth. It can be very difficult to admit that we are wrong. This can be a major factor in why some do not come to faith in God.

And it goes beyond mere intellectual pride in the case of belief in an all-powerful God. To admit that God is greater than we are is to admit that we are less than God. In an age and culture dominated by humanistic philosophy, it has come to be assumed by many that there is no need for God. Some may admit that God exists in some abstract way, but are not prepared to put their opinions in subjection to the claims of that same all-powerful God. "If that is the way God is, I certainly do not want to worship him." Belief in a New Age pantheistic God (something akin to the "Force" in the *Star Wars* movies) is a result of people being unwilling to accept that they are truly much smaller than God. The New Age philosophy, an offshoot of Hindu and Buddhist religion, teaches that God is you and you are God. It does not take a lot of humility to accept this proposition.

So there is an intellectual pride that might cause one to reject clear evidence for the Bible, and there is an emotional pride that is unwilling to put anyone else on the throne. Those who would seek to use evidence, such as that contained in this book, to convince people to accept the Biblical truth would do well to keep these factors in mind. As Jonathan Swift said, "It is impossible to reason a person out of something they were not reasoned into the first place."

In the great majority of cases, the reason people reject the well established evidence in support of the Bible is not because the evidence is not strong enough, but because of pride or an emotional response to a life experience. Perhaps this is why God tells us, through Peter, to "Always be prepared to give an answer to everyone who asks you to give the reason for the hope that you have. But do this with gentleness and respect, keeping a clear conscience, so that those who speak maliciously against your good behavior in Christ may be ashamed of their slander" (1 Peter 3:15,16). A quick, intelligent, intellectually consistent answer may not be sufficient. The qualities of gentleness and respect for those who do not agree are absolutely key as well. And one could add a measure of patience on top of the gentleness and respect. The key to overcoming intellectual pride or emotional barriers to belief in the truths presented in the Bible is found in the good behavior of the believers. This is a difficult teaching to accept, but it is God's truth. Chapter nine will treat this issue more thoroughly.

Besides, it would be fair to admit that Christians are equally susceptible to the weaknesses described above. We may very well believe what we believe for emotional reasons ourselves. Perhaps those who would accuse us of turning to Christianity as a crutch to help us in our insecurity may have at least a bit of a point. Or perhaps it is possible that for some of us our belief is based primarily on a decision we have made many years ago, which we cling to tenaciously at this point, out of a form of intellectual pride. Have you discontinued challenging your own beliefs, dooming yourself to a shallow faith?

Perhaps one would argue that it is better to believe in the right things for the wrong reasons than to believe in the wrong things for the right reasons. This may even be a valid argument up to a point, but faith based on emotion or pride is like a house built on sand. When the storms of life's difficulties or of persecution crash up against such a house, will it stand? When a person experiences much success in a worldly sense, it can become a reason for pride in self. In this case, will faith based on intellectual pride be able to withstand worldly pride? Very likely it will not.

As described above, some are unable to accept the obvious evidence for the Bible because of some sort of negative experience they have had surrounding Christianity. Conversely, some turn to Christ at least largely because of some sort of positive spiritual experience. Faith that is based on experience alone is necessarily shaky faith. A solid faith built on a foundation like a house on a rock will include elements of experience, of emotion, of spiritual insight and of intellectual knowledge. This book is intended primarily to address the last category. It would be well advised for anyone who comes to faith in God based on an emotional, an experiential, a spiritual or an intellectual experience to dig deeper and wider into all the categories, laying a foundation that will never be shaken.

CONCLUSION

The evidence that Jesus worked the most amazing "miracles, signs and wonders" is overwhelming, both from the internal evidence in the Bible and from external sources: even sources who were avowedly enemies of Christianity. These miracles were not of the sort one hears about today. The miracles did not involve trivialities such as getting a better job or partially improved health. Jesus raised the dead, gave sight to people who had been born blind, created food out of thin air, walked on water...the list could go on. Jesus often did these things in the most open possible forums, in front of hundreds or even thousands of viewers, some of who were his avowed enemies. Jesus performed miracles to verify his claims, to offer witness to his message and often simply to help a person for whom he felt a deep compassion.

Jesus, Son of God, worker of miracles.

For Today

1. What do you think might be the difference between the three terms, "signs, wonders and various miracles" (Hebrews 2:3,4)? If you are really ambitious, you could look up the Greek words for the three categories and try to do more than just guess.

2. List two miracles other than those mentioned in this chapter that would be examples of wonders Jesus performed to verify a claim. Also, find two examples of a miracle that was performed largely due to the faith of an individual who sought Jesus' help. Lastly, find two miraculous works of Jesus that appear to have been done primarily to help meet a need.

3. Can you think of a reasonable scenario (whether you believe in the scenario or not) to explain the gospel accounts and still conclude that Jesus did not work miracles?

4. Assuming you have faith in Jesus Christ and in the Bible as the Word of God, what sort of basis (emotional, experiential, spiritual or intellectual) do you tend to lean on? How might you broaden the basis of your belief?

5. What did Jesus show about himself through the miracle recorded in Matthew 17:25-27?

Author's note: An excellent reference on the subject of miracles is the enlightening little book by C. S. Lewis, *Miracles* (Harper, San Francisco, California, 2001).

Chapter Three
The Ultimate Miracle

Extraordinary claims require extraordinary proof.

–David Hume

In chapter two we looked at the miracles that Jesus performed, examined evidence that Jesus really did work these miracles and considered what they imply about the miracle-worker himself. However, we did not consider the ultimate miracle—the resurrection of Jesus Christ from the dead.

Now, wait a minute. Did Jesus do this miracle? Did he raise himself from the dead, or did the Father raise his son from the dead? We will let the theologians work out this question because it really does not matter who did it. No matter who "did" it, the resurrection of Jesus Christ from the dead is truly the greatest and most important miracle recorded in the Bible.

One purpose of this chapter is to show why this particular event is so central both to the message of the Bible and to its reliability and inspiration. More importantly, the purpose is to very carefully consider whether the resurrection of Jesus Christ from the dead, as recorded in the New Testament, really happened. We will see that there is a lot riding on this question.

BEYOND A REASONABLE DOUBT

Before attempting to accomplish these goals, we need to consider how difficult a task is before us. The case for the resurrection of Jesus Christ requires the absolute highest standard of proof.

By way of illustration, consider four scenarios. In each case, someone will make a claim and we will ask what standard of proof is required to believe the claim. First, imagine you are at home and your roommate/spouse or whatever comes in all excited and proclaims that he/she received a bill in the mail today. Hmm...You would probably wonder why all the excitement. You certainly would not be demanding proof of the claim.

The second scenario involves yourself and the same person. This time, your excited friend is announcing that he/she has found a two-pound bag of chips for only $1.19. Wow! Let's tell the neighbors right away. Would this claim stop you in your tracks? What standard of proof would you require?

The third scenario is just a bit more interesting. This time imagine your partner excitedly proclaims that she has won $10,000,000 in the lottery. This time, your head perks up a bit. It perks up quite a bit, in fact. You would check her face for sincerity, and probably ask to see the winning ticket—not necessarily because you do not trust her, but because you don't want to make too great a fool of yourself if you admit you believe her and it turns out she was pulling your leg. You would want some proof. Within a few seconds or perhaps a few minutes, you would be jumping up and down, or perhaps just giving some high fives, depending on your personality.

The fourth scenario is the one to focus on. This time, your loved one pronounces that he has seen a cow with six legs. In this scenario you would give a deeply incredulous look and immediately demand proof. If you were to not demand proof, it would reveal more about you than about your friend. Not demanding evidence would imply that you are a very gullible person.

Unfortunately (or perhaps fortunately) the resurrection of Jesus is most like the fourth scenario. Only a fool would simply believe someone has been raised from the dead without some very strong evidence to support the claim. The first scenario represents a claim about something that is so mundane and expected that absolutely no proof is required. Bills come in the mail more days than not.

The second scenario—the one with the chips—requires just a bit more proof. One does not see a two-pound bag of chips for $1.19 every day. It is amazing (using the word very loosely) to find chips that cheap. You might not exactly demand proof, but it is so surprising to find chips this cheap, you just might sneak a peak at the receipt to make sure your friend is not mistaken. If you were to become convinced, you probably would not dance up and down the street, declaring the amazing discovery to all within earshot, but you would be sure to tell a few friends about the great price on chips at the store.

The lottery scenario is quite different. The chances of claiming such a big payoff in the lottery is less than one in a million for sure. This would be a very unexpected result, especially if your friend had the good sense not to play the lottery. But assuming that she did buy a few lotto tickets occasionally, the claim about the lottery is still so unexpected that you would definitely want proof before believing it. Cruel practical jokesters have been known to pull off elaborate schemes to convince their friends that they won the lottery, only to say they were

The Ultimate Miracle

joking. The point is this. Winning the lottery is a very unlikely event, but no matter how unlikely it is, it still is definitely possible. A possible but very unlikely event requires a good deal of evidence in order to be believed.

However, the scenario with the six-legged cow is a different animal altogether. Cows simply do not have six legs! In this case, your assumption would be that your friend either made a mistake or has been deceived by some sort of optical illusion. It is impossible for cows to have six legs. Well, maybe it is not impossible, but it certainly is unheard of. You would require some pretty convincing proof. A picture might help, but with modern technology, pictures can be faked. A few other eyewitnesses would certainly help, especially if their descriptions all corroborated one another. However, there is only one completely convincing form of evidence. If you could see the cow for yourself—if you could walk around her and touch her, you would be completely convinced that your friend had actually seen a cow with six legs.

Such is the case with the resurrection of Jesus Christ from the dead. According to common experience and even common sense, it is simply unbelievable that Jesus Christ was raised from the dead on the third day. The chances of winning the lottery may be one in ten million. The odds against a person being raised from the dead are certainly much greater than that. One might even say it is impossible—a miracle. In order to convince the skeptic, very strong evidence is required indeed. To quote a well-known skeptical scientist, "If you hear hooves clip-clopping down a street, it could be a zebra or even a unicorn—but before you assume anything other than a horse, you should demand a minimal standard of evidence."[1] The more unlikely the claim, the stronger the evidence that is required in order to substantiate it.

Besides this, the burden of proof lies with the believer, not the skeptic. Reason would tell us that the skeptic does not need to prove his or her case against the resurrection of Jesus. Because a claim of resurrection lies so far outside of normal experience, it is unfair to require the non-believer to prove that the resurrection story is bogus. It is not right to charge the skeptic with being closed-minded for not believing in the resurrection. The skeptic would reply, "Open-minded is fine, but I do not want to be so open-minded, my brains fall out. Give me some proof."

There is an additional factor that makes the burden of proof on the believer heavy. This is brought out by the illustration used above. In the fourth scenario, when your friend claimed that he had seen a cow with six legs, you had every reason to expect strong evidence. A picture

---

[1]. Richard Dawkins, from an essay in *"A Brief History of Science,"* (The Ivy Press, East Sussex, England, 1998) p. 10.

would be nice, and eyewitnesses could be very helpful, but there was one kind of evidence that would be very convincing. If one could actually go to see the cow up close and personal, that would be by far the most convincing proof of this very far-fetched claim.

Unfortunately, in the case of the resurrection of Jesus from the dead, we do not have access to such proof. Because the event (if it did indeed occur) happened almost two thousand years ago, it is not possible to go back to Israel to investigate the claim directly. Besides, all the eyewitnesses are long dead. At first glance, this might seem like an overwhelming burden of proof. In the end, we will let the evidence speak for itself.

So the job that remains is to prove beyond a reasonable doubt that Jesus Christ was in fact raised from the dead on the third day. Because of the nature of the claim, the task is not simply to show that this is the *most likely* explanation of the facts surrounding his death. The resurrection of the dead is so far from normal experience that one must prove beyond a doubt that it is the *only* reasonable explanation of the facts. To quote from the eighteenth-century British philosopher and skeptic, David Hume, "One must ask if the present evidence for the alleged event is so strong that any other explanation of the evidence would be even more miraculous."

A DIFFICULT JOB, BUT AN IMPORTANT JOB

The burden of proof for supporting belief in the resurrection of Jesus is great, but the importance of the assignment is great as well. On this issue hangs all of Christianity. Let it be said again. All of Christianity rests on the issue of the resurrection of its founder, Jesus Christ. This is not an overstatement. Consider the radical statement of the apostle Paul.

> And if Christ has not been raised, our preaching is useless and so is your faith. More than that, we are then found to be false witnesses about God, for we have testified about God that he raised Christ from the dead. But he did not raise him if in fact the dead are not raised. For if the dead are not raised, then Christ has not been raised either. And if Christ has not been raised, your faith is futile; you are still in your sins. Then those also who have fallen asleep in Christ are lost. If only for this life we have hope in Christ, we are to be pitied more than all men (1 Corinthians 15:14-19).

According to Paul, if Jesus Christ was in fact not raised from the dead, then the apostles and the writers of what we now call the New

Testament are liars. In that case, the entire gospel message along with the writings of the New Testament is a scam. Paul continues by stating that if the resurrection is a lie, then Christianity is a lie, in which case anyone who has been living the Christian life has been living a lie. Given the incredible sacrifice and commitment required of a true disciple of Jesus, Paul concludes that if the resurrection is a lie, then the Christian is to be pitied above all men. If Christ is not raised, then why not "eat, drink and be merry, for tomorrow we die."

Perhaps at first Paul's declaration that Christians are to be pitied more than all men if the resurrection claim is a hoax seems a bit farfetched. Isn't Paul overstating his case just a bit?

Paul's statement is certainly diametrically opposed to the claim of the famous philosopher and mathematician Pascal, who made what is commonly known as Pascal's wager. Pascal made what at first glance may appear to be a perfectly logical challenge to the unbeliever. In essence he claimed that even if one could not decide for sure whether or not a creator exists, it is better to believe than not to believe. The argument is that if the Creator exists and one does not believe then one may be in big trouble. The reverse of the argument, according to Pascal, is that even if one believes in God and it turns out that he does not exist, nothing is lost. There is nothing to be lost in believing, whether that belief is based on truth or not, but there is a lot to be lost in unbelief if God actually does exist.

Typical First Century Hebrew Tomb, Mount Carmel, Israel (Photo by Julie Geissler)

Whether or not the logic of Pascal holds up in scholastic circles, Paul, a claimed eyewitness to the resurrection, states clearly that Pascal's wager is wrong, at least in the case of Christianity. Given the great sacrifice of time, energy, fortune, emotional energy and the like required of a disciple, Paul states that if all this is given over to a lie, then we are to be pitied more than all men. What a cruel fate it would be to give one's whole life to a hoax.

History would give us a number of examples of people giving their all for something that does not exist. Coronado and others spent their life's energy searching for El Dorado—the City of Gold, when no such city existed. Henry Hudson and many others gave their lives searching for a Northwest Passage that did not exist. Hundreds of similar stories could be cited. However, there is a key difference between these examples and the Christian life. With both the search for El Dorado and for the Northwest Passage, even in seeking a nonexistent goal, Coronado and Hudson gave some sort of meaning to their lives. Both opened up large areas to exploration. In the end, what they accomplished was at least as significant as that for which they were searching.

One might argue similarly for Christianity. Even if it is not really true, then at least the Christian life is better than the alternative. Even if one does not go to heaven, at least life down here was better for having believed, yet Paul is saying that if the resurrection is a lie, then the Christian claim is the cruelest of hoaxes.

There are some other New Testament passages that back up this claim. In 1 Peter 1:3-4 one finds the statement, "In his great mercy, he has given us new birth into a living hope through the resurrection of Jesus Christ from the dead, and into an inheritance that can never perish, spoil or fade—kept in heaven for you." Hope certainly is at the heart of Christianity. The resurrection of Jesus Christ provides that hope. However, if Jesus Christ was not raised, then that hope is a false hope. In fact, it is a cruel hope. The greater the sacrifice to obtain some sort of a hope, the more cruel it becomes if false. Christianity is the ultimate illustration of this principle.

Another supporting example is found in Acts 17:31, "For he [God] has set a day when he will judge the world with justice by the man he has appointed. He has given proof of this to all men by raising him from the dead." This is clearly a reference to Jesus Christ. The Christian life is lived in the assumption that our every action will be brought into a final judgment before God. According to the passage just referred to, the resurrection is the ultimate proof of this. In fact, if Jesus was not raised, then neither will there be a judgment day, so "eat, drink and be merry, for tomorrow we die."

To reinterate, in this chapter, we will be looking at the validity of the claim that Jesus was raised from the dead. Bear in mind what is at stake here. If the claim is true, then without question, only the worst of fools would not accept the gospel message, with all that is implied therein. If it is a false claim, then Christianity is not left as a nice religion. It is not "one of many paths to the same end," as some religious persons might claim. If Jesus Christ was not indeed raised from the dead, then Christianity is a lie and a cruel hoax. Its followers are deceived and are to be pitied above all men.

JUST THE FACTS, MA'AM, JUST THE FACTS

The above subtitle is a reference to one of the author's favorite old-time TV shows. However, the reference may date me just a bit. It comes from the show *Dragnet*, a 1960s and 1970s police docudrama in which its leading character, the deadpan police detective Joe Friday, would often ask emotional crime victims for "just the facts."

It is time to consider the question, so let us look at a few undisputed historical facts relating to the validity of the resurrection. What do we know about the resurrection that even the most die-hard of skeptics would have to admit is true, unless they were simply not aware of what is known from historical records?

First of all, one can be sure without a doubt that Jesus is in fact an historical figure. Some would actually want to paint the entire person of Jesus as a myth. As recently as the twentieth century, no less a figure than the philosopher Bertrand Russell (a strident atheist, by the way) would boldly claim that, "Historically, it is quite doubtful whether Christ ever existed at all, and if He did, we do not know anything about him."[2] In reality, all this quote does is prove the extreme bias of Bertrand Russell. This bias is so off the charts that it should cause the intelligent reader to question the validity of anything Russell might say.

For an uneducated person to claim that the historicity of Jesus as a person is a myth would be forgivable, but for someone as educated as Bertrand Russell to make such a claim is extremely irresponsible. Russell was certainly well aware than no reputable historian would doubt the existence of Jesus any more than they would question the reality of Julius Caesar. Arguably, there is as much material evidence for the existence of Jesus Christ as any other ancient historical figure. One could mention the great number of words about Jesus in the Encyclopedia Britannica or a few of the dozens of historians from the first two centuries AD who refer to his life and what he did. It is no exaggeration to state that anyone who claims not to believe that Jesus existed is either

---

2. Bertrand Russell, *Why I Am Not a Christian and Other Essays on Religion and Related Subjects*, (Simon and Schuster, New York, 1957), p. 16.

extremely ignorant of history or so biased that the wise listener would do well to turn their ear in another direction.

Another fact of history that would be accepted by even the most strident skeptic (assuming that they do not have the kind of extreme bias exhibited by Bertrand Russell) is that Jesus Christ was in fact crucified outside Jerusalem by the Roman authorities under Pontius Pilate. If Jesus was not crucified, then he also was not raised from the dead, so this is an important point.

One can be sure that Jesus was crucified as recorded in the Bible because historians with no stake in believing this claim have recorded the event. For example, one can quote from Cornelius Tacitus, who lived from AD 55-120. Tacitus is generally considered to be one of the most important and reliable historians of ancient Rome. In addition, in those of his writings that are relevant to early Christianity, Tacitus was not writing about events of the distant past. He wrote concerning events that had occurred in his own lifetime, or at most a couple of generations before he lived. Tacitus wrote two extensive historical works, *Annals*, covering Roman political history from the death of the emperor Augustine in AD 14 to the end of Nero's reign in AD 68, and *Histories*, which began with the death of Nero and continued to the death of Domitian in AD 96. To quote from Tacitus concerning Jesus:

> "But not all the relief that could come from man, not all the bounties that the prince could bestow, nor all the atonements which could be presented to the gods, availed to relieve Nero from the infamy of being believed to have ordered the conflagration, the fire of Rome. Hence to suppress the rumor, he falsely charged with the guilt, and punished with the most exquisite tortures, the persons commonly called Christians, who were hated for their enormities. Christus, the founder of the name, was put to death by Pontius Pilate, procurator of Judea in the reign of Tiberius: but the pernicious superstition, repressed for a time, broke out again, not only through Judea, where the mischief originated, but through the city of Rome also."[3]

Despite his desire to defame the Christian religion, Tacitus unwittingly provided strong historical evidence to support the claims of Christianity. This pagan enemy of the Christians recorded the crucifixion of Jesus Christ under Pontius Pilate.

Another Roman writer who reported a few details regarding the early church was Lucian of Samosota. Lucian was a social critic who wrote sarcastically of Christians. In one of his commentaries, he said:

---

3. Cornelius Tacitus, *Annals*, XV, 44.

The Ultimate Miracle

"The Christians, you know, worship a man to this day—the distinguished personage who introduced their novel rites, and was crucified on that account.... You see, these misguided creatures start with the general conviction that they are immortal for all time, which explains the contempt of death and voluntary self-devotion which are so common among them; and then it was impressed on them by their original lawgiver that they are converted, and deny the gods of Greece, and worship the crucified sage, and live after his laws."[4]

Obviously, Lucian wrote with malice toward Christians in general, but fortunately for us, he recorded for future ages an independent commentary on Christian character, as well as relating the event of Jesus' crucifixion.

Other pagan writers from the first two centuries could be called as witnesses to the fact that Jesus Christ was crucified in Jerusalem. Another source of evidence to support the fact of the crucifixion is Jewish writings of the first two centuries AD. The most famous of these comes from the Jewish historian, Josephus who was referred to previously. In his book *Antiquities*, Josephus records concerning Jesus, "...and when Pilate, at the suggestion of the principal men among us, had condemned him to the cross, those that loved him at the first did not forsake him."[5] Being a Jew, Josephus had no motive to support the Christian position, but he does faithfully report that Jesus was crucified under the orders of Pontius Pilate, supplying the additional information that it was under pressure from the Jewish leaders.

Another source of Jewish sentiment is found in the Talmud—a collection of commentaries to the Hebrew Bible written primarily in the first two centuries AD. Of course, the Talmud was not written about Jesus, but in it one can find some statements which refer to him. For example consider a passage in the Babylonian Talmud:

> It has been taught: On the eve of the Passover they hanged Yeshu. And an announcer went out in front of him, for forty days (declaring): "He is going to be stoned, because

---

4. Lucian of Samosota, *The Death of Peregrine*, (Translated by Fowler and Fowler, The Clarendon Press, 1949) pp. 11-13. The two quotes above are found in Josh McDowell's book *The New Evidence That Demands a Verdict*, (Thomas Nelson Publishers, Nashville, 1999). A more complete list of very early pagan authors who referred to Jesus Christ and to his crucifixion can be found in this reference.

5. Flavius Josephus, *Antiquities*, (Ward, Lock, Bowden & Co., New York, 1900) XVIII, 33.

he practiced sorcery and enticed and led Israel astray. Anyone who knows anything in his favor, let him come and plead in his behalf." But not having found anything in his favor, they hanged him on the eve of the Passover.[6]

It is clear in this passage from the Talmud that Yeshu refers to Jesus and that hanging refers to crucifixion (see Galatians 3:13). Besides this, the Jewish author provides independent confirmation of the biblical claim that Jesus was crucified on the eve of the Passover.

In summary, the clear testimony of history is that Jesus Christ was in fact crucified in Jerusalem under the authority of the governor Pontius Pilate, on the eve of the Passover, as recorded in the New Testament scripture.

There is a third historical fact that is relevant to the crucifixion. This very significant fact is that the claim of Jesus Christ having been raised from the dead was made publicly in Jerusalem almost immediately after the event. The apostles and other followers of Jesus in the same city where the events occurred declared the resurrection openly. It was proclaimed at the same time and place where the eyewitnesses to the events, including the Roman officials and soldiers, as well as the Jews who did not accept Jesus' teaching, had every opportunity to bring forth evidence to the contrary. This fact will be very important in establishing the truth of the resurrection.

The Bible records the first time the resurrection was publicly declared, in front of thousands of people. This event, which occurred seven weeks after the execution of Jesus, is recorded in Acts chapter two. "This man was handed over to you by God's set purpose and foreknowledge; and you, with the help of wicked men, put him to death by nailing him to the cross. But God raised him from the dead, freeing him from the agony of death, because it was impossible for death to keep its hold on him" (Acts 2:24,25). To the skeptic, the simple fact that Peter's sermon is recorded in the Bible does not supply sufficient proof that the resurrection was openly and publicly preached within a very short time of the supposed event. In fact, there have even been some critics of Christianity who have argued, despite what is written in Acts 2, that the resurrection claim was not made for a number of generations after the death of Jesus. The arguments of these Bible critics is that a group of disciples of Jesus who wanted to build up his reputation with those they were attempting to convert made up the resurrection story. Unfortunately for the Bible critic, this scenario simply cannot be reconciled with the facts.

---

6. From the Babylonian Talmud, *Sanhedrin*, 43a

There has simply never been a time when the Christian church did not have the resurrection as a central part of the message of the gospel. In fact, a brief survey of the book of Acts will prove to the reader that an account of the resurrection is a significant part of every recorded gospel sermon. The well-prepared skeptic might argue that Acts and the other books of the New Testament were either not written until well into the second century AD, or that they were changed to reflect the newly developing resurrection claim. However, during the twentieth century, this charge was completely discredited by discoveries of increasingly ancient actual copies of the New Testament documents. The oldest reliably dated partial manuscript of the New Testament, known as the Rylands papyrus, has been dated at 130 AD, about fifty years from the writing of the gospel of John. We will explore the integrity of the New Testament text in chapter six, but suffice it to say that with the evidence in hand, it is inconceivable to the knowledgeable scholar of the Bible that such a key doctrine as the resurrection of Jesus Christ from the dead could have been added in at a later date.

There are references to the resurrection from extra-biblical sources such as Josephus.[7]

> ...when Pilate, at the suggestion of the principal men among us, had condemned him to the cross, those that loved him at the first did not forsake him; for he appeared to them alive again the third day; as the divine prophets had foretold these and ten thousand other wonderful things concerning him. And the tribe of Christians so named from him are not extinct at this day.

In addition, early Christian writings, some from as early as the end of the first century, provide proof that the resurrection was preached since the beginning of Christianity. For example, one could quote Ignatius (AD 50-115), the bishop of Antioch, a protégé of the apostle John, from his epistle to the Trallians, "He was crucified and died under Pontius Pilate. He really, and not merely in appearance, was crucified, and died, in the sight of beings in heaven and on earth, and under the earth. He also rose again in three days..." Is anyone willing to support the claim that Ignatius waited for his teacher, John, to die, and then made up a bogus account of the resurrection, going against all the other teachers in the early church?

Besides this fact, one can take note of the day of Christian worship. From the inception of the New Testament church, the disciples began meeting on the first day of the week—Sunday to commemorate the

---

7. Josephus, *Antiquities*, xviii.3.3.

resurrection of Jesus Christ. There is no credible evidence for the early church ever meeting for their principle worship of the week on any other day. If the resurrection was not pronounced by the eyewitnesses from the very beginning, how can one account for the fact that the church has met since its very beginnings on Sunday to commemorate this very event?[8]

So there is no reasonable doubt that the resurrection was publicly proclaimed in Jerusalem in the immediate aftermath of the event. Claims to the contrary are not based on careful consideration of the facts.

The last fact of history we will consider that is relevant to the question of the resurrection of Jesus is the most significant of the four. The fact is that the tomb in which Jesus was laid was empty on the third day. It may seem a bold move to claim this as historical fact, but given the assumption that Jesus was crucified in Jerusalem on the eve of the Passover, as proven above, there is no logical alternative. The tomb where Jesus' body was laid was empty on the third day.

How can one claim this to be a fact? That is easy. If the tomb had not been empty, then as soon as the disciples began to proclaim the resurrection of Jesus, the Jews would have simply escorted people over to the tomb to show them the body. This did not happen. The reason this did not happen is simple. The tomb was empty. In fact, the Jews who in later times attempted to explain away the resurrection never raised the claim that the tomb was not empty.

How did the tomb become empty? That is the subject of the rest of this chapter, but the undeniable fact (undeniable to those willing to consider the facts) is that the tomb where Jesus' body was laid was empty.

To summarize, the facts of history are these: Jesus did live, he was crucified in Jerusalem under the authority of Pontius Pilate on the eve of the Passover, his resurrection was publicly declared in Jerusalem almost immediately after the event, and the tomb where his body was laid was empty on the third day.

THERE HAS GOT TO BE ANOTHER EXPLANATION

Now we can proceed to the heart of the question. What is the most reasonable explanation of the facts? Remember that the explanation

---

8. A brief survey of the writings of the early church fathers will support this claim. A number of references to early church writings can be cited for the interested reader. These would include Cyril C. Richardson, *Early Christian Fathers*, (The Macmillan Company, New York, 1970); and Maxwell Staniforth, *Early Christian Writings*, (Penguin Books, 1968).

that Jesus was resurrected requires an extra strong measure of proof, as such an explanation is outside the range of normal events.

We will proceed by considering possible alternative explanations of the facts. Historically, there have only been a fairly small number of alternative explanations that skeptics of Christianity have raised. Each of these explanations will be considered in turn, but to summarize, these attempted explanations of the facts are listed below.

1. The stolen body theory.
2. The swoon theory.
3. The mass hallucination theory.

Other explanations could be listed, but they are either variations of the three listed above or are so unreasonable as not to deserve separate treatment.

Where should one look for the most carefully considered arguments against the resurrection? One could look to Jewish writers. Historically, the Jews have had the most at stake in disproving the resurrection of Jesus Christ to their people. If Jesus was in fact resurrected, then the only reasonable alternative for a Jew would be to accept him as the Messiah he claimed to be. Therefore, it is a good idea to ask what has historically been the Jewish answer to the resurrection.

The answer is that the Jewish response to the resurrection claim has been to invoke the stolen body theory. For example, in Justin Martyr's defense of Christianity in the second century AD, he mentions a Jewish opponent whom he quotes as saying "one Jesus, a Galilean deceiver, whom we crucified; but his disciples stole him by night from the tomb, where he was laid, when unfastened from the cross, and now deceive men by asserting that he has risen from the dead and ascended into heaven."[9] Jewish medieval literature also repeated the charge that the disciples stole Jesus' body. For this reason, we will consider this alternative first.

ALTERNATIVE #1: THE STOLEN BODY THEORY

Again, the idea is to explain the facts that almost any open-minded person would concede are true. Jesus was crucified in Jerusalem, his body was interred in a tomb, but three days later, it was no longer there. Almost immediately afterward, the disciples of Jesus were openly declaring that he was raised from the dead. One obvious approach to an explanation of the facts is that someone stole Jesus' body from the tomb. Is this a reasonable explanation of the facts?

---

9. Justin Martyr, *Dialogue Against Trypho*, 108

The answer to this question, of course, would depend on whom one would accuse of snatching the body. Was it the Roman soldiers? Could it have been the Jewish opponents to Jesus? Or might some of Jesus' followers have stolen the body? In order to answer this question, some of the details surrounding the crucifixion and burial are relevant. These details will be taken from the gospel accounts of the events in question.[10]

A number of facts recorded in the gospels are relevant to the stolen body theory. First, Jesus declared publicly that he would be killed and raised on the third day. His opponents were well aware of this fact, and did all they could to prevent a faked resurrection. For example, Jesus said to the crowds in Matthew 12:40, "For as Jonah was three days and three nights in the belly of a huge fish, so the Son of Man will be three days and three nights in the heart of the earth." Or one could mention Jesus' discussion with his disciples in Matthew 16:21, "From that time on Jesus began to explain to his disciples that he must go to Jerusalem and suffer many things at the hands of the elders, chief priests and teachers of the law, and that he must be killed and on the third day be raised to life." (Also see Matthew 17:22,23, Matthew 20:17-19, Mark 10: 32-34, Luke 18:31-33, and John 16:16.)

Because those who conspired to have Jesus killed were well aware of his prediction that he would be resurrected from the dead, they did everything humanly possible to prevent Jesus' disciples pulling off some sort of hoax:

> The next day, the one after Preparation Day, the chief priests and the Pharisees went to Pilate. "Sir," they said, "we remember that while he was still alive that deceiver said, 'After three days I will rise again.'" So give the order for the tomb to be made secure until the third day. Otherwise, his disciples may come and steal the body and tell the people that he has been raised from the dead. This last deception will be worse than the first. "Take a guard," Pilate answered. "Go make the tomb as secure as you know how." So they went and made the tomb secure by putting a seal on the stone and posting the guard (Matthew 27:62-66).

---

10. Admittedly, the facts mentioned in this section are not as strongly attested to in historical accounts outside the Bible as those listed above. In chapter six of this book, it will be shown that the New Testament stands as one of the most reliable, if not *the* most reliable historical document of the ancient world we have. In a nutshell, the gospel writers give such specific details in their accounts and those details hold up so well to historical scrutiny, that one would do well to simply take the accounts of the events surrounding the crucifixion at face value. The reader who feels uncomfortable with this claim may want to read chapter six first and come back to this chapter afterward.

The Ultimate Miracle

Little did they know at the time that they would be helping provide strong support for belief in the resurrection. It is ironic that in attempting to ensure that the body could not be stolen, the enemies of Jesus provided great proof that the body was in fact not stolen.

Besides, this was no ordinary guard that was posted in front of the tomb of Joseph of Arimathea, where Jesus' body was laid. This was a cohort of the most hardened soldiers in the world at that time: Roman legionnaires! A very large stone was rolled in front of the tomb, and a number of heavily armed Roman soldiers stood a twenty-four hour guard in front of the tomb.

So who stole the body? Was it the Jews? What possible motive would they have had? No one has ever proposed a reasonable motive for the Jewish leaders to steal Jesus' body. They were the same ones who had Pilate post a guard. Even if someone could come up with some sort of convoluted motive for the Jews to steal the body, as soon as the resurrection was claimed by the followers of Jesus, surely they would have promptly produced the body and put an immediate stop to the public preaching of the resurrection.

Would the Roman soldiers steal the body? This idea is even more outlandish. What would be the motive? According to historical accounts of Roman military discipline, the soldiers themselves were liable to death if they failed in their charge to guard the tomb, so they certainly had a heavy disincentive to stealing the body, or to let anyone else steal the body, for that matter. The Romans certainly would not want to steal Jesus' corpse. The last thing they wanted was another Messiah story to stir up the Jews in rebellion against Rome. It certainly was not the Jewish opponents of Jesus or the Romans who stole the body, if indeed the body was stolen.

The fact is that the only conceivable people with a motive to steal the body from the tomb would have been the disciples of Jesus. The stolen body scenario, then, comes down to this. Did followers of Jesus steal his body from the tomb? We will break this question down into three parts:

1. Would they have stolen the body?
2. Could they have stolen the body?
3. Did they steal the body?

WOULD THEY HAVE STOLEN THE BODY?

Would the followers of Jesus have stolen his body? That is a good question. Given how difficult it would have been to steal the body of Jesus from a well-guarded tomb, the disciples would need to have had a very strong motive. Joseph of Arimathea, a believer in Jesus, chose the internment location, so it could not have been because they simply wanted to move it to another gravesite. The only conceivable motivation for Jesus' followers to steal the body was in order to allow them to deceive the people into believing in the resurrection. The reason the chief priests and Pharisees had Jesus' tomb guarded was to prevent just such a deception (Matthew 27:62-66).

From what we know about the apostles, is there any chance they would have decided to fake a resurrection? From the gospel accounts it is extremely doubtful that the apostles even had the resurrection in mind when Jesus died. One finds the followers of Jesus scattering and hiding out in secret locations after the crucifixion. The disciples were a frightened and demoralized band of idealists. The whole idea of a group of them gathering around and hatching a plot to steal the body under these circumstances goes absolutely counter to what we know of their psychological state, as well as their character. From what we know of Peter, it is inconceivable to think of him gathering around himself some of the apostles and proposing: "Hey guys, I have an idea. Now that they have killed Jesus, let's take advantage of the situation and steal his body. Then we will pretend he raised from the dead."

Even if there were some evidence to support the idea that they stole the body (there is absolutely none), it would be next to impossible to convince a jury that these men would have hatched such a plot. Although both Jesus and his followers were at different times accused of lying, no one could ever make a charge of deceit stick. Whether one accepts their teaching or not, a charge of deceit will simply not hold up. There is no evidence that these men and women were deceitful.

Even if one could grant the possibility that these followers, avowedly honest as they were in every other situation, might for some unknown reason hatch a deceitful plot, one could still reasonably ask whether they would. What is the motive? Why would they want to steal the body? What could they hope to gain by claiming that Jesus was resurrected from the dead? To do so would obviously have gone against the clear teaching of their leader, who commanded scrupulous honesty. Besides, even if they could pull off such a hoax, the only possible result for them would ultimately be persecution, torture and death.

Again, even if one could accept, as unlikely as it would be, that the apostles might have launched a deceitful conspiracy to pretend Jesus was raised from the dead, surely at least one of them would have relented upon pain of death. A number of the other apostles were martyred as well. Church tradition holds that all the apostles died a martyr's death except John. None of the apostles ever recanted their story. One can be absolutely assured that if they had, the Jewish leaders would have paraded the turncoat through Judea in order to discredit the resurrection claim. This is not even counting hundreds of other witnesses to the resurrection, none of whom ever recanted, even on pain of death. Is it even conceivable that dozens of people would go to the grave for a blatant lie? Can anyone believe such a thing? No way.

COULD THEY HAVE STOLEN THE BODY?

So, the followers certainly would not have stolen the body. But even if they would have, could they have? Assuming the impossible—that the apostles hatched a plot to steal Jesus' body—could they have pulled it off? By what means could they whisk the body of Jesus away?

Remember that there was a guard of Roman legionnaires in front of the tomb. Besides, there was a large stone blocking the entrance. What does the skeptic propose? Did the apostles, along with a few allies, attack a number of Roman soldiers, the most well-trained and best equipped fighters in the world at that time? What would they use to fight these men? Stones? Sticks? Swords? Would they do this without any armor? Besides, even if one could imagine this battle for the body of Jesus occurring, where were the slain Roman soldiers? Surely there would have been some evidence of this fierce struggle. Surely they would have had casualties as well. Remember these are the same men who fled in fear when Jesus was arrested. Could a pitched battle between a ragtag group of poorly armed Jews and a group of Roman soldiers occur on the outskirts of Jerusalem without anyone ever even noticing? The evidence clearly shows the apostles incapable of such a bold and deadly attack.

Most skeptics will concede that this idea is ludicrous. Perhaps, they retort, the disciples bribed the soldiers to help them remove the body and conspired with them to cover up the deed. At least this one has a veneer of believability to it, but let us look closely at this scenario. This is the story the Jewish leaders attempted to promulgate, as recorded in Matthew 28:11-15.

> While the women were on their way, some of the guards went into the city and reported to the chief priests everything that had happened. When the chief priests had met with the elders and devised a plan, they gave the soldiers a large sum of money, telling them, "You are to say, 'His disciples came during the night and stole him away while we were asleep.' If this report gets to the governor, we will satisfy him and keep you out of trouble." So the soldiers took

the money and did as they were instructed. And this story has been widely circulated among the Jews to this very day.

How much money would be required to bribe a company of Roman soldiers? The death penalty was at stake here. Justin Martyr recorded all the offenses for which Roman soldiers were liable to the death penalty. These included desertion, inciting mutiny, leaving the night watch and deserting one's post, among other similar offenses. To accept this scenario to be true, one must believe that the disciples were able to come up with enough money to bribe an entire group of soldiers who would be willing to risk imprisonment at the least, or possibly even death. Would any amount of money suffice for such an end? Did the followers of Jesus have such a huge amount of money? Besides, would Jesus' followers do such a thing? Of course not. This would run absolutely counter to everything they were taught by their beloved leader, Jesus Christ.

On the contrary, the version of the story recorded in the New Testament as quoted above is far more believable. First, the Jewish political leaders had sufficient political clout with the Roman government to protect the soldiers from punishment for the crime of falling asleep at their post. Certainly the Roman soldiers were well aware of this fact, and of the fact that Jesus' followers had no such influence with the Romans. Second, they had access to large resources of money to make a successful bribe. Third, history records that the Jewish leadership was not beyond using deceit, bribery and intimidation to achieve their desired goals. None of these are true of the followers of Jesus. Whose story is believable?

DID THEY STEAL THE BODY?

So, the disciples would not have stolen the body, and even if somehow they did want to do it, they could not have pulled it off. The third question is, even if they would have (already proven impossible) and even if they could have (also already proven impossible), did they do it? Did the followers of Jesus steal his body? The answer, again, is an emphatic no! Even if, against all odds, one could be logically convinced that the disciples would hatch a resurrection conspiracy, and even assuming that they could either militarily defeat the Roman guard and move the stone, or perhaps come up with enough money to bribe the soldiers to risk their lives and form a conspiracy; still, one can prove that they did not do it.

What is the evidence to support this claim? First, there is the appearance of the tomb on that fateful Sunday. What was left behind in

The Ultimate Miracle

the tomb? The book of John records that when Peter and John came upon the tomb they found the stone rolled away and a pile of linen strips lying there. The only conceivable reason for John to record such a detail is because it is what actually happened. According to Jewish custom, when a body was prepared for burial, it was wrapped in strips of linen. When the empty tomb was discovered, the linen strips were lying there, but not the body.

When they stole the body, would the disciples have taken the time to remove the linen strips? Why would they do this? The body would have significant decomposition by this time, and besides, these men had all fled in fear of death. Would they be willing to chance death, just to steal a body? Members of the jury, do you believe this story? Would a group of insecure, nervous conspirators take the time to unwrap a body, especially given that it would already be decomposing? Would they want to transport the body of the most recognizable person in Jerusalem uncovered through the countryside just to perpetrate a hoax?

There is an even stronger argument to prove that the disciples did not steal the body. Jesus was alive after the event. The strongest proof of all that his body was not stolen is that Jesus was not even dead. Over five hundred eyewitnesses were able to see Jesus and many were able to speak with him alive during the weeks after he was killed. Isn't this the strongest possible evidence? Not just a few people, but well over 500 eyewitnesses.

> For what I received I passed on to you as of first importance: that Christ died for our sins according to the Scriptures, that he was buried, that he was raised on the third day according to the Scriptures, and that he appeared to Peter, and then to the Twelve. After that, he appeared to more than five hundred of the brothers at the same time, most of whom are still living, though some have fallen asleep. Then he appeared to James, then to all the apostles, and last of all he appeared to me also, as to one abnormally born (1 Corinthians 15:3-7).

In his letter to the Corinthian church, written within one generation of the death of Jesus, Paul spoke of the existence of hundreds of witnesses to the resurrection as common knowledge. To the skeptical, he in effect said, "Go ask the witnesses for yourselves if you do not believe me." Remember that Paul made this statement in the same context as his statement quoted earlier that if Jesus was not raised, then the believer's faith is in vain.

What is the skeptic to do with over five hundred eyewitnesses? The number of eyewitnesses is so compelling that Jesus being alive after the crucifixion could easily have been included in the list of "facts" earlier in this chapter. It was only left off because no extra-Biblical source specifically mentions the number of eyewitnesses.

Besides, these eyewitnesses are generally of the highest possible quality. They are not prison inmates seeking lighter sentences in return for sympathetic treatment. Not at all! On the contrary, these witnesses are the seed of the New Testament church: the most honest, law-abiding, sacrificial, unselfish people the Roman Empire ever witnessed. Most of them were in fear for their lives because of potential persecution. Persecutors especially targeted eyewitnesses, yet there is no record of even one eyewitness recanting their story. If even one eyewitness were to later come out and admit that the supposed appearances of Jesus after his death were all a hoax, one can be absolutely certain that the enemies of the early church would have paraded that person throughout Judea. There is no record of such a person or of any Jewish opponent of Christianity even claiming there was such a person. This is despite the fact that some of the witnesses were killed for their faith.

Would anyone die for something they know to be a lie? Would hundreds do the same? Is there any answer to this argument?

In desperation, the skeptic might argue that Paul is the only one who claimed all these eyewitnesses. He or she might argue that Paul invented the existence of hundred of witnesses. This argument does not work. Obviously, Paul was making such a claim before people who had access to at least some of the witnesses he mentioned. How else could he have challenged his readers to check it out for themselves? Besides, Paul was certainly not the only biblical writer to record these events. One could mention Matthew, Mark, Luke, John and Peter. Anyone who would claim that Paul made up the story of the hundreds of eyewitnesses simply must be ignorant of the facts of the case. It would be like someone reading in a history book about the genocide in Cambodia under the Pol Pot regime and claiming that the story was made up.

Whatever one's view of the resurrection account, the claim that Jesus' body was stolen is unsupportable. Attempting to explain the fact of the empty tomb by invoking the claim that the disciples stole the body inescapably runs into the fact that there is no way these followers of Jesus would have stolen the body. Besides, even if they wanted to, it would have been very unlikely for them to accomplish it. And even if they would have and could have, the fact is that they did not. Jesus was alive and appearing before witnesses in the days immediately after his crucifixion. Skeptics can write books or produce movies based on the stolen body theory, but a fable repeated a thousand times is still a fable.

ALTERNATIVE #2: THE SWOON THEORY

Let us move on to the second most commonly mentioned alternative explanation to the resurrection. This is what is most often referred to as the swoon theory. Historically, Jewish antagonists to Christianity have not generally mentioned this alternative, for reasons that will be seen shortly, but skeptics have attempted to bring forth this "theory" off and on since the time of the enlightenment. J. N. D. Anderson, a lecturer in Oriental Law at the University of London and an expert in studies of the resurrection, has claimed that the first recorded mention of this theory is by Karl Venturini in the eighteenth century. He also mentions that some Muslim groups have made a habit of using this argument.[11]

There are a few variant versions of the theory, but the essence of these arguments can be summed up as follows: Yes, Jesus was crucified outside Jerusalem under the orders of Pontius Pilate. However, after six hours on the cross, he passed out ("swooned"). Although he had gone unconscious, the Roman soldiers in charge of the execution mistook him for dead and cut him down from the cross. His disciples dragged him off, still unconscious, failing to notice that he was actually still breathing, and had him placed in the tomb of Joseph of Arimathea. Upon being laid in the cool tomb, Jesus awakened. After gathering strength for several hours, Jesus removed his grave clothes, moved back the stone and, without being detected by the soldiers guarding the tomb, snuck off. Later, he found some of his disciples in hiding and claimed to have been raised from the dead.

Perhaps the reader is already saying to himself, "Come on, give me a break," but it bears keeping in mind that some have taken this theory seriously. In fact, Hugh Schoenfield wrote a book entitled *The Passover Plot* that proposes a variant of this theory. This book has made the rounds among certain skeptics of Christianity. In this book, Schoenfield makes the claim that the entire crucifixion scene was a conspiracy on the part of Jesus so that he could falsely claim to have been raised from the dead, and therefore to be the Messiah. According to the author, the wine vinegar offered to Jesus while on the cross contained a drug that would cause him to become temporarily unconscious. The purpose of the drug was to allow him to fake his own death and ultimately to fake his resurrection. In the ending of the *Passover Plot*, Jesus' well-planned conspiracy was thwarted when, contrary to his plan, a soldier thrust a sword into Jesus' side, ending his life. This might make for an interesting novel if it were not written with deliberate intent to deceive the poorly informed and gullible critic. It is an obvious attempt to

---

11. J.N.D. Anderson, *Christianity, The Witness of History,* (Tyndale Press, London, 1969).

enforce a preconceived opinion into a set of historical facts with which it is completely inconsistent.

Is the swoon theory believable? Let us consider the facts. The reader is invited to read one of the gospel accounts of the resurrection, recorded in Matthew, Mark, Luke or John. Before his crucifixion, Jesus was severely beaten in front of the Sanhedrin (Matthew 26:67) and flogged by the Roman guard (Matthew 27:26). It is well known that flogging at the hands of the Romans could leave its victim near death. After the flogging, Jesus was severely beaten about the head with rods (Matthew 27:30). Although documents external to the Bible do not record these events, the careful and specific details in the gospel accounts, so easily refutable to any of the early readers of Matthew and the other gospels, can only be explained as an accurate rendering of the events. After undergoing these tortures, Jesus was too weak to carry the cross bar on which he was to be impaled. A bystander was called to carry it to the place of the execution. Does Schoenfeld really believe Jesus would have been willing to undergo all this in order to be able to fake his own resurrection?

Presumably, Jesus was not far from death when he was crucified, which would do much to explain the fact that he only suffered on the cross for six hours, compared to the typical twelve to twenty-four hour time span of a crucifixion before death occurred. So here we have Jesus, already dead on the cross, but the gospel writers provide more details of the scene.

> Now it was the day of Preparation (for the Passover), and the next day was to be a special Sabbath. Because the Jews did not want the bodies left on the crosses during the Sabbath, they asked Pilate to have the legs broken and the bodies taken down. The soldiers therefore came and broke the legs of the first man who had been crucified with Jesus, and then those of the other. But when they came to Jesus and found that he was already dead, they did not break his legs. Instead, one of the soldiers pierced Jesus' side with a spear, bringing a sudden flow of blood and water. The man who saw it has given testimony, and his testimony is true. He knows that he tells the truth, and he testifies so that you also may believe (John 19:31-35).

The Roman execution detail was well acquainted with death by crucifixion. When the Jews requested that the crucifixions be ended quickly out of reverence for the coming Passover, the guards agreed to end it by breaking the legs of the prisoners. Apparently, it was common knowledge that if the legs of someone being crucified were broken, they would no longer be able to push themselves up, and would soon die of suffocation. When the soldiers came to Jesus, they saw that he was already dead. A person hanging limp and unsupported from a cross would die of suffocation within just a few minutes. In other words, a person who "swooned" while undergoing crucifixion would die in very short order unless he were to revive from the swoon at least sufficiently to push up with his feet on the nails in order to catch a breath. Would anyone doubt the witness of these Roman soldiers who were experts on death by crucifixion?

However one feels about the soldier's ability to know the difference between the living and the dead, one of them thrust a spear into the side of Jesus. Before the crucifixion, Jesus was already near death. Next he was hung and killed on the cross, and now he received, in addition, a wound that, if left untreated, almost certainly would have killed him.

John provides one significant additional detail that seals the case. When the sword was thrust into Jesus' side, a mixture of blood and water came out. According to medical authorities, this is a sure sign that his blood serum had already begun to separate out. Apparently, Jesus was stabbed in the heart or at least in the region around the heart. The separation of "blood and water" is something that occurs soon after death. John provided a medical detail, the significance of which he probably was not even aware. Has anyone ever come forth to claim that John's eyewitness account is anything other than truthful? Why would John have recorded such a minute detail if it were not true? Why include details in an account that other eyewitnesses who were still alive could refute?

Now, Jesus had already been killed twice over. Whatever small amount of blood remained to circulate at the time of his death had already flowed out of his body due to the sword wound. Next, Jesus' body was wrapped multiple times in linens that covered him from head to foot. Of course, according to the swoon theorists, the women who lovingly performed this funeral rite failed to notice that Jesus was actually still alive, despite the fact that his body was surely undergoing *rigor mortis*. The swoon theory now has Jesus, already nearly dead due to a series of the most serious beatings, then killed on the cross, then given another wound that would have killed him, then being tightly wrapped with cloths that completely covered his face, finally reviving from being killed twice over. Of course, all this happened after his body was laid in the tomb for over a day, having gone without water for over forty-eight hours.

After all this, according to the swoon theory, Jesus had the strength to remove a stone that three healthy adult women were unable to move (Mark 16:3), and managed to sneak past an armed cohort of Roman guards. No one can take this theory seriously!

Consider the words of one medical authority:

> Clearly, the weight of historical and medical evidence indicates that Jesus was dead before the wound to His side was inflicted and supports the traditional view that the spear, thrust between his right ribs, probably perforated not only the right lung but also the pericardium and heart and thereby ensured His death. Accordingly, interpretations based on the assumption that Jesus did not die on the cross appear to be at odds with modern medical knowledge.[12]

It seems that the only way to refute this statement is to assume that the gospel writers were lying when they reported such details as the bursting of blood and water from the wound in Jesus' side. However, this inevitably brings one back to the question, why would John and others deliberately report a specific detail that could be so easily refuted? Normally, when a deceiver creates a lie, they provide as few details as possible so the facts can't be substantiated.

The swoon theory simply does not add up. It is easy to see why most careful critics of Christianity have not used this idea in order to discount the resurrection. It is only effective when used with people who are either predisposed to disbelieve the resurrection or who are ignorant of the recorded events surrounding the resurrection.

ARGUMENT #3 THE MASS HALLUCINATION THEORY

There have been other attempts to refute the claim of resurrection of Jesus Christ from the dead. However, the quality of these arguments decline rapidly. Consider, for example, the mass hallucination theory. According to this theory, all the appearances of Jesus after his death on the cross were visions. In other words, Jesus did not appear before the supposed witnesses to the resurrection, they only thought he had. According to the mass hallucination theory, these visions were some sort of a psychological effect. People who have proposed this idea have assumed that out of some sort of wishful thinking, and under the extreme pressure of persecution, the followers of Jesus had what was in effect a hallucination or a "vision" of a resurrected Jesus.

To be honest, this idea has so little credibility that it probably does not deserve a lot of attention. Nevertheless, let us define terms. One could define a vision as an effect in which the brain of an individual

---

12. William D. Edwards, MD, et al. "On the physical Death of Jesus Christ," *Journal of the American Medical Association*, 255:11, 1986.

The Ultimate Miracle

receives a signal of an image for which there is no corresponding physical object producing that image. Is this what happened to the witnesses of the resurrection? Is this a reasonable explanation of the facts of the resurrection?

Consider what happened during one of these "visions," as recorded in the gospel of Luke.

> While they were still talking about this, Jesus himself stood among them and said to them, "Peace be with you."
>
> They were startled and frightened, thinking they saw a ghost. He said to them, "Why are you troubled, and why do doubts rise in your minds? Look at my hands and my feet. It is I myself! Touch me and see; a ghost does not have flesh and bones, as you see I have."
>
> When he had said this, he showed them his hands and feet. And while they still did not believe it because of joy and amazement, he asked them, "Do you have anything here to eat?" They gave him a piece of broiled fish, and he took it and ate it in their presence (Luke 24:36-43).

Is it possible to touch a vision? Do visions eat fish? Unless those who recorded the gospel accounts were simply lying, these details cause the mass hallucination theory to fall apart of its own weight. However, the whole idea of the hallucination theory is that they were mistaken, but not lying. And even if one could somehow be convinced that those who recorded Jesus eating fish and being touched by the disciples were lying, the mass hallucination theory still would not work, because the mass hallucination theory pre-supposes that the gospel writers actually believed that Jesus appeared before them. Besides, what is one to do with the empty tomb? If hundreds hallucinated the resurrection of Jesus simultaneously, there still is the empty tomb to explain.

There is more that could be said against the mass hallucination theory. Putting aside for a moment the physical contact some had with the resurrected Jesus or the claim that he ate fish in front of the disciples, one could perhaps become convinced that a single person, under the extreme stress of the death of their leader, might somehow have a visual hallucination of Jesus. However, is it even remotely believable that two persons could have the same visual hallucination at the same time? Are there any examples of this kind of event in history? What about all the apostles having more or less the identical hallucination at the same time? Is there precedence for such an event? Most telling of all, is there any way at all to conceive of five hundred persons at once having identical visions of Jesus after his death? Surely these people compared notes after seeing Jesus. Have over five hundred persons of very different psychological makeup ever simultaneously had the same vision?

As mentioned above, other theories to explain away the resurrection have been proposed, but these are either so far out as to not bear mentioning, or are essentially rehashed versions of the theories already mentioned. For the person who desires to look into this further, the author would recommend the book *The New Evidence That Demands a Verdict*.[13]

SUMMARY

It is true that the onus of proof for the resurrection lies with the believer. Besides, the level of proof required is great, because the resurrection of a person who is dead is certainly not within the range of events that one would normally consider possible. However, there are a number of reliable and objective historical facts in this case. These would include the crucifixion of Jesus, the fact that the resurrection was preached by the original witnesses in Jerusalem almost immediately after the event, and the fact of his tomb being empty on the third day. Given the facts that are known, one is left with only one legitimate explanation. Jesus Christ was raised from the dead on the third day.

The facts scream out this conclusion, but so do the lives of the original witnesses. One day Peter was cowering in a courtyard in fear of a servant, denying he even knew Jesus Christ. A few weeks later he was declaring in the boldest possible terms before the Jewish ruling council, "Judge for yourselves whether it is right in God's sight to obey you rather than God. For we cannot help speaking about what we have seen and heard" (Acts 4:19,20). The only event that can explain this radical transformation is the resurrection of Jesus from the dead. Is there any other conceivable way to explain the lives of the apostles after the death of Jesus if one cannot assume that they were completely convinced he had been raised from the dead? And they should know, because they were eyewitnesses of the fact.

---

13. Josh McDowell, *The New Evidence That Demands a Verdict*, (Thomas Nelson Publishers, Nashville, 1999). This book represents a significant improvement on the two earlier editions of *Evidence That Demands a Verdict*, which some readers may be familiar with. Also of interest by McDowell is *The Resurrection Factor*, (Here's Life Publishers, San Bernardino, California, 1981). The author acknowledges help in this section from these sources.

The Ultimate Miracle

Despite the scattering of references listed above, it is exceedingly difficult to find anyone willing to produce a carefully reasoned argument against the resurrection of Jesus Christ. It would appear that the same God who raised his son from the dead did a very good job of creating a case for us to believe it.

It would be difficult to improve on the statement of Thomas Arnold, a former professor of history at Oxford and famous author of a three volume set, *History of Rome*:

> I have been used for many years to study the histories of other times, and to examine and weigh the evidence of those who have written about them and I know of no one fact in the history of mankind which is proved by better and fuller evidence of every sort, to the understanding of a fair inquirer, than the great sign which God hath given us that Christ died and rose again from the dead.

In summary, the only reasonable conclusion of the matter is that Jesus Christ was indeed resurrected from the dead. What will you do in response to this fact?

For Today

1. Why should the resurrection of Jesus Christ require such strong supporting evidence?

2. Can you think of, or have you heard of, any other reasonable arguments against the fact of the bodily resurrection of Jesus from the dead? How would you respond to those arguments?

3. If you have come to believe in the resurrection, what does this event mean to you?

4. If you have not come to believe in the resurrection, what kind of evidence would be sufficient for you to be able to accept the truth of the Biblical claim?

Chapter Four
We Should Have Known It Was Coming

> *Everything must be fulfilled that is written about me in the Law of Moses, the Prophets and the Psalms.*
>
> *—Jesus Christ*

During his ministry in Palestine, Jesus was often challenged on the issue of authority. The religious leaders of his day demanded that Jesus state on what authority he based his teachings. In general, he would let the evidence of the miracles speak for themselves, but on one occasion Jesus replied to his hearers concerning his authority: "You diligently study the Scriptures because you think that by them you possess eternal life. These are the Scriptures that testify about me, yet you refuse to come to me to have life" (John 5:39,40).

In this passage, when Jesus spoke of the Scriptures, he was obviously referring to the Old Testament. Jesus claimed that when the Jews read the Old Testament Scriptures, they were reading about him. Jesus was saying, in effect, "From reading the Scriptures, you should have known I was coming, and you should have recognized me when I came." On what basis could Jesus make such a claim?

A related passage is found in Luke 24:44, in which Jesus was speaking to his disciples. "This is what I told you while I was still with you: Everything must be fulfilled that is written about me in the Law of Moses, the Prophets and the Psalms." Now, this is an amazing claim. The three divisions of the entire Hebrew Bible were the Law of Moses, the Prophets and the Psalms. Therefore, Jesus was telling his followers that when they read the Old Testament, they were reading in detail about him. Jesus boldly claimed to have fulfilled all the prophecies in the Old Testament concerning the Messiah[1].

It is not as if the Jews in Jesus' day were unaware that their scriptures predicted the coming of a Messiah. It was understood by most Jews that God had foretold the sending of a savior for his people. There were many different ideas about the Messiah: that he would be a military ruler, something like David, or a "suffering savior" as implied

---

[1]. In addition to the historical messianic prophecies discussed in this chapter, one could mention hundreds of historical prefigures, foreshadows, types and antitypes relating to Jesus Christ in the Old and New Testaments. These are discussed in detail in the book, *From Shadow to Reality*, (Illumination Publishers, Spring, Texas, 2004).

by such passages as Isaiah 53, or a priestly savior. Some had their own unique concept of the Messiah. In Luke 24:44, Jesus was claiming that he fulfilled every one of the prophecies about the Messiah.

So what are these prophecies? How do we know they were truly prophecies about the Messiah? How do we know Jesus really fulfilled the prophecies? Whether he did or did not fulfill these prophecies, what does that say about the man Jesus Christ? These questions are the subject of this chapter.

It would be helpful to put the prophecies of the Old Testament into an historical context. What is the history of prophecy? "Prophets" have been known in all ages of history. In the context of ancient cultures, a prophet was one who proclaimed the will of "the gods" to the people. Often, such prophets would attempt to verify their teachings by making some sort of verifiable prediction of the future. Whether or not the predictions of the prophet came true were an indication of his or her reliability. This predictive aspect of prophecy is the connotation most familiar to the western mind.

In their time, the prophets of Israel were seen primarily as spokesmen for God, "forth-tellers," rather than "fore-tellers." Their primary message was "thus says the Lord." Nevertheless, with all the important prophets of Israel, an element of predictive prophecy is found as well.

The prophets of Israel were not unique in this. One could use the example of the prophets of Baal, as mentioned often in the Old Testament. Perhaps the most famous of prophets from the ancient world were the Oracles of Delphi. The Oracles were women who lived at the Greek temple dedicated to Apollo in the city of Delphi. The temple was built on the site of a cave out of which produced sulfurous fumes. It was at this cave that the Oracles performed their rites. Those who sought guidance in a personal, civic or military venture would travel to Delphi for a prophecy. Scholars note that the ceremonies of the priestesses may have included ecstatic utterances, not completely unlike modern-day speaking in tongues.

The most famous prophecy of the priestesses of Delphi was the one they made to Croesus, the king of Lydia. Croesus came to the Oracle to ask advice on whether to attack the armies of Persia. The priestess gave a typically enigmatic reply, "Croesus will destroy a great empire." Unfortunately for Croesus, the empire destroyed in the war was Lydia, not Persia. Alexander the Great also reportedly consulted the prophetesses at Delphi before his epic-making crossing of the Dardanelles Straits, which ultimately led to his conquests of almost the entire known world. In this case, the Oracles seemed to have correctly predicted success for Alexander.

When one looks at the advice/prophecy given by the Oracles at Delphi, a familiar pattern will emerge. These prophecies seem to have been either vague in what they predicted, or to have involved predictions that were by no means earth-shaking surprises. The statement of the priestesses of Delphi to Croesus could have been taken either way. Predicting success for Alexander was not exactly a huge shot in the dark, as he was the son of the greatest military leader of his day.

Other prophets throughout history have been claimed as foretellers. One might mention the Frenchman Nostradamus, mystic, astrologer and practitioner of black magic. Nostradamus probably is the most well known supposed prophet of the modern world. He lived from 1503-1566 AD. As an astrologer to the king of France, he once issued a prophecy that seemed to predict accurately the king's death in a jousting contest. This cemented Nostradamus' reputation as a prognosticator. Nostradamus published a long series of rhymed quatrains that have been variously interpreted as predicting a wide range of events including the French Revolution, the rise of Hitler, the assassination of John F. Kennedy, and the attempted assassination of Pope John Paul I in 1978. However, a simple review of these poems makes the interpretations that have been read into them dubious. For example, consider the quatrain that has been cited as Nostradamus' prediction of the assassination of John F. Kennedy:

The great man will be struck down in the day by a thunderbolt,
The evil deed predicted by the bearer of a petition:
According to the prediction another falls at night,
Conflict in Reims, London and pestilence in Tuscany.
(Century 1, Quatrain 27)

After the fact, believers in Nostradamus have seen details in common with the assassination of JFK. A bullet struck JFK ("a thunderbolt"), Jean Dixon predicted JFK's assassination ("predicted by a bearer of a petition"), and someone also assassinated JFK's brother the night of his primary victory in California ("another falls at night"). However, it would not be difficult for historians to find dozens of historical events that could be fit into this rather vague poem.

Those who want to see Nostradamus as a prophet can find sufficient evidence by scanning his hundreds of quatrains and trying to fit them into current events. As a more recent example, almost immediately after the destruction of the twin towers in New York on 9/11/2001, an e-mail made the rounds purporting to show that Nostradamus had prophesied the event. The supposed quatrain of Nostradamus is as follows:

"In the year of the new century and nine months,
From the sky will come a great King of Terror...
The sky will burn at forty-five degrees.
Fire approaches the great new city..."
"In the city of York there will be a great collapse,
2 twin brothers torn apart by chaos
while the fortress falls the great leader will succumb
third big war will begin when the big city is burning"

The problem with this hoax is that this "quatrain" was actually put together by taking two separate passages of Nostradamus out of context and joining them together. The first line is loosely based on the text;

"The year 1999, seventh month,
From the sky will come a great King of Terror.
To bring back to life the great King of the Mongols
Before and after Mars to reign by good luck.
(Quatrain 10, Century 72)

The next section is taken from a quatrain applying to a completely different century that reads:

"At forty-five degrees, the sky will burn,
Fire approaches the great new city,
Immediately a huge, scattered flame leaps up
When they want to have verification from the Norman."

The rest of the "quatrain" which made the rounds was probably filled in by the one who created the e-mail. The point of mentioning this hoax is not so much to debunk the claim as to show that the "prophecies" of Nostradamus are vague enough that, if taken out of context, they can be used to "predict" almost any world event. The French astrologer Nostradamus would appear to fit into a pattern. He made one very famous successful prediction, but one that was actually pretty easy to foresee. King Henry II of France was killed in a joust as was predicted by Nostradamus. Bear in mind, however, that Henry II was already noted for jousting and that jousting was an extremely dangerous sport. Beyond that, he made extremely vague predictions that could be variously interpreted. We will see that the statements of the Old Testament prophets concerning the Messiah are radically different from this pattern.

The assassination of JFK brings us to the person who is probably the best know "prophet" of the twentieth century, at least to Americans—Jean Dixon. In 1963, Dixon successfully predicted that John Kennedy would be shot. This one prediction made her reputation and her career as a psychic. Is there any chance that Jean Dixon made a lucky guess? Given the facts of the Cuban missile crisis, the assassination attempts on Castro sponsored by the Kennedy regime and the public commitment under the leadership of Robert Kennedy to bring down the leaders of American organized crime, this prediction was not exactly a huge shot in the dark. After this one dramatic prediction (admittedly, it was pretty dramatic), Dixon never made another major successful prediction. Yet, she remained America's most famous supposed prophet for a generation. The pattern repeats itself: one successful but easily predictable guess, followed by a number of either very vague predictions or ones that anyone might guess anyway. "I predict that there will be a big scandal in the White House next year." As we will see, this pattern bears no relationship whatever to the predictions of the Old Testament prophets.

One could move on to the prophets of today. The "prophets" employed by the National Enquirer and similar publications make their yearly predictions. There will be scandal in the White House and unrest in the Middle East. The stock market will go up. This stuff is to be taken as seriously as the Farmers' Almanac and its "prophecy" of the weather for the coming year.

Comparing modern-day prophecies with those in the Bible, especially with the prophecies in the Old Testament, is an entirely different matter. Consider the command given to Israel concerning the prophets:

> You may say to yourselves, "How can we know when a message has not been spoken by the Lord?" If what a prophet proclaims in the name of the Lord does not take place or come true, that is a message the Lord has not spoken. That prophet has spoken presumptuously. Do not be afraid of him (Deuteronomy 18:21-22).

The prophets in the Old Testament made predictions, both about events in the short term, and events in the distant future. Most typically, their short-term prophecies did not make it into the biblical text. Those who were consistently able to get it right when predicting events in their own time were accepted as true prophets. Is there any modern-day "prophet" who is able to meet this standard? Does the National Enquirer publish last year's predictions at the beginning of the new year and evaluate their accuracy? Do they fire anyone who makes a false prediction? What would you guess?

But this brings us back to the subject at hand. Jesus claimed openly to the Jewish people that the Old Testament was written about him. He openly and boldly claimed that all the prophecies written about the Messiah were written about him, and that he fulfilled those prophecies in his own lifetime. This claim is quite testable. It is either true or it is not. In claiming to be the fulfillment of the Old Testament passages about the Messiah, Jesus threw down the gauntlet. If his claim was true then without a doubt the following are true:

1. Jesus is the Messiah.
2. God inspired the Old Testament.

The question is, will the claims of Jesus to have fulfilled all the prophecies of the Messiah stand up to objective scrutiny?

OUR APPROACH

In order to approach this question, we will consider the kinds of questions a skeptical inquirer might ask, which would include the following:

1. Are there really specific prophecies about the coming Messiah in the Bible, or are we simply reading what happened to Jesus into vague passages in the Old Testament that in reality are not prophecies at all?

2. If there are in fact some bona fide Old Testament prophecies of a coming Messiah, when were they written?

3. Did Jesus really fulfill these prophecies? How do we know? Is there independent confirmation outside the biblical text?

4. Is there any chance Jesus was aware of the Messianic prophecies and simply made sure he fulfilled them in order to lend credence to his claims?

The first question is very important. Using the vague sorts of "prophecies" such as those found in the writings of Nostradamus as an example, this is a very legitimate question for a skeptic to ask of the biblical prophecies. How do we really know the Old Testament prophet is making a statement about the future? How do we know we are not simply scanning the Scriptures, looking for some passage that we can conveniently mold and interpret to fit our preconceived intent, which is to claim that Jesus fulfilled all the prophecies of the Messiah?

It may be fairly easy to convince those who already believe, but if the argument is not strong enough to convince a hardheaded but fair-minded skeptic, it is really not a good argument. We will look carefully at the context of a number of Old Testament passages, asking whether or not they clearly are messianic prophecies. The method to be used is to ask whether a Jew who lived before the time of Jesus would have been likely to interpret the scripture in question to be a prophecy of the Messiah. There are some passages in the Old Testament that most Christians would interpret as prophesying the Messiah, but which do not pass this test. We will attempt to systematically restrict our study to passages that even the skeptic would probably concede would naturally be interpreted by the Jewish audience as being about the Messiah.

Another aspect of this first question that a skeptic might raise is the question of whether it might be possible that the early church may have changed certain passages in the Old Testament in some sort of subtle way to improve the case for claiming that these verses were prophecies of the Messiah. The answer to this question is quite simple. The Jews have had ultimate possession of the original Hebrew manuscripts of the Old Testament. The Old Testament is the Hebrew Bible. The almost unbelievable meticulousness of Jewish scribes throughout the centuries at maintaining the integrity of the Hebrew text of the Old Testament is legendary, as will be shown in detail in chapter six. There is absolutely no way that the Jewish scholars would have allowed the text of the Hebrew Bible to be changed to fit some sort of Christian agenda. Both Jew and Gentile alike read the same prophecies, even today.

The next question is crucial to the argument as well. When were these supposed biblical prophecies written down? If Jean Dixon had predicted all the way back in 1945 that John Kennedy would eventually become president, and be assassinated in 1963, that would have truly been a spectacular prophesy! If Nostradamus had stated in the sixteenth century that a country in the newly-discovered continent of North America would eventually become independent, that it would become a democratic state, which elects its national leader, and that one of its leaders, named Kennedy, would be assassinated some time near the middle of the twentieth century, now that would be a prophecy to make your hair stand up!

As illustrated above, clearly the date of authorship of these prophecies is important. A specific statement about a person made several hundred years before he was born would be strong evidence for even the most hardened skeptic that something unusual is going on, assuming the date of writing could be clearly established.

Let us address the question of date of authorship immediately. When was the Old Testament written? When were the specific books such as Isaiah, Psalms and Micah, books that will be used in this section, written? In general that is a tough question, as we clearly do not have the original manuscripts. The specifics of this question will be dealt with carefully in chapter six of this book. However, to answer question number two above, it is only necessary to prove that, whatever the actual dates of authorship, the messianic passages were at least a few hundred years old at the time Jesus made the claim to have fulfilled all the prophecies of the Messiah. It turns out that this is a simple task.

The task was made easy, in part, by the discovery in the 1940s of what are commonly known as the Dead Sea Scrolls. These scrolls were originally discovered by some shepherd boys in a group of caves in the desert hill country west of the Dead Sea. Eventually, hundreds of manuscripts were discovered in large clay vessels scattered in a number of caves. Many of the parchments were of Jewish writers from the Essene sect, but a significant number were Old Testament manuscripts. These scrolls have been dated to somewhere between 250 BC and AD 50. One scroll, known as Isaiah A, was discovered. This scroll contains the entire book of Isaiah, except for a few words. It has been dated to 100 BC. One fragment of Exodus has been dated to the early second century BC. From the evidence of the Dead Sea Scrolls, one can state conclusively that all or nearly all the Old Testament was written well before 100 BC.

That is fine, but one can go further. It just so happens that the entire Old Testament was translated into Greek, in a translation referred to as the Septuagint version, some time in the late third and the early second century BC. This was the Greek Old Testament in use in the time of Christ. Using this fact, one can be certain that the Old Testament was complete in more or less its present form by 200 BC. Allowing sufficient time for the Old Testament books to be distributed and evaluated by the Jewish rabbis carefully enough for them to be accepted by consensus as inspired books would push the date of authorship back even further.

In short, given the evidence of the Dead Sea Scrolls and the Septuagint translation of the Hebrew Bible, one can state with certainty that the Old Testament has been around in more or less its present form since at least 300 BC. To push the date of authorship back to the actual writing of the separate Old Testament books is a more difficult task, some of which will be left for chapter six. However, for the purposes of this chapter, the case is sufficient. Whether Isaiah was written in 750 BC or in 400 BC does not change the argument to be presented here. The entire Old Testament was written hundreds of years before the ministry of Jesus Christ.

The third question is also essential to the argument. How can one be sure that the prophecies were actually fulfilled by Jesus Christ in his lifetime? Is it possible that the writers of the New Testament simply read the Old Testament, discovered the apparent foreshadowing of a Messiah, and wrote the gospel accounts to make it appear as if Jesus had fulfilled the prophecies? For the Bible believer that is an easy question. The acts of Jesus are recorded in the New Testament. One need simply read in the New Testament what he did and the events that occurred around him to check out whether Jesus fulfilled the prophecies of the Messiah found in the Old Testament. But then again, the Bible believer probably already believes Jesus is the Messiah anyway, so how is one to convince the skeptic?

The skeptic (quite reasonably) asks: "How can I be sure Jesus really fulfilled the supposed prophecies in the Hebrew Bible?" The simple answer is that many of the prophetic fulfillments are a matter of historical record. Some, but not all, of the events concerning the Messiah as prophesied in the Old Testament Scripture were realized in the life of Jesus Christ as recorded in numerous histories, both of Christians and of non-Christians. In general, the specific prophecies chosen for consideration in this chapter will fit this pattern. As we go through the various Messianic prophecies, care will be taken to point out whether or not the relevant events are recorded in external historical sources, or whether one must count on Biblical accounts to confirm that Jesus did in fact "fulfill [what is] written about me in the Law of Moses, the Prophets and the Psalms" (Luke 24:44).

Jesus fulfilled many of the prophecies about the Messiah, as confirmed by ancient historical records. Others are only confirmed as recorded in the New Testament. In the latter cases, the readers must decide for themselves. Eventually, the evidence for the historical trustworthiness of the New Testament writers becomes overwhelming (see chapter seven). At some point only those who are simply unwilling to accept the obvious facts would continue to harbor significant doubts about the historical reliability of the gospel accounts. With the accumulated weight of evidence as presented in this book, the case for accepting as fact that Jesus fulfilled the messianic prophecies should speak for itself. Again, let the reader decide.

The last question mentioned above which a skeptic might ask is an interesting one. It certainly is a logical one—one that Bible critics through the centuries have often raised. If one is prepared to concede that the Old Testament writings precede the life of Jesus by many years, and that Jesus did in fact do many of the things the Messiah was supposed to do, is it not possible that Jesus more or less faked the whole thing? Assuming that Jesus wanted to claim to be the Messiah, and that he was a careful student of the Hebrew Bible, could he have kept a mental list of prophecies required to claim to be the Messiah and check them off one by one as he went along? Imagine Jesus saying to himself, "Ok, the Messiah is supposed to ride into Jerusalem on a donkey. I had better take care of that one on this trip." Or imagine Jesus calling Peter over: "Peter, would you please go out and find a donkey for me? Why? Please, just do what I ask, OK." To an inquirer not well acquainted with either the character of Jesus or the nature of Old Testament prophecy, this might seem like a perfectly logical alternative. However, this viewpoint will very rapidly become untenable as the specific prophecies are considered. We will see that this challenge to the messianic claims of Jesus is absolutely illogical in the face of the specific prophecies. For some of the messianic prophecies, there is simply no way Jesus could have manipulated events in order to trump up a claim to be the Messiah.

To summarize, if it can be shown by careful consideration that most or all of the Old Testament was written before 300 BC, that external historical records confirm Jesus' claim to have fulfilled a number of prophecies found in the Old Testament, and that there is no way that Jesus could have manipulated the situation to make himself appear to be the Messiah, the reader will be left with only one reasonable conclusion: Jesus is the Messiah and the Bible is inspired by God. We will proceed now to a point-by-point look at a number of specific messianic prophecies.

EARLY EDITION

In recent years, the CBS network has featured an upbeat drama series titled "Early Edition." This show has an interesting plot line. The main character, Gary Hobson, is delivered tomorrow's edition of the Chicago Tribune at his doorstep every morning, before the events described in the paper actually happen. He has the option of using the information to bet on the horses or sporting events and make himself filthy rich, or to help people avoid the tragedies in their lives reported in the paper. Of course, Hobson's sidekick is urging him to compromise "just a little bit" and go for the bucks, but the humble and noble main character sticks to his guns and uses his miraculous paper to help people.

In the Bible, we have an "Early Edition" of a most dramatic kind. We are not talking about predicting tomorrow's events. We are not talking about Jean Dixon predicting next year's election outcome either. We are talking about the equivalent of an Early Edition for a newspaper in the year 2525 or beyond! And this is not some sort of vague prediction, such as "the stock market will go up next year." It is more like literally finding a newspaper for a date seven hundred years in the future, replete with minute details. We are talking very specific and very far in the future. It would be like someone predicting today that in the year 2735 the country of Guatemala will become the dominant world power and having it come true. There is absolutely nothing to compare with this in human experience or even in the wildest of human fantasies.

ISAIAH 53:1-12

As a first example of just such a specific and far-seeing prophecy, consider Isaiah 53:1-12.

> Who has believed our message
> and to whom has the arm of the Lord been revealed?
> He grew up before him like a tender shoot,
> and like a root out of dry ground.
> He had no beauty or majesty to attract us to him,
> nothing in his appearance that we should desire him.
> He was despised and rejected by men,
> a man of sorrows and familiar with suffering.
> Like one from whom men hide their faces
> he was despised, and we esteemed him not.
> Surely he took up our infirmities
> and carried our sorrows,
> yet we considered him stricken by God,
> smitten by him and afflicted.
> But he was pierced for our transgressions,
> he was crushed for our iniquities;
> the punishment that brought us peace was upon him,
> and by his wounds we are healed.
> We all, like sheep, have gone astray,
> each of us has turned to his own way.
> and the Lord has laid on him the iniquity of us all.
> He was oppressed and afflicted,
> yet he did not open his mouth;
> He was led like a lamb to the slaughter,
> and like a sheep before her shearers is silent,
> so he did not open his mouth.
> By oppression and judgment, he was taken away.
> And who can speak of his descendants?
> For he was cut off from the land of the living;
> for the transgression of my people he was stricken.
> He was assigned a grave with the wicked,

and with the rich in his death,
though he had done no violence,
nor was there any deceit in his mouth.
Yet it was the Lord's will to crush him and cause him to suffer,
and though the Lord makes his life a guilt offering,
He will see his offspring and prolong his days,
and the will of the Lord will prosper in his hand.
After the suffering of his soul,
he will see the light of life and be satisfied;
by his knowledge my righteous servant will justify many,
and he will bear their iniquities.
Therefore I will give him a portion among the great,
and he will divide the spoils with the strong,
because he poured out his life unto death,
and was numbered with the transgressors.
For he bore the sin of many,
and made intercession for the transgressors.

Since this is the best known of the Messianic prophecies let us first consider how one can be sure this is a prophecy about the Messiah. It so happens that many of the Jews themselves, even before the time of Jesus, considered this passage to be a prophecy about the Messiah. It is sometimes referred to as describing the suffering Messiah. Not all Jews agreed that this was a messianic prophecy, but that was primarily because they saw it as inconsistent with their own mistaken view of the Messiah. Some saw the Messiah as a conquering general who would be sent by God to establish his physical kingdom, bringing back the glory days of King David. They could not conceive of a humble, suffering Messiah. In fact, some groups, the Essenes among them,[3] actually believed in two separate "Messiahs," one being the conquering general, and the other being the suffering Savior.

Because many Jews themselves considered Isaiah 53 a prophecy of the Messiah even before Jesus' ministry, it is difficult to support

---

3. The Essenes were a conservative, ascetic sect of Judaism that flourished in Judea principally from the first century BC into the first century AD. They removed themselves from the general society of their fellow Jews to live in communes under very harsh conditions. It was the Essenes who preserved many of their own writings, as well as a good number of Old Testament manuscripts, which were eventually discovered in the caves where they were stored. These are the Dead Sea Scrolls. Some of the extra-biblical writings of the Essenes seem to indicate a belief in two separate Messiah-like figures, one of whom could be described as a suffering savior, as found in Isaiah 53, the other being a kingly Messiah. Some even see a third, priestly Messiah, in the writings of the Essenes. For further study on this subject, see William Sanford LaSor, *The Dead Sea Scrolls and the New Testament*, (William Eerdmans, Grand Rapids, Michigan, 1972)

the claim that Christians simply read the details of Jesus' life into the scripture, so that they could claim Jesus to be the Messiah.

Besides, even if we did not have a record of Jewish teachers referring to this writing as being about the Messiah, it still bears the marks of a messianic prophecy on its own. Consider such phrases as "my righteous servant" (v. 11), "the Lord has laid on him the iniquity of us all" (v. 6), and "by his wounds we are healed" (v. 5).

Perhaps most telling is the phrase "He grew up before him like a tender shoot, and like a root out of dry ground" (v. 2). This phrase can be understood in the light of Isaiah 11:10. "In that day, the Root of Jesse will stand as a banner for the peoples; the nations will rally to him and his place of rest will be glorious." In Isaiah eleven, "the Root of Jesse" is a reference to King David, the son of Jesse. This passage is clearly about the Messiah, as it implies that a still future "Root of Jesse" (i.e. the Messiah) will rise up again to raise the banner of Israel, returning glory to Jerusalem, the "place of rest" of King David. The Root in Isaiah 11 is the root in Isaiah 53.

Speaking of "the Root," one could mention Psalm 80:14,15: "Watch over this vine, the root your right hand has planted, the son you have raised up for yourself." Again, one sees the Messiah referred to in the Old Testament as "the root." It is interesting that some Jews saw two different Messiahs in Isaiah 53 (the suffering Messiah) and in Isaiah 11:10 (the saving general), as they are both referred to as "the root." Of course, when these various prophecies were fulfilled in Jesus, the meaning of these Old Testament scriptures all became clear.

Let us return to Isaiah 53. This passage is certainly about the Messiah. We are not ripping it out of its context. When was this passage written? Isaiah was a prophet to Israel during the reigns of the kings of Judah; Uzziah, Jotham, Ahaz and Hezekiah. An approximate date of writing for Isaiah 53 is 730 BC. Remember that if one is unwilling to accept the conservative date of the book, even most liberal scholars must accept that it was written at least three hundred years before the life of Christ. This was not a prophecy about the near future when Isaiah wrote the passage, to say the least. To put it in context, 750 years ago, the crusades were in full swing. Columbus' voyage was still almost two hundred and fifty years in the future.

Consider now some of the specific predictions about the life and death of the Messiah as described in Isaiah 53. According to this prophecy, the Messiah will:

1. Be despised and rejected by men (v. 3)

2. Be pierced for man's sin (v. 5)

3. Be silent before his accusers (v. 7)

4. Be cut off: have no descendents (v. 8)

5. Be buried with the wicked and the wealthy (v. 9)

6. See his offspring (despite v. 8), and prolong his days (v. 10)

In order to fulfill all the prophecies about the Messiah, Jesus had to be despised and rejected by men. Well, that certainly was true. The fact that Jesus was despised and rejected is a matter of common knowledge, both from Scripture and from historical record. Perhaps the most telling example of this is found in Luke 23:18-24, in which the Jewish mob shouted, "Crucify him! Crucify him!" The crowd preferred that Pilate release a violent criminal rather than let Jesus go free. Jesus certainly fulfilled this prediction about the Messiah.

In addition, the Messiah had to be pierced. This is a clear (future) reference to the poignant event recorded in John 19:33, when the soldier pierced the side of Jesus with the spear. Was Jesus the only Jew ever to be despised and rejected, as well as to be "pierced"? Probably he was not, but according to Isaiah 53, the Messiah must also be silent when oppressed and afflicted, similar to the way a lamb is docile before her shearers. One could guess that it would be next to impossible to find a single Jew who was despised, rejected, pierced, and yet silent before his persecutors. It is well known, of course, that Jesus refused to defend himself when he was tried before the Sanhedrin. Those not acquainted with this episode can find an account in Mark 14:55-65, which describes how the high priest demanded that Jesus answer to the false charges that were laid before him. "But Jesus remained silent and gave no answer."

Besides this, the Messiah had to be without human descendants. Of course, Jesus never married or had children, as history can confirm (putting aside the highly dubious claims of Dan Brown in *The Da Vinci Code*). In addition, the Messiah had to be buried "with the rich." This certainly would apply to Jesus, who was buried in the carved-out tomb of Joseph of Arimathea, a wealthy Jew (John 19:38). At the same time, Jesus was killed along with two wicked men, amazingly fulfilling both aspects of the phrase "He was assigned a grave with the wicked, and with the rich in his death." In the ancient world this seeming paradox would have been particularly striking.

Lastly, according to Isaiah, the Messiah would "see his offspring and prolong his days." At first glance, it might appear that Isaiah was contradicting himself, because he had already said that the Messiah would be cut off, without descendents. However, if one considers the resurrection of Jesus from the dead, the meaning is clear. The descendants Isaiah refers to are the spiritual brothers and sisters who would join Jesus in the kingdom of God (Mark 3:34,35).

Is this luck? Is coincidence a possibility? Isaiah predicted that the Messiah would be despised and rejected, pierced, silent before his accusers, without human descendants, and buried with the rich. And Isaiah predicted all this almost eight hundred years before the events. It is doubtful that any Jewish person in all of history (other than Jesus Christ) has ever fulfilled all these conditions.

The skeptic must be given his chance to rebut. How do we know Jesus really did all these things? The fact that Jesus was despised and rejected, as well as the fact that he was buried with the rich and killed before having any children is a matter of historical record. In this case one is not left with the Bible proving itself. Besides, is there any reason to question the accuracy of John's account of the piercing of Jesus' side? Why would John have included such a specific detail in his account if it were not true? The enemies of the church who were eyewitnesses to the crucifixion would easily have proved such a detail incorrect.

The skeptic is not done with questions. Perhaps Jesus read Isaiah 53, and, wanting to fake being the Messiah, made sure he fulfilled all the prophecies found there. Could Jesus have arranged to be despised and rejected? Jesus once called the Pharisees and teachers of the Law "hypocrites," "white-washed tombs," and even a "brood of vipers." To the casual observer, it certainly could be claimed that Jesus went out of his way to be despised and rejected. Also, knowing the prophecy, could Jesus have chosen to remain silent when accused in order to be able to make a false claim of being the Messiah? Given that his life was at stake, the charge is conceivable, but extremely difficult to believe.

When one considers the prophecy about the Messiah being pierced, the charge that Jesus may have arranged to fulfill all the prophecies becomes absurd. Can one picture Jesus making sure he died really quickly on the cross so that he could be stabbed, rather than having his legs broken when the Jews ask for the victims to be killed early? Would anyone propose that while Jesus was on the cross he might have said to one of the soldiers, "Please make sure you stab me after I die. I want to fulfill the prophecies."?

We have seen that Isaiah 53 is a bona fide messianic prophecy, that it was written hundreds of years before the events occurred, that some of the fulfillments are a matter of historical record and that Jesus could not conceivably have arranged to see that he did all these things. Isaiah 53 alone could prove the case, but there is much more.

PSALM 22:15-18

The greatest number of prophecies of the Messiah is recorded in the Psalms. Arguably, the best example is found in Psalm 22.

> My strength is dried up like a potsherd,
> and my tongue sticks to the roof of my mouth;
> you lay me in the dust of death.
> Dogs have surrounded me,
> a band of evil men has encircled me,
> they have pierced my hands and feet.
> I can count all my bones;
> people stare at me and gloat over me.
> They divide my garments among them
> and cast lots for my clothing (Psalm 22:15-18).

According to the Hebrew manuscript, David wrote the twenty-second psalm. This would be King David, who ruled the united kingdom of Israel from about 1010-970 BC. It is impossible to prove that David was the actual author, but there is no particular reason to doubt the biblical claim. If one can assume he was the writer of this poem, then it was written over one thousand years before the time of Jesus Christ. In any case, it certainly was written hundreds of years before Jesus was killed. Again, we are not dealing with a prediction for the coming year, to say the least! Besides, as we will see, this prophecy involves the minutest details of events that occurred around the death of Jesus Christ. It would be something like one of us successfully predicting what a particular person will eat on some day in the year 3060. Unlike the quatrains of Nostradamus, this is no veiled, vague and obscure poem that could be applied by one's imagination to any of a great number of historical events.

How can one be certain this is a prophecy of the Messiah? Unlike most of the other scriptures we will be looking at, this passage contains no clear-cut reference to the Messiah that would have been unmistakable to the Jews before the fact. It is the details of the events themselves that prove this to be a prophetic utterance about the Savior.

Let us, then, skip right to the details. First, in Psalm 22:15, David describes his strength drying up, and his mouth being extremely dry. If this were the whole story, one could claim that it was David writing about himself. Certainly David felt this way at one time or another as he fled from the persecutions of King Saul. However, it just so happens that the description could also apply to Jesus while on the cross.

> Later, knowing that all was now completed, and so that the Scripture would be fulfilled, Jesus said, "I am thirsty."
> A jar of wine vinegar was there, so they soaked a sponge in it, put the sponge on a stalk of the hyssop plant, and lifted it to Jesus' lips (John 19:28,29).

Again, the parallels between Psalm 22:15 and the events of Jesus' death is interesting, but if that were the whole story it would prove nothing. However, consider Psalm 22:16. Here, David describes being surrounded by evil men and having his hands and his feet pierced. Did anything like this ever actually happen to David? That would be hard to believe. Imagine how David must have felt when he penned these words. He must have wondered what in the world he was talking about! In the light of history, there is absolutely no doubt what God, through David, was referring to. Is there any doubt the prophecy refers to the crucifixion?

It is very interesting to note that when King David lived, crucifixion was yet to be invented. The first historical record of an execution style similar to crucifixion is found in the writings of the Persians around the year 400 BC. This was more than six hundred years after David lived. Even then, the execution did not involve nailing to a cross, but to a stake. It was only the Romans who created the modern (for them) method of crucifixion by piercing the hands and the feet on a cross.

How did the writer of Psalm 22 know about crucifixion hundreds of years before it even existed? The skeptic must answer this question. And how did one of the writers of the Old Testament know the Messiah would be crucified? Does this passage leave any doubt about whether Jesus was who he claimed to be? Perhaps the skeptic can hold out against this psalm referring to the Messiah, but by the time we are done, this stand will become absolutely untenable. This is a blow-away scripture! The skeptic simply cannot rationally deny it refers to crucifixion. "They have pierced my hands and my feet...." He or she reflexively resorts to the idea that the Psalm was written after the event, but is immediately reminded that there is no doubt it was written at least three hundred years before Christ, and probably hundreds more.

To emphasize this point, let us continue to Psalm 22:17. Here the writer enigmatically declares, "I can count all my bones; people stare and gloat over me." Again, there is no particular event in King David's life that would appear to apply to this description. However, a glance at the gospel accounts makes the interpretation clear. Those who stood around the cross during the crucifixion stared and gloated at Jesus. "You who are going to destroy the temple and build it in three days, save yourself! Come down from the cross, if you are the Son of God" (Matthew 27:40). However, what about the reference to counting all his bones? Again, a search of the gospel accounts answers this question.

As mentioned previously, the gospel writers unanimously describe Jesus as dying relatively quickly from the crucifixion (for good reason). Jesus was crucified at about the third hour and died at about the ninth hour of the day. Soon thereafter, the Jewish leaders asked that the executions be terminated out of respect for the Jewish feast of the Passover. The soldiers broke the legs of the two thieves who were crucified along with Jesus. They did this knowing that a crucified person who could no longer push himself up by his nailed feet would die of suffocation in a matter of minutes. When they came to Jesus, he was already dead, so they did not break his legs. This must be what the prophet was referring to when he declared, "I can count all my bones." Again, the Old Testament prophet got an exact and very specific prediction correct, hundreds of years before the event. Could this be luck or coincidence?

If you think it is impressive that David got the specific mode of death of the Messiah right, be prepared to be even more impressed! Consider verse eighteen. "They divide my garments among them and cast lots for my clothing." According to the prophet, the Messiah will have his garments divided up. No, actually, his garments will be gambled for. Which is it? Did they go "one for me, one for you, one for you," or did they gamble, with a winner-takes-all? It almost seems that the writer is contradicting himself. A glance at John 19:23,24 will solve the dilemma.

> When the soldiers crucified Jesus, they took his clothes, dividing them into four shares, one for each of them, with the undergarment remaining. This garment was seamless, woven in one piece from top to bottom.
> "Let's not tear it," they said to one another. "Let's decide by lot who will get it." So this is what the soldiers did.

Yes, the soldiers divided up his clothes, and yes they gambled (cast lots) for the most valuable of his items of clothing, because to divide it up would have been to reduce its value.

How did David get this one right? One might wonder if there has ever been any other situation in all of history for which all the attributes described in Psalm 22 would apply. The psalmist correctly predicted the minutest conceivable detail of the death of the Messiah over one thousand years before it happened. There is no comparison to the modern-day "prophet" predicting the stock market to go down next year, or Nostradamus and his very vague verses.

Again, the skeptic deserves his hearing. We know Psalm 22 was written many hundreds of years before the events in Jesus' life. How do we know for sure that these things really happened to Jesus? Could the New Testament writers simply have made up a story that conveniently matched Psalm 22? The simple answer is no. The crucifixion of Jesus is one of the most well documented events of ancient history. One could argue that the details about the bones not being broken and the garments being gambled for are only recorded in the New Testament. However, David got the fact that the Messiah was to be crucified correct. It is not a big step to accept the veracity of the eyewitnesses concerning the breaking of the legs of the two thieves and the soldiers gambling over Jesus' clothes.

In the light of these prophecies, could Jesus have faked being the Messiah? Could he have arranged to fulfill these prophecies? Jesus certainly did not have control over whether they stoned him or crucified him (unless, of course, Jesus was God). Assuming Jesus was aware of Psalm 22, it would nevertheless be hard to imagine that he advised the soldiers on how to divide up his clothing. One thing we can say for sure, Jesus definitely did not arrange for them to leave his legs unbroken. He was dead already! Let us give up this idea that Jesus might have arranged circumstances so as to appear to have fulfilled the prophecies of the Messiah. It just does not work.

So far, the Messiah must be despised and rejected, pierced, silent when accused, without human descendants, buried with the wealthy, and have his days "prolonged," despite being cut off. Besides this, he must be very thirsty right before he dies, he must be crucified, and he must have his persecutors both divide and gamble for his clothing. He also must be able to "count all his bones." Jesus' claim to have fulfilled all that was written about the Messiah is looking viable.

ZECHARIAH 11:10-13

Now we will examine a prophecy given by Zechariah to Israel. Zechariah was a priest and prophet who ministered to God's people in the period during and immediately after their exile in Babylon. The prophecy itself was written in 520-518 BC. The Bible critic may not accept this date, but we know for sure that it was written over three hundred years before the death of Christ, which is sufficient to make the case at hand. There are actually a number of messianic prophecies in Zechariah, but we will focus on Zechariah 11:10-13.

> Then I took my staff called Favor and broke it, revoking the covenant I had made with all the nations. It was revoked on that day, and so the afflicted of the flock who were watching me knew it was the word of the Lord.
>
> I told them, "If you think it best, give me my pay; but if not, keep it." So they paid me thirty pieces of silver.
>
> And the Lord said to me, "Throw it to the potter"—the handsome price at which they priced me! So I took the thirty

pieces of silver and threw them into the house of the Lord to the potter.

It is fun to speculate what Zechariah must have thought about what he was writing. Surely he must have asked himself what was the meaning of this seemingly very cryptic passage he wrote down. In the light of the gospel accounts, all is made crystal clear.

According to our outline, however, we must first ask how one can be sure this is a prophecy concerning the Messiah. Consider the opening phrase of the passage quoted. "Then I took my staff called Favor and broke it, revoking the covenant I had made with all the nations." This implies that the passage refers to an event through which the Old Covenant (i.e. the Law of Moses) would be supplanted by a New Covenant. There are a number of Old Testament passages that seem to connect the revoking of the Old Covenant and the bringing in of a New Covenant with the Messiah.[4] Besides, when describing the event, God is quoted as saying he was sold for thirty pieces of silver. With historical hindsight, one can see that God was describing himself as the savior being sold for a pittance. This is certainly a prophecy of the Messiah.

Zechariah eleven describes an interesting situation. One can detect someone accepting some pay, but only reluctantly. ("If you think it best, give me my pay, but if not, keep it.") And what was his pay? His pay was thirty pieces of silver, to be exact. What was the payment for? Apparently, it was used to, in some sense, buy God! Did the person accept the payment? No, it was thrown into the Lord's house, to the potter (whatever that means). Is there some specific detail here?

When one looks to the New Testament to see how this messianic prophecy was fulfilled, the events in Zechariah are described with such exact detail, that the reader must be reminded that this prophecy and the fulfillment are separated by about five hundred and fifty years. Some of the details relating to the fulfillment of prophecy are found in Matthew 26:14-16.

> Then one of the twelve—the one called Judas Iscariot—went to the chief priests and asked, "What are you willing to give me if I hand him over to you?" So they counted out for him thirty silver coins. From then on Judas watched for an opportunity to hand him over.

Jesus was betrayed for thirty pieces of silver. Not twenty-nine, not thirty-one—thirty. Right away, the skeptic will cry foul. How do we

---

4. For example, Jeremiah 31:27-37

know it was really thirty pieces? If it were not really thirty pieces, what possible motivation would the gospel writer have to make up this detail? There were dozens of eyewitnesses to this event. If the gospel writers were to lie about this detail, they would have been setting themselves up to be discounted. No one ever came forward to deny this statement of the gospel writer. There is only one reasonable explanation. Jesus was sold for thirty pieces of silver. There is simply no accounting for this fact. God inspired the Bible. What else can one conclude?

Did Judas happily take his money and run? Not exactly. After Jesus was arrested, Judas returned to the chief priests.

> When Judas, who had betrayed him, saw that Jesus was condemned, he was seized with remorse and returned the thirty silver coins to the chief priests and the elders. "I have sinned," he said, "for I have betrayed innocent blood."
>
> "What is that to us?" they replied. "That's your responsibility."
>
> So Judas threw the money into the temple and left. Then he went away and hanged himself.
>
> The chief priests picked up the coins and said, "It is against the law to put this into the treasury, since it is blood money." So they decided to use the money to buy the potter's field as a burial place for foreigners. That is why it has been called the field of Blood to this day (Matthew 27:3-8).

Where did Judas throw the coins? He threw them into the temple—the house of the Lord—exactly as prophesied by Zechariah. Now that is spectacular. How did Zechariah know that? The answer is simple. God told him. There is no other conceivable answer, unless one is willing to charge Matthew with lying. But again, what is the motivation for Matthew to provide such detailed, impeachable evidence if it is a lie?

The part in Zechariah 11 about the potter ("I took the thirty pieces of silver and threw them...to the potter.") appears to be very obscure until one looks at Matthew 27. Because of a regulation concerning "blood money," the Jewish temple officials refused to take the betrayal money and put it back into the treasury. Is it just a coincidence that they bought the potter's field with the money? If you are prepared to accept that this is a coincidence, then no amount of evidence will be able to convince you.

Could Jesus have arranged to have these prophecies fulfilled? If he was God he could, but as a man he was not even present when these transactions were taking place. What possessed the chief priests to set thirty pieces of silver as the price? They certainly were not motivated to help Jesus fulfill the prophecy in Zechariah! One can only imagine the Bible skeptic becoming quiet at this point. Did the temple officials use the money for the potter's field in order to help Jesus fulfill the messianic prophecies? The last thing in the world they wanted was for Jesus' followers to be able to claim that he was the Messiah.

WHERE WILL THE MESSIAH COME FROM?

The Old Testament provided some very specific information about where the Messiah was to come from. In fact, at one point in his ministry, some of Jesus' enemies attacked those who were claiming Jesus was the Messiah, by pointing out that Jesus came from Galilee, when everyone knew that the Messiah was supposed to be from Bethlehem (John 7:41,42).

It turns out that the critic whose words were recorded in John chapter seven was not exactly correct, as we will see. However, the Old Testament passage he was referring to is Micah 5:2.

> But you, Bethlehem Ephrathah, though you are small among the clans of Judah, out of you will come for me one who will be ruler over Israel, whose origins are from of old, from ancient times."

To put this passage in an historical perspective, Micah was a contemporary of Isaiah. This prophecy was recorded around 750 BC. There is no question that the Jews considered this a messianic prophecy. It very clearly refers to a time of God coming to his people.

It is interesting to note that there were actually two towns with the name Bethlehem in Palestine. It just so happens that Jesus was born in Bethlehem Eprathah, the one referred to in the prophecy. Apparently, according to this prophecy, the Messiah must be born in Bethlehem. Jesus certainly fulfilled this one. This is a matter of historical record. One need not rely simply on the Bible to confirm that Jesus fulfilled this prediction.

Did Jesus manage to arrange this one? Hmmm...Are we to picture Mary, saying, "My son could be the Messiah, I must go to Bethlehem for his birth? No, actually, it was Augustus Caesar who arranged for Jesus to fulfill this prophecy. It was he who called for a census in that part of the Roman Empire at the time Mary was pregnant with Jesus. By the way, the calling of this census is recorded in history as well.

There is a reason that the Messiah was to be from Bethlehem. King David's family was from the town of Bethlehem. There are a number of Old Testament prophecies which state that the Messiah was to be a direct descendent of David.[5] Actually, Jesus was a direct descendent of David, both through his mother and through Joseph. In fact, that is why Mary and Joseph were in Bethlehem in the first place. When Augustus called the census, everyone was asked to go to his or her ancestral home. The atheist may find this difficult to swallow, but it would seem that through God's sovereignty he inspired Augustus to call for a census in his eastern realms at just the correct time to cause Jesus to be born in Bethlehem.

This is not the whole story on where the Messiah was to be born and raised. The critic mentioned above from John chapter seven was only partially correct about where the Messiah was to be from. More on this is found in Isaiah 9:1.

> Nevertheless, there will be no more gloom for those who were in distress. In the past he humbled the land of Zebulun and the land of Naphtali, but in the future he will honor Galilee of the Gentiles, by the way of the sea, along the Jordan.

At first, this is not obviously a prophecy about the Messiah, but when one looks down the page just a bit the case is made.

> For to us a child is born, to us a son is given
> and the government will be on his shoulders.
> And he will be called Wonderful Counselor, Mighty God
> Everlasting Father, Prince of Peace.
> Of the increase of his government and peace
> there will be no end.
> He will reign on David's throne and over
> his kingdom,
> establishing and upholding it with justice and
> righteousness from that time on and forever.
> The zeal of the Lord Almighty will accomplish this
> (Isaiah 9:6,7).

There is probably no passage in the entire Old Testament that is more obviously about the Messiah than Isaiah 9. God is to honor the land of Zebulun and the land of Naphtali. What is this referring to? Zebulun and Naphtali are two of the original twelve tribes of Israel who were allotted land after the conquests under Joshua. If one compares a map showing the approximate boundaries between these two tribes

---

5. For example, Isaiah 9:7, Jeremiah 23:5, Jeremiah 33:15 and Ezekiel 34:22,23

(many Bibles have a map of the approximate territories of the tribes at the back), with a map showing the location of Nazareth, one will discover that the little town of Nazareth is right on the border between these two territories.

According to Isaiah 9, the Messiah is to be from Galilee, in the region right around Nazareth. How many people would meet both requirements: having been born in Bethlehem Ephrathah (Micah 5:2), but actually caming from Galilee, in the region right around Nazareth (Isaiah 9:6,7)? Probably only a very small number of people in all history would meet these two qualifications simultaneously. Jesus was one of them. Did Jesus arrange for his parents to raise him in Nazareth? Does anyone question the historical fact that Jesus was a Galilean? How did Isaiah know that the Messiah would be from the region around Nazareth? How, in seeming contradiction, did Micah know he would be from Bethlehem? How can the skeptic explain away this prophecy?[6]

WHEN WILL THE MESSIAH LIVE?

There are a few passages in the Old Testament that predict the actual time of the coming of the Messiah to God's people. In order for Jesus to make good on his claim to have fulfilled all that was written about the Messiah, he had to take care of these details as well. He had to be born in the right place and at the right time. Let us consider two prophecies concerning the timing of the coming of the Messiah.

Both of these prophecies will be found in Daniel. The book of Daniel was written over the fairly long life span of Daniel, some time between 600 BC and 530 BC. The date of writing of Daniel is perhaps the most controversial of all the Old Testament books, but suffice it to say that because the book is found in the Septuagint translation, it is easy to show it was written a few hundred years before the time of Christ.

The first prophecy we will look at is found in Daniel 2:36-45. The context of this particular passage is important. It would be helpful for the reader to read the entire second chapter of Daniel. To summarize, Nebuchadnezzar, the king of Babylon, had a very vivid and frightening dream. He threatened to kill all his wise men and sorcerers unless they could interpret his dream. Unfortunately for the sorcerers and wise men, he refused to tell them the dream, which made it difficult to interpret it! After praying to God, Daniel told Nebuchadnezzar exactly what he had dreamed. At the same time, Daniel gave him the interpretation of the dream he had received from God.

---

6. Another prophecy, Hosea 11:1, also places the Messiah in Egypt as a child (see Matthew 2:13-15). This passage is not quite so clearly about the Messiah, so is not dealt with in detail here.

The vision of Nebuchadnezzar was of a giant statue in four parts. There were a head of gold, arms and an upper torso of silver, a lower torso of bronze and legs of iron. After seeing this awesome statue, Nebuchadnezzar had seen a huge rock being cut out "but not by human hands." This rock struck the statue, smashing it to dust. Because Daniel was able to accurately reveal the dream that Nebuchadnezzar had had, the king was well prepared to accept the interpretation that followed. Daniel gave Nebuchadnezzar the interpretation of the dream.

>..."You are the head of gold. After you, another kingdom will rise, inferior to yours. Next, a third kingdom, one of bronze, will rule over the whole earth. Finally, there will be a fourth kingdom, strong as iron—for iron breaks and smashes everything—and as iron breaks things to pieces, so it will crush and break all the others...
>
> "In the time of those kings, the God of heaven will set up a kingdom that will never be destroyed, nor will it be left to another people. It will crush all those kingdoms and bring them to an end, but it will itself endure forever. This is the meaning of the vision of the rock cut out of a mountain, but not by human hands—a rock that broke the iron, the bronze, the clay, the silver and the gold to pieces."

Daniel claimed that God had given him the interpretation of the dream. The history of the world in the next several centuries after Daniel ultimately proved this claim to be true. Daniel told Nebuchadnezzar that the four parts of the statue represented four great kingdoms that would rule the world. We will examine this prophecy in more detail in chapter five, but to summarize, the four kingdoms were Babylon (the head of gold), Persia (the torso of silver), Greece (the belly and thighs of bronze) and Rome (the legs of iron).[7]

The prophecy predicts that "in the time of those kings," in other words during the time of the domination of the Roman Empire, God will set up a kingdom that will never be destroyed. One can assume that the Jewish readers were well aware what kingdom God (through Daniel) was talking about. This is the Kingdom of God—the one to be inaugurated by the Messiah. To put a fairly long explanation very simply, Daniel prophesied that the Messiah would come to Israel during the time of Rome. Daniel did not say it in these exact words. He probably did not even know of Rome (although in the sixth century

---

7. This dream and its interpretation are described in much more detail in my book on Daniel, *Daniel, Prophet to the Nations*, (Illumination Publishers, Spring, Texas, 2005) pp. 93-104.

BC, Rome did exist as a very minor city-state in a relatively primitive Italy). However, that is essentially what one can infer Daniel said when one reads Daniel two with historical hindsight. In the time of those (Roman) kings, God will set up a kingdom.

Jesus said he "must fulfill all that is written" about the Messiah. Daniel prophesied that the Messiah would come during the time of Rome. Jesus obviously fulfilled this requirement. The fact that Jesus came to Israel during the time of Rome is certainly a matter of historical fact. And what about the skeptic's question about whether Jesus could have simply arranged to fulfill as many of the prophecies as possible so he could mount a claim to be the Messiah? If Jesus were just a man trying to claim to be the Messiah, he would not have been able to arrange to fulfill this one. It is hard to have an effect on the date of one's own birth!

Daniel chapter two brings to mind the question of what the Jewish people are waiting for today. Even if they reject Jesus, the Old Testament clearly stated that the revived Kingdom of God was to be established during the time of Rome. If someone were to come to Israel today and claim, like Jesus did, to be the fulfillment of all prophecies of the Messiah, it would be impossible to establish the claim.

Actually, there is a prophecy in Daniel that is much more exacting about the date of the coming of the Messiah. Daniel two tells us that the Messiah must appear in Israel during the time of the ascendancy of Rome. Did you know that God, through Daniel, prophesied the actual year of the coming of the Messiah to Jerusalem?

The prophecy just mentioned is found in Daniel 9:24-25. In order to establish the context of this prophecy it would be helpful to read the entire chapter nine of Daniel. In this chapter, Daniel had been reading from the prophet Jeremiah, when he discovered that the period of the captivity of God's people in Babylon was supposed to endure for seventy years. As Daniel read Jeremiah, he realized that the seventy years were just about up. He then prayed to God, petitioning him to help his people. Daniel reported that after this prayer, he was given a vision of the angel Gabriel, who told him:

> "Seventy 'sevens' are decreed for your people and your holy city to finish transgression, to put an end to sin, to atone for wickedness, to bring in everlasting righteousness, to seal up vision and prophecy and to anoint the most holy.
>
> "Know and understand this: From the issuing of the decree to restore and rebuild Jerusalem until the Anointed One, the ruler, comes, there will be seven 'sevens' and sixty-two 'sevens.' It will be rebuilt with streets and a trench, but in times of trouble" (Daniel 9:24,25).

There is no doubt that this is a prophecy of the Messiah. In fact, the Hebrew word Messiah literally means "the Anointed One." Surely the Jewish reader would see the Messiah in the phrase, "the Anointed One, the ruler" who was to come to "restore and rebuild Jerusalem." In this vision given to Daniel, God revealed several hundred years before the fact when the Messiah was going to come to Jerusalem. In one's first reading, this prophecy may appear to be a bit obscure, but a careful reading combined with a little historical background makes the interpretation straightforward.

There are two crucial aspects to understanding this prophecy. First, one must understand the meaning of the seventy "sevens." Second, the exact meaning of the phrase, "the decree to restore and rebuild Jerusalem" must be explained.

What does the phrase "seventy 'sevens'" refer to? First, seventy "sevens" is seventy times seven, which is four hundred ninety. Second, the phrases, "Seventy 'sevens'...to finish" and in Daniel 9:26, "After sixty-two 'sevens' the Messiah will be cut off," clearly imply that the sevens are periods of time. Could this be 490 months? 490 days? 490 years? 490 weeks? Or could this be some sort of symbolic language for an indefinite period of time? It would be fair to say that from the context of this scripture alone, this question would be difficult to answer with certainty. However, if one considers that Daniel chapter two already informed us that the Messiah was to come to Israel during the time of Rome, only one possibility seems reasonable. The Messiah is to come to Jerusalem 490 *years* after the decree to restore and rebuild Jerusalem. Four hundred and ninety months is about forty-one years, and the time of Rome was much farther off than that in Daniel's day.[8]

The next thing, then, is to establish the date of the decree to restore and rebuild Jerusalem. Cyrus "the Great" of Persia defeated Babylon in the year 539 BC, allowing the captivity of Israel to end. The Persians issued a number of decrees in the following years that could be described as restoring Israel to Jerusalem (see my book on Daniel for more details on this). Of those, the one that could most accurately be described as a decree to actually restore and rebuild the city of Jerusalem was that issued by the Persian ruler Artaxerxes in 458 BC. You may want to get out your calculator on this one. If you calculate when 490 years after the year 458 BC falls, you will get the answer AD 32. Actually, your calculator will be off by one year because there was no year AD 0. Therefore, the correct answer is AD 33. It does not require a

---

8. Admittedly, this argument is somewhat simplified. To see the argument worked out more fully, see John Oakes, *Daniel, Prophet to the Nations*, (Illumination Publishers, Spring, Texas, 2005), pp. 152-164.

Bible expert to realize the significance of this answer. It would appear that, Daniel predicted when Jesus Christ would be crucified. Daniel predicted that somewhere around AD 33, God would provide a way to "put an end to sin, to atone for wickedness...and to anoint the most holy." This is not smoke and mirrors. The author did not make up the part about the decree to restore and rebuild Jerusalem being issued in 458 BC. In fact, it is found in Ezra 7:12-26, in which the year of the reign of Artaxerxes is clearly stated.[9]

Remember our outline. A prophecy will be proven genuine, even to the skeptic, if it meets four criteria. The Old Testament passage must be clearly about the Messiah, and it must have been written hundreds of years before the prophesied event. Both are certainly true about Daniel 9. Besides, the fulfillment of the event must be a matter of historical record, found in ancient texts other than the Bible. Although one could argue plus or minus two or three years for the date of his death, the fact that Jesus lived and died almost exactly 490 years after the decree to restore and rebuild Jerusalem is an historical fact. Last, one can ask if there is any way Jesus, knowing the Old Testament, could have arranged to fulfill the prophecy in order to allow him to falsely claim to be the Messiah. If Jesus were just a man, it would have been really difficult for him to arrange to be alive at the right time to fulfill this prophecy. At the risk of being redundant, it seems fair to ask the skeptic how they can explain away Daniel chapter nine.

The fact is that there are dozens of other prophesies of the Messiah scattered throughout the Old Testament that were fulfilled in the life of Jesus Christ. The interested reader is invited to search through some or the entire list in the following table. This list represents only a fraction of those that could be mentioned. However, surely the examples already used are sufficient to make the case.

Let us summarize the prophecies listed in this chapter. In order for anyone to be able to make the claim, as Jesus did, to be the realization of everything written in the Hebrew scripture about the Messiah, that person must:

    Be despised and rejected by men
    Be pierced
    Be silent when accused
    Have no physical descendants

---

9. Actually, there is a little bit of wiggle room in the dates, because the context of Ezra 7 allows for a date of either 459 or 458 BC for the decree. Besides, it is difficult to establish the exact year of the death of Jesus Christ. One can conservatively estimate the date of the crucifixion somewhere between 29 and 32 AD. Again, more details on this can be found in my book on Daniel.

Be buried with the rich
Be extremely thirsty at the time of his death
Be crucified
Have people divide his garments among them
Have people gamble for his clothing
Be sold for thirty pieces of silver
Have his blood money returned and used for the potter
Be born in Bethlehem
Be raised in Galilee somewhere near Nazareth
Be born in the time of Rome
Die somewhere around AD 33.

One can choose any five of these requirements at random to create a list for which there is only one person in the entire history of the world who has experienced all five in their own lifetime. Amazingly, several different writers who recorded their prophecies over a span of several hundred years made these predictions. Every one was written several hundred years before Jesus Christ was born. There is simply no other possible explanation. Jesus Christ is the Messiah and the Old Testament contains writings that are inspired by God.

In my own personal experience, I have heard some willing to debate the Lord, liar or lunatic argument. I met people who would at least put up some sort of reasoned argument against the biblical miracles or against the resurrection of Jesus, but up until now, I have never met anyone who is willing to even engage in a reasoned argument against the prophecies of the Messiah. There is no leg for the argument to stand on. The only thing the skeptic is left with is the choice either to accept the truth or to close his or her mind and simply refuse to accept the obvious truth and the implications that come along with that truth.

How could this happen? How could someone absolutely refuse to accept something that has been proven beyond a reasonable doubt? How can theologians stand before their defenseless students and spout forth nonsense about the Bible being a work of man? One might as well ask why someone dying of cancer would refuse treatment. One could similarly ask why that crazy guy Harry Truman (no relationship to the past President) refused to leave Mount St. Helens when it was about to blow up. One could ask how the general public in Germany could ignore the mass extinction of the Jews amongst them.

In general, what we believe has more to do with emotion than cold logic. When something that is true threatens our feeling of self-worth or of self-preservation, it is ignored easily enough. Those who believe in the Bible should be patient with those who do not accept the seemingly obvious implications of Scripture. We too have been guilty of accepting as true things that which now seem foolish to us. In fact, we are probably making a similar mistake in some area of our lives even now. Patience and compassion are called for.

In this chapter we have looked at a number of prophecies of the Messiah that found their fulfillment in Jesus Christ. In the next section, we will look at a number of other prophecies found throughout the Bible. Be prepared to be impressed with the Word of God.

OLD TESTAMENT PROPHECIES OF THE MESSIAH

Genesis 3:15	Psalms 78:2	Isaiah 49:6
Genesis 12:3	Psalms 110:1	Isaiah 55:4
Genesis 49:10	Psalms 132:11	Jeremiah 23:5,6
Deuteronomy 18:15	Isaiah 2:3,4	Daniel 7:13,14
Deuteronomy 21:23	Isaiah 7:14	Zechariah 3:8-10
Psalms 2:2	Isaiah 9:6	Zechariah 6:12
Psalms 16:8-10	Isaiah 11:10,11	Zechariah 9:9,10
Psalms 31:5	Isaiah 25:6-9	Zechariah 13:1
Psalms 68:18	Isaiah 28:16	Malachi 3:1
Psalms 69:21	Isaiah 40:10-11	

For Today

1. It would appear that the case for the Old Testament is made. Is there anything even remotely equivalent to the fulfilled prophecy in the Bible to be found in the scriptures of other world religions? (You may need to do some thinking or asking around on this one.)

2. In view of your answer to the first question, can the belief that various world religions are just different paths to the same truth be maintained?

3. Can you think of something in the course of your life that at one time you strongly resisted believing despite a mountain of evidence in its favor? Why were you unwilling at the time to accept what now seems painfully obvious?

4. In this section, arguments based on probability were avoided because they can be very subjective. However, if you are a bit into math, you can try this exercise. Try to obtain a very rough estimate of what fraction of all people in the history of the world have been crucified. Then try to estimate the fraction of all people in the world who have lived in the area around Galilee near the border of Zebulun and Naphtali. Last, attempt to estimate the fraction of all people who have had no descendants despite reaching adulthood. Multiply these fractions. Do you already have a number small enough that by random chance not a single person ever in the history of the world would have had all three things happen to them?

Challenge: Choose three other messianic prophecies in the Old Testament from the table in this chapter. Find their fulfillment in the New Testament and analyze them by the same criteria as used in this chapter (when written, why messianic, is it historical and could Jesus have arranged it).

Chapter Five
Visions of the Future

> *If what a prophet proclaims in the name of the Lord does not take place or come true, that is a message the Lord has not spoken.*
>
> *– Deuteronomy 18:21*

Think for a minute back to the first century. What do you think the typical gospel sermon was like? Did the early evangelists principally made an appeal to the emotions of their hearers? Was the message of the apostles a diatribe against the pagan religion of the day? The book of Acts is the most reliable source available for the very early history of the Christian church. A brief survey of a number of the sermons recorded in Acts will yield an outline something like this:

1. Jesus Christ fulfilled the prophecies of the Messiah found in the Scriptures (the Old Testament, of course, being the only "Scriptures" at the time).
2. Jesus proved himself to be the Son of God by the miracles he worked, and especially by being raised from the dead.
3. Through the death of Jesus on the cross, God provides a way for your sins to be forgiven.
4. Therefore, repent and put your faith in Jesus Christ.

It is interesting to consider that the earliest evangelists stressed evidence for faith in Jesus Christ in their public sermons. They did this much more than is typically done today. Why might that be?

A common misconception is that the average person in the time of Christ was extremely emotional and superstitious—much more so than today. Some skeptics would even argue that the extreme tendency toward superstition of the ancient peoples would explain how the early church was able to pull off convincing people that Jesus was raised from the dead. It is interesting to note that the early gospel preachers relied more strongly on reason and evidence in their evangelistic appeals than most of their counterparts in the twenty-first century. Perhaps we need to reconsider our stereotype that the people in the ancient world, especially in the time of Rome, were more prone to emotional, superstition-laden argument than we are. In fact, given the influence of Greek culture, with its emphasis on reason and logic, perhaps the shoe is really on the other foot. Do the facts bear out a claim that the earliest believers in Jesus Christ were gullible and easily convinced? The answer, in general, is no.

What about those to whom the Old Testament writings were originally addressed? Were they an extremely emotional and superstitious lot—easily believing in whatever crackpot came along with a new religious theory? From the modern perspective, the cultures in the ancient Near East may appear more prone to superstition and emotionalism, at least before the influence of the Greeks, with their emphasis on logical argument and rhetoric. It is interesting however, that in reading the Old Testament, one finds a picture of God being careful to provide solid evidence to his people regarding the reliability of the revelations he was bringing to them. Consider, for example, Deuteronomy 18:21, 22:

> You may say to yourselves, "How can we know when a message has not been spoken by the Lord?" If what a prophet proclaims in the name of the Lord does not take place, or come true, that is a message the Lord has not spoken. That prophet has spoken presumptuously. Do not be afraid of him.

In this passage God was telling his people, through Moses, how to test the validity of the message coming from a prophet. The sayings of a prophet were to be considered as coming from God if the things that he predicted actually come to pass. Evidently, the Jews were expected to consider carefully the validity of whatever message they heard, in order to decide whether it was from God or not. Although describing future events was not the primary role of the prophets of Israel, it was apparently something they would do on occasion; partly to prepare God's people for future events, but also to provide evidence to support believing that the prophet was speaking for God. With a few exceptions,[1] the near-term predictions of the Old Testament prophets were usually not recorded in the Bible. However, God decreed through Moses that those who were to be accepted as prophets of God had to pass a very rigorous test. One hundred per cent of their short-term predictions had to come true for them to be accepted as true messengers of

---

1. 2 Chronicles 18:9-27 would be one example.

God. If they predicted rain and instead a drought occurred, or if they predicted military victory and a defeat ensued, the supposed prophet was to be ignored. Surely none of the so-called modern-day prophets would be able to pass this test!

In this chapter, we will be looking at a number of prophetic passages in both the Old and the New Testaments. These will be prophecies of things not directly related to the coming of the Messiah, as messianic prophecies have already been covered in the previous section. Some will be prophecies of the distant future, while others will be of things fulfilled within one generation of the message. Some of these will meet the rigorous standards described in the previous chapter (definitely written hundreds of years before, certainly prophetic, confirmed by historical account outside the Bible), while others will rely on events recorded in the Bible. All will contribute to a growing conviction that the entire Bible is the inspired Word of God.

OLD TESTAMENT PROPHECIES THAT WERE FULFILLED DURING OLD TESTAMENT TIMES

A number of books on Christian apologetics cover prophecies of the Messiah. Few cover Old Testament prophecies that were fulfilled during Old Testament times. This is partly because messianic prophecies provide such compelling evidence. Another factor is that prophecies of the Messiah involve historical events with which many readers are already at least somewhat familiar. The prophecies included in this section may well involve historical events about which the reader is not familiar. Nevertheless, they provide further convincing evidence for the inspiration of the Bible. In addition, they offer helpful insight into how the Jewish readers of the Old Testament were convinced that God inspired the writings of the prophets.

Although we do not have access to the conversations in which the ancient Hebrew scholars discussed what writings to include in their Bible (the Old Testament), it is easy to imagine them taking note in their discussions of some of the fulfilled prophecies to be mentioned here. Almost certainly those who discussed what writings were to be considered inspired by God kept the standard of Deuteronomy 18:21, 22 in mind. Did all the predictions of this prophet come true, as far as we know?

THE DESTRUCTION OF ISRAEL AND JERUSALEM

In the book of Deuteronomy, one can find stern warnings to the Israelites against turning away from the one true God and turning toward idols. In chapter twenty-eight of Deuteronomy, God warned his people that if they were disobedient to the law delivered to them by Moses:

> The Lord will drive you and the king you set over you to a nation unknown to you or your fathers. There you will worship other gods, gods of wood and stone. You will become a thing of horror and an object of scorn and ridicule to all the nations where the Lord will drive you (Deuteronomy 28: 36,37).

God, through Moses, then listed a number of consequences of disobedience. Further down, he continued:

> The Lord will bring a nation against you from far away, from the ends of the earth, like an eagle swooping down, a nation whose language you will not understand, a fierce-looking nation without respect for the old or pity for the young. They will devour the young of your livestock and the crops of your land until you are destroyed. They will leave you no grain, new wine, or oil, nor any calves of your herds or lambs of your flocks until you are ruined. They will lay siege to all the cities throughout your land until the high fortified walls in which you trust fall down. They will besiege all the cities throughout the land the Lord your God is giving you. Because of the suffering that your enemy will inflict on you during the siege, you will eat the fruit of the womb, the flesh of the sons and daughters the Lord your God has given you (Deuteronomy 28:49-53).

> The Lord will send you back to Egypt on a journey I said you should never make again. There you will offer yourselves for sale to your enemies as male and female slaves, but no one will buy you (Deuteronomy 28:68).

The fulfillment in history of Moses' prophetic words is a familiar thing to those who are well versed in Old Testament biblical history. For some, the fact that these words of Moses were fulfilled to the letter is so familiar that they may easily miss the astounding nature of the prophecy and its exact fulfillment. For those less knowledgeable of the relevant Near Eastern history, some background information will be helpful.

The events recorded in Deuteronomy occurred around 1400 BC. We depend for the details of the story on the record in the Bible, but at least the broad outline of the events surrounding the Hebrews entering and conquering significant parts of Palestine are confirmed by archaeological record (see chapter seven for more on this). After entering the Promised Land, the Hebrew people were not politically unified. They were organized primarily along the lines of the twelve tribes, with occasional periods of at least partial unity under the Judges. However, as prophesied by Moses, the Israelites eventually set a king over themselves. The first king was Saul the Benjamite. Upon his death, King David came to power, establishing a dynasty that lasted for over four hundred years. David built a powerful nation, over which he ruled personally from about 1010 to 970 BC. Political and spiritual unity proved to be short-lived. By the reign of David's grandson Rehoboam, corruption in both government and religion led to the division of the kingdom into the Northern Kingdom (known as Israel, Samaria or Ephraim) with its capital at Samaria, under King Jeroboam and his successors, and the Southern Kingdom (Judah), with its capital at Jerusalem, under the Davidic kings.

The Northern Kingdom was spiritually more corrupt than the Southern. It never fully accepted worship of Jehovah, but rather mixed worship of Jehovah God with obeisance to Baal and other pagan gods. For this reason (at least from the biblical perspective), the Northern Kingdom was completely destroyed in 722 BC by the Assyrian armies under Shalmanezer. Samaria was leveled, and thousands of captives were taken as slaves and scattered to various points in the vast Assyrian Empire. These events are recorded in 2 Kings 17. They are confirmed by archaeological finds in Nineveh, the capital of Assyria.

Although idolatry was a major problem in Judah as well, the Southern Kingdom kept at least the form of correct worship generally much more faithfully than did Ephraim. Nevertheless, as the Jews in Judah slipped further into idolatry, the Babylonians under King Nebuchadnezzar finally conquered them. Jerusalem was defeated in 605 BC, and many were carried as slaves into captivity. At that point, Jerusalem began paying tribute to Babylon. However, in 597 BC, the king rebelled and the city was again attacked and put under siege by Nebuchadnezzar. This time, the king was taken into captivity along with thousands of Israelites. A puppet king was left in his place. When this king rebelled, Nebuchadnezzar attacked again. This time, the temple was destroyed and Jerusalem was finally leveled in 586 BC.

Nevertheless, a small remnant of Jews remained behind under a governor who was not of the Davidic dynasty. Foolishly, a minority of the remnant rebelled even against this authority as established by Nebuchadnezzar. Out of fear of the returning armies, the majority of the remnant fled in the opposite direction, into Egypt, in hopes of finding safe haven there. These events are recorded in 2 Kings 25 and Jeremiah 52. Again, separate Babylonian records substantially confirm the biblical record.

Visions of the Future

Imagine one of the Israelite refugees in Egypt pulling out a manuscript including what we now call Deuteronomy 28 and considering the fate of Israel. Imagine him or her thinking "if only we had listened to the warnings of Moses." The prophecy of Deuteronomy 28 had been fulfilled in exact detail. As prophesied, the Israelites put a king over themselves ("and the king you set over you," v. 36). In addition, exactly as prophesied, God sent them and their king into exile in a country with which they were not even familiar. At the time of the conquest of Palestine under Joshua, the Israelites were very familiar with Egypt, but at that time the Assyrian Empire did not yet even exist, and Babylon was a distant and at least temporarily insignificant city. Later, however, the name Assyria became synonymous with ferocity and cruelty ("a fierce-looking nation without respect for the old or pity for the young" v. 50). Both the Assyrians and Babylonians conquered Israel by a strategy of laying siege to the major cities ("They will besiege all the cities throughout the land the Lord your God is giving you" v. 52). During the siege of Samaria, the famine became so extreme that some of the Jews actually resorted to cannibalism of their own children. This gruesome fact is recorded in 2 Kings 6:24-31 ("Because of the suffering that your enemy will inflict on you during the siege, you will eat the fruit of the womb, the flesh of the sons and daughters the Lord your God has given you" v. 53). Perhaps most astonishingly of all, Moses accurately prophesied the part about the last remnant fleeing into Egypt ("The Lord will send you back in ships to Egypt on a journey I said you should never make again" v. 68).

Fortunately for Israel, and for God's plan to bless his people, the prophecy did not end with Deuteronomy 28:68.

> When all these blessings and curses I have set before you come upon you and you take them to heart wherever the Lord your God disperses you among the nations, and when you and your children return to the Lord your God and obey him with all your heart and with all your soul according to everything I command you today, then the Lord your God will restore your fortunes and have compassion on you and gather you again from all the nations where he scattered you. Even if you have been banished to the most distant land under the heavens, from there the Lord your God will gather you and bring you back. He will bring you to the land that belonged to your fathers, and you will take possession of it (Deuteronomy 30:1-5).

Of course, God's prophetic promise of blessing to his people upon their repentance was fulfilled as well, even after they had been scattered across the Near East. After a seventy-year period of exile for God's people under the Babylonians, God allowed the Persian general Cyrus to conquer Babylon. Almost immediately after his victories, Cyrus decreed a general return of the Jews to their homeland in order to rebuild their nation (see Ezra 1:2-4 for an excerpt from that decree). With the support and help of Cyrus and his successors, thousands of Israelites returned to the Promised Land, rebuilding the temple and the city of Jerusalem. The prophecy was fulfilled to the letter. As one scans the spectrum of human history, are there any other examples of a people who was conquered and totally scattered, but who later returned in numbers to their original homeland under the protection of a new conquering power?

The author cannot think of any.[2] The prophecy in Deuteronomy 30 is very specific. It is also very unlikely by the standard of human history. However, God brought it to pass. Good job, God. It is worth bearing in mind that approximately 900 years separated the prophecy in Deuteronomy 28-30 and its complete fulfillment. That would be equivalent to a prediction made somewhere around AD 1100 being fulfilled today.

REBUILDING JERICHO

There is another interesting Old Testament prophecy that can be found in the book of Joshua. This prophecy may not have had such a great impact on the stage of world history, but it is an amazing example of specific prophetic fulfillment. At the time of the destruction of Jericho, the leader of God's people, Joshua, made the following statement:

> "Cursed before the Lord is the man who undertakes to rebuild this city, Jericho: At the cost of his firstborn son will he lay its foundations; at the cost of his youngest will he set up its gates" (Joshua 6:26).

One might read the book of Joshua and pass through this prophecy without paying it great notice. Unfortunately, a few hundred years later, an Israelite made the same mistake. In I Kings 16:26 there is a record of a man named Hiel of Bethel who, in the time of King Ahab (around 860 BC), rebuilt the city of Jericho. This was somewhere around five hundred years after the prophecy of Joshua. Perhaps Hiel was unaware of the prophecy, or perhaps he figured that five hundred years was long

---

2. With the possible exception of the return of the Jews to their ancient homeland in Palestine in the past century.

enough for God to forget the warning he had made through Joshua. Whatever the reason for Hiel not taking heed of the solemn oath from Joshua, the Bible records that at the time of laying the foundation of Jericho, the unfortunate man lost his first-born son Abiram. Despite this tragic loss, Hiel continued to build Jericho, "and he set up its gates at the cost of his youngest son Segub" (I Kings 16:34). Will we make the same mistake as Hiel, or will we take heed to the Word of God?

THE GREATNESS OF BABYLON

Another very interesting prophecy that was both recorded and fulfilled during Old Testament times is found in the book of Isaiah, chapter 39. Here one finds recorded the visit of an envoy from the city of Babylon to King Hezekiah in Jerusalem. Hezekiah reigned in Jerusalem from 716 to 687 BC. At the time of the envoy's visit, Babylon was a major city, but it had no independent political power at all. It was subject to the mighty Assyrian Empire. Hezekiah took the envoys on a tour of his palace, showing them his storehouse of gold, silver, spices and other treasures. Despite the fact that Babylon was politically powerless at the time, Isaiah made what must have seemed an amazing prophecy to Hezekiah at that time.

> Then Isaiah said to Hezekiah, "Hear the word of the Lord Almighty: The time will surely come when everything in your palace, and all that your fathers have stored up until this day, will be carried off to Babylon. Nothing will be left, says the Lord. And some of your descendants, your own flesh and blood who will be born to you, will be taken away, and they will become eunuchs in the palace of the king of Babylon" (Isaiah 39:5-7).

This prophecy/prediction of Isaiah would be roughly equivalent in the modern context to someone predicting that sometime around a hundred years from now, the city of Houston and the state of Texas will rise up and rebel against the United States, form its own independent power, and conquer Mexico. Would anyone believe a prediction like this? Yet, this is essentially what happened. Sure enough, in the year 612 BC, about one hundred years after the prophetic statement of Isaiah, Nabopolassar, a Babylonian general, along with Cyaxares, the leader of the Medes, rose in rebellion against Assyria and destroyed its capital of Nineveh. Seven years later Nabopolassar's successor, Nebuchadnezzar, conquered Judah, taking off to Babylon the treasure that had been so proudly displayed by Hezekiah.

There is more to the specific fulfillment of this prophecy. Remember that Isaiah had said that some of Hezekiah's own flesh and blood descendants would be taken away and become eunuchs in the palace of the king of Babylon. Unfortunately, this is exactly what happened. In 605 BC, Hezekiah's great grandson King Jehoiakim payed tribute to Nebuchadnezzar, and a number of captives/hostages were taken to Babylon. Later, Jehoiakim rebelled against Babylon. Soon after, he died and was succeeded by his son, Hezekiah's great, great grandson, Jehoiachin. Nebuchadnezzar returned and put Jerusalem under siege. The city wall was breached, Jehoachin fled, and was captured. He and many of his family and palace eunuchs were carried into captivity in Babylon. This tragedy occurred in 597 BC in dramatic and specific fulfillment of the prophecy of Isaiah. These events are recorded in 2 Kings 24, 25 as well as in 2 Chronicles 36.

Isaiah wrote down his prophecy of these events over one hundred years before they happened. To add to the illustration above, this would be like a modern-day prophet adding to his or her prediction for Texas that at the time Texas conquers Mexico, the great, great grandson of Vincente Fox (the former president of Mexico) will be in power, and that he will be taken to Houston and kept in captivity there, along with his family. Let us face the facts here. This amazing prophecy shows that God spoke through Isaiah.

SEVENTY YEARS OF CAPTIVITY

The prophet Isaiah foretold the destruction of Jerusalem. His successor Jeremiah lived through the tragic events foretold by Isaiah. God gave Jeremiah the unenviable task of prophesying the destruction of Jerusalem while the city was surrounded by Nebuchadnezzar's troops. To say the least, the leaders of Jerusalem were not pleased when Jeremiah advised the people to give up and surrender to their hated enemies, the Babylonians. In order to shut him up, they threw him down to the bottom of a deep well and left him for dead.

Jeremiah prophesied doom to Jerusalem saying, "thus says the Lord." Actually, it would not have required a miraculous prophetic ability for Jeremiah to predict that the end was near for Jerusalem when a seemingly insurmountable army surrounded the city. Probably even Jean Dixon could have gotten that one right. However, during this crisis, Jeremiah was able to prophesy a return to greatness for God's people.

Therefore the Lord says this: "Because you have not listened to my words, I will summon all the peoples of the north and my servant Nebuchadnezzar king of Babylon," declares the Lord, "and I will bring them against this land and its inhabitants and against all the surrounding nations. I will completely destroy them and make them an object of horror and scorn, and an everlasting ruin. I will banish from them the sounds of joy and gladness, the voices of bride and bridegroom, the sound of millstones and the light of the lamp. This whole country will become a desolate wasteland, and these nations will serve the king of Babylon *seventy years*.

"But when the *seventy years* are fulfilled, I will punish the king of Babylon and his nation, the land of the Babylonians, for their guilt," declares the Lord (Jeremiah 25:8-12, emphasis added).

God caused this prophecy to be fulfilled to the letter. In the year 605 BC the first part of this prophecy was realized (during Jeremiah's lifetime) as Nebuchadnezzar surrounded the city and Jehoiakim was forced to surrender. The seventy years of captivity had begun. Almost seventy years later, while reading Jeremiah in the city of Babylon, Daniel, one of the original captives taken in 605 BC, read this passage.[3] He stood in the city that had been captured by the Persian general Cyrus just that year. He did a little math, and realized that the restoration of Israel was imminent. Daniel began to pray.

Sure enough, just as Isaiah had prophesied, seventy years after the captivity, and after the destruction of Jerusalem, the Babylonian Empire was destroyed, and Cyrus decreed the return of the Jews to Jerusalem. Daniel read from Jeremiah "In the first year of Darius," which is the first year after the capture of Babylon, or around 538 BC. This was the year Cyrus issued his decree, allowing the Jews to return to Jerusalem (Ezra 1:2-4). The Jewish remnant probably arrived in Jerusalem in the year 536 or 535 BC, seventy years after the captivity in 605 BC.[4]

How did Jeremiah know such an overwhelming force as that of the mighty Babylonian Empire would only last for seventy years? And how did he know that the Jewish remnant would return to Jerusalem seventy years after the captivity had begun? The answer is obvious.

---

3. Daniel 9:1-3

4. For a more careful discussion of the date of the captivity and the return, see Sir Robert Anderson, *Daniel in the Critic's Den,* (Kregel Publications, Grand Rapids, Michigan, 1990), pp. 153-159, and John M. Oakes, *Daniel, Prophet to the Nations,* (Illumination Publishers, Spring, Texas, 2008).

CYRUS THE SAVIOR OF ISRAEL

If Daniel had read Isaiah carefully, he could even have known ahead of time who it was that would conquer Babylon. Arguably, Isaiah 44:28-45:2 and 45:13 are the most specific of all Old Testament prophesies.

> ...who says of Cyrus, 'He is my shepherd
> and will accomplish all that I please;
> he will say of Jerusalem, "Let it be rebuilt,"
> and of the temple, "Let its foundations be laid."
>
> "This is what the Lord says to his anointed,
> to Cyrus, whose right hand I take hold of
> to subdue nations before him
> and to strip kings of their armor,
> to open doors before him
> so that gates will not be shut:
> I will go before you and will level the mountains;
> I will break down gates of bronze
> and cut through bars of iron.
> I will give you the treasures of darkness,
> riches stored in secret places,
> so that you may know that I am the Lord,
> the God of Israel, who calls you by name.
> For the sake of Jacob my servant,
> of Israel my chosen,
> I call you by name
> and bestow on you a title of honor,
> though you do not acknowledge me.
>
> "I will raise up Cyrus in my righteousness:
> I will make all his ways straight.
> He will rebuild my city
> and set my exiles free,
> but not for a price or reward,
> says the Lord Almighty" (Isaiah 44:28-45:4 and 45:13).

Cyrus, later known as Cyrus "The Great," completed his meteoric rise to power as the head of the great Persian/Mede Empire in 550 BC. It was not until 539 BC that he was able, with the help of his Median allies, to conquer the city of Babylon, ultimately freeing the Jews from their captivity there. How did Isaiah know the name of Israel's deliverer some time before 700 BC? For Isaiah to correctly guess in the 700s

BC that the politically powerless Babylonians would rise to power and destroy Assyria is quite remarkable. When he then went on to predict that God's people would be delivered from captivity after seventy years, that was right up there on the amazement level scale. But when Isaiah got the name of the still-unborn general who would conquer Babylon and release God's people from enslavement over one hundred and fifty years before it happened, well, what can one say about that?

The skeptic has only one conceivable fallback in this situation, which is to claim that Isaiah 44 and 45 is a later insertion after the fact. Of course, they have no reliable evidence to support their claim. The main thing they have is their conviction that the Bible must be the work of man. A more reasonable explanation of the facts is that this amazing prophecy of Isaiah was part of the reason that the book ultimately became an accepted part of the Hebrew scripture. God virtually forced the hand of the scribes and teachers. That God inspired Isaiah must have been obvious to anyone reading it from the time of the restoration of Israel onward.

There are actually a few details in Isaiah's prophecy besides the simple naming of Cyrus as the deliverer of Israel. This passage specifically says that Cyrus will say of Jerusalem, "Let it be rebuilt," and "Let its foundation be laid." The historically unique fact that Cyrus carried out a policy of returning exiles to their homelands to rebuild their nations has already been mentioned. In 2 Chronicles 36:23 one can find one of Cyrus' decrees:

> The Lord, the God of heaven, has given me all the kingdoms of the earth and he has appointed me to build a temple for him at Jerusalem in Judah. Anyone of his people among you—may the Lord his God be with him, and let him go up.

Perhaps by this time Cyrus had been shown a copy of Isaiah! In fact Cyrus, as well as his successors, actually offered significant amounts of money from their treasuries to support the rebuilding of the Temple and of the city of Jerusalem.

The prophecy also states that Cyrus will subdue nations and open doors before him so that gates will not be shut. It so happens that when Cyrus conquered Babylon, he had his armies divert the Euphrates River. Once the riverbed ran nearly dry, his armies marched right into the city and opened its gates almost without a fight.

God, through Isaiah, also predicted in Isaiah 45:4 that he would call Cyrus by name (he certainly did that), and that he would give him a title of honor, even though he would not acknowledge the name of Jehovah. In Isaiah 45:13, God specifically declares that Cyrus will "rebuild my city" (i.e. Jerusalem), and "set my exiles free, but not for a price or reward." Cyrus did indeed set the exiles free, for no obvious financial or even political reward. This seldom-mentioned prophecy is surely one of the most amazing in all of scripture.

A great number of other Old Testament prophecies fulfilled during the time of the Old Testament could be cited, but the examples used here should provide plenty of evidence for the inspiration of the Bible. Besides, they may give insight into how the Old Testament books were selected in the first place. These writings all passed the test of Deuteronomy 18:22-23.

OLD TESTAMENT PROPHECIES FULFILLED "BETWEEN THE TESTAMENTS"

There are also a number of prophecies found in the Old Testament whose fulfillment are found, not in the Bible, but rather in the pages of history. This is especially true of those Old Testament prophecies that were fulfilled in the period "between the Testaments."[5]

With the completion of the book of Malachi, somewhere around 435 BC, a period of biblical silence reigned for over four hundred and fifty years. This was certainly not a period in which God was not working—far from it. However, for a period of several centuries, no new revelation from God in the form of Scripture was revealed. The time of the prophets appeared to have ceased. Of course, the situation changed when, in the most dramatic fashion, John the Baptist appeared to Israel out of the desert wearing clothes of camel's hair. But that is another story.

For what must have seemed an extremely long time to the Jews, prophecy ceased. Many must have felt the glory days were over forever. However, God had not ceased speaking to his people. During the time between the Testaments he spoke to them through the amazingly specific historical fulfillment of prophecies, year after year. Despite the lack of new revelation from God, these fulfilled prophecies provided a steady stream of proof to faithful Israel that the God who spoke through the prophets was definitely still at work in the world. The faithful Jew between the Testaments could watch as empire rose and fell, as kings came and went, as times of peace and of persecution passed exactly as predicted by the prophets, including stunningly exact details that showed the sure fingerprint of God.

As the Jews could see prophecy fulfilled in their day, proving God's working in their world, so we can see marvelous evidence of the

---

5. A very readable source which will bring alive some of the prophecies in Daniel is Charles F. Pfeiffer, *Between the Testaments* (Baker Books, Grand Rapids, Michigan, 1959).

inspiration of God's word. Although we do not have the immediate impact of seeing God's words fulfilled in specific events of our day, we do have the advantage of historical perspective, allowing us to study the facts of history in light of Biblical prophecy from a distance that allows us to get the big picture of how God works through people and events and the movements of history.

There are dozens of Old Testament prophecies that were fulfilled in the time between the Testaments. For the sake of simplicity and clearness of presentation, we will focus only on those found in the book of Daniel. For a wider description of prophecies from Jeremiah, Isaiah, Ezekiel and other books that were fulfilled during this time, the book *Evidence That Demands a Verdict* is recommended.[6]

The book of Daniel has a theme similar to that of its New Testament equivalent—Revelation. It was written in order to provide encouragement to God's people to remain faithful no matter what the pressure from the world to conform to its ungodly standard of behavior. More specifically, Daniel was written to encourage the Jews in the time between the Testaments who were to undergo an unprecedented level of persecution, especially under the infamous ruler Antiochus Epiphanes.[7] Of course, Daniel contains actual events in the life of Daniel, Shadrach, Meshach and Abednego that are a great encouragement to remain faithful despite persecution. However, it is the predictive prophecies and visions of Daniel that are relevant to this discussion.

Put simply, the visions of Daniel provide a detailed record of the political history of the Near East for the six hundred years *after* the death of Daniel. There is no other writing in the history of mankind that is even remotely like Daniel. It is in a literary genre by itself: history books of the future!

In fact, we have already looked at two examples. We have already seen that Daniel predicted the fact that Jesus would come to Jerusalem during the time of the Roman influence in Palestine. He even predicted the year that Jesus Christ would be killed, almost six hundred years before it happened. That is amazing, but there is more.

---

6. Josh McDowell, *Evidence That Demands a Verdict*, (Here's Life Publishers, San Bernardino, California, 1972), pp 265-323. This volume includes specific prophecies concerning the fate of Tyre, Sidon, Gaza, Samaria, Edom, Nineveh, Babylon and others. There is a lot of good information here. Unfortunately, in the updated *New Evidence That Demands a Verdict*, McDowell leaves out this material.

7. For a more thorough treatment of this theme, see John M. Oakes, *Daniel, Prophet to the Nations*, (Illumination Publishers, Spring, Texas, 2008). This book has a much more thorough treatment of the predictive prophecies in Daniel. It also provides a good amount of the historical background needed to completely understand the visions of Daniel.

NEBUCHADNEZZAR'S DREAM

Consider, for example, Nebuchadnezzar's dream as interpreted by Daniel in the second chapter of his book. We have already glanced at this chapter in the context of discussing messianic prophecy. We will look at it in more detail now. Daniel two is an account of Nebuchadnezzar, the king of Babylon and conqueror of Jerusalem. In the second year of his reign (i.e. about 603 BC), Nebuchadnezzar had an extremely vivid dream that disturbed him greatly. He called upon his astrologers as well as various mystics and wise men to interpret his dream on pain of death. Apparently, he did not trust his own "seers." In order to assure the accuracy of their dream interpretation, he refused to tell them the dream itself. Under threat of death, Daniel prayed to God for help in interpreting the dream, and God answered his prayer. With God's help, Daniel told Nebuchadnezzar in specific detail the dream he had had, and provided the interpretation of the dream.

> "You looked, O king, and there before you stood a large statue—an enormous, dazzling statue, awesome in appearance. The head of the statue was made of pure gold, its chest and arms of silver, its belly and thighs of bronze, its legs of iron, its feet partly of iron and partly of baked clay. While you were watching, a rock was cut out, but not by human hands. It struck the statue on its feet of iron and clay and smashed them. Then the iron, the clay, the bronze, the silver and the gold were broken to pieces...
>
> "This was the dream, and now we will interpret it to the king.... You are the head of gold.
>
> "After you, another kingdom will rise, inferior to yours. Next, a third kingdom, one of bronze, will rule over the whole earth. Finally, there will be a fourth kingdom, strong as iron—for iron breaks and smashes everything—and as iron breaks things to pieces, so it will crush and break all the others. Just as you saw that the feet and toes were partly of baked clay and partly of iron, so this will be a divided kingdom; yet it will have some of the strength of iron in it, even as you saw iron mixed with clay. As the toes were partly iron and partly clay, so this kingdom will be partly strong and partly brittle, and just as you saw the iron mixed with baked clay, so the people will be a mixture and will not remain united, any more than iron mixes with clay.
>
> "In the time of those kings, the God of heaven will set up a kingdom that will never be destroyed, nor will it be left

to another people. It will crush all those kingdoms and bring them to an end, but it will itself endure forever" (Daniel 2: 31-44).

In interpreting the dream, with God's help, Daniel provided a quick outline of the history of the Near East for the next two thousand years! He also prophesied the coming of the kingdom of God. Daniel told Nebuchadnezzar that the head of gold was the empire/kingdom of Babylon. Because Nebuchadnezzar was the emperor of Babylon, Daniel said it in a complimentary way: "You are the head of gold." Babylon held sway over a large part of the Near East from about 610 BC until 538 BC. Probably to avoid offending Nebuchadnezzar, Daniel downplayed the importance of the kingdom represented by the chest and arms of silver, because it was to defeat Babylon. The empire that conquered Babylon was the dual Persian/Median Empire, under the leadership of Cyrus. Persia ruled the greater part of the known world for just over two hundred years. The chest of silver was Persia.

The Persian Empire was destroyed in 331 BC by the armies of Alexander the Great. Alexander founded an empire that included all of former Persia, plus Egypt and Greece. Daniel accurately predicted that Alexander and his Greek successors would "rule over the whole (known) earth." That was quite a prediction, given that it was made almost three hundred years before the appearance of Alexander on the scene. The belly and thighs of bronze in Nebuchadnezzar's dream were Greece.

It would appear, though, that Daniel's interpretation focused primarily on the fourth kingdom—the iron kingdom. It does not require a historical specialist to decide what ancient empire would best be described as being made of iron, which "breaks and smashes everything." Sure enough, exactly as predicted by Daniel, beginning in about 170 BC, and ending in the battle of Actium in 31 BC, Rome completely destroyed all remnants of the Hellenic empires established by the armies of Alexander the Great.

As vividly depicted by Daniel, Rome was the most powerful empire in all of human history. Yet, also as described by Daniel, it was to be "a divided kingdom." After centuries of world dominance, Rome separated into Eastern and Western empires. Constantine established Constantinople (also known as Byzantium or as the modern Istanbul) as an alternative eastern capital for the empire during his reign (AD 306-337). The Roman Empire was finally permanently divided after AD 395. How did Daniel know about all this in 603 BC?

Even the part in the dream about the feet, partly of iron and partly of baked clay, was played out in history exactly as described by Daniel. After separation, the Western Empire, centered in Rome, proved to be very fragile. "Barbarians" such as the Goths, Vandals and others attacked it repeatedly. Finally, the last Western Roman emperor was deposed and Rome was sacked in AD 476. The Western half of the Roman Empire was the "clay" part of the legs.

The case with the Eastern Empire, commonly known as Byzantium, was quite different. This was the part made, in Daniel's words, of iron. The Eastern Roman Empire endured for over one thousand years after Rome was divided. Byzantium was the power that protected Europe against the attacks of the Arabs for many centuries, finally bowing to defeat at the hands of the Ottoman Turks on May 29, 1453. Daniel's amazing prophecy described, in outline, the history of Western Asia, Northern Africa, and Southern Europe for two thousand years. This will surely help the nonbeliever see the reliability of the Bible!

After outlining in brief the history of the world for the next two millennia, Daniel went on to describe how during the time of Rome, God would establish a spiritual kingdom that would endure forever. This has already been described in the section on messianic prophecy. It is worth remembering that the church, the kingdom of God, has certainly outlasted the Roman Empire that fought so fiercely to destroy it. One can only imagine how the members of the church in the first two centuries took heart from Daniel chapter two.

BEASTLY DREAMS

If Daniel chapter two provides a broad historical outline of the future, then Daniel chapters seven and eight fill in the details. In chapter seven Daniel described a vision in which he saw four great beasts coming "up out of the sea": a lion, a bear, a leopard and a fourth beast, which Daniel described as "terrifying and frightening and very powerful." It had large iron teeth; it crushed and devoured its victims and trampled underfoot whatever was left" (Daniel 7:7).

The four beasts of Daniel seven are the four parts of the giant statue in Daniel two: Babylon, Persia, Greece and Rome. The first beast (v. 4), the lion, is Babylon, whose leader Nebuchadnezzar was given "the heart of a man." The second beast (v. 5), the bear, was Persia. The bear had three ribs in its mouth, which were the three great kingdoms which Persia conquered: Babylon, Lydia and Egypt. Daniel even got the number of ribs in the Bear's mouth correct. The third beast (v. 6), the leopard, was Greece, under Alexander the Great and the Greek dynasties who succeeded him to power. These successors just happened to number four ("The beast had four heads."). There is no doubt, however, that this vision primarily focused on providing God's people information about the fourth beast—the terrible beast— Rome. It would be very helpful if the reader will read all of Daniel seven to get the context.

Daniel was given an interpretation of the vision of the four beasts by a heavenly being. The interpretation follows:

> "I, Daniel, was troubled in spirit, and the visions that passed through my mind disturbed me. I approached one of those standing there and asked him the true meaning of all this.
>
> "So he told me and gave me the interpretation of these things: 'The four great beasts are four kingdoms that will rise from the earth. But the saints of the Most High will receive the kingdom and will possess it forever—yes, forever and ever.'
>
> "Then I wanted to know the true meaning of the fourth beast, which was different from all the others and most terrifying, with its iron teeth and bronze claws—the beast that crushed and devoured its victims and trampled underfoot whatever was left. I also wanted to know about the ten horns on its head and about the other horn that came up, before which three of them fell—the horn that looked more imposing than the others and that had eyes and a mouth that spoke boastfully. As I watched, this horn was waging war against the saints and defeating them, until the Ancient of Days came and pronounced judgment in favor of the saints of the Most High, and the time came when they possessed the kingdom.
>
> "He gave me this explanation: 'The fourth beast is a fourth kingdom that will appear on earth. It will be different from all the other kingdoms and will devour the whole earth, trampling it down and crushing it. The ten horns are ten kings who will come from this kingdom. After them another king will arise, different from the earlier ones; he will subdue three kings. He will speak against the Most High and oppress his saints and try to change the set times and the laws. The saints will be handed over to him for a time, times and half a time" (Daniel 7:15-25).

Daniel received this vision in 553 BC, during the reign of Belshazzar, emperor of Babylon. In it, he was shown in amazing detail the persecution of the church in the first century AD, over six hundred years in the future. This is unbelievable! This is unexplainable (unless, of course, the Bible is inspired by God).

Rome was the indescribably horrible beast in the vision. Just as Daniel described, Rome broke and crushed all nations that stood before it. But what about the ten horns in the vision? These are the first ten emperors of Rome: Augustus, Tiberius, Caligula, Claudius, Nero, Galba, Otho, Vitellius, Vespasian and Titus. Actually, the vision focuses on the eleventh horn, "the other horn that came up, before which three of them fell." This horn (or king) was the eleventh emperor of Rome: Domitian. Domitian was the first systematic persecutor of the church. Before his reign, sporadic local persecutions had broken out, but his was the first official empire-wide policy to try to stamp out this new sect. He reigned from AD 81-96. Over four hundred years before the event, Daniel predicted that the eleventh emperor of Rome would start a great persecution against the saints!

So what did this "eleventh horn" do? Domitian, through his father, overthrew three emperors who ruled simultaneously—Galba, Otho and Vitellius, fulfilling the words of the prophecy "he will subdue three kings."[8] And what about the phrase, concerning this eleventh horn, that he "had eyes and a mouth that spoke boastfully."? Contemporaries of Domitian were unanimous in describing his as being extremely boastful. He was even more arrogant than his predecessors, which is saying a lot. This is exactly as described by Daniel. He was so prideful that he even had the Roman calendar changed so that the month of October was called Domitianus! The way Daniel described Domitian's calendar-changing efforts in his vision, the eleventh horn would "try to change the set times." Fortunately, after Domitian died, his successors went back to calling it October.[9]

In verse 25, the angel also told Daniel that the eleventh horn would change "the laws." Again, this is exactly what Domitian did. During his reign Domitian threw out the entire Roman legal system (one of the greatest legal systems ever created) and inserted his own it its place. Immediately after his death, the Roman senate threw out Domitian's legal system in favor of the original Roman law.

The angel who interpreted the vision to Daniel went on to describe how the "other horn" would oppress the saints for "a time, times and half a time." In apocalyptic literature, three and a half "times" represents a limited period of persecution. Of course, this is exactly what happened. Domitian was the first to systematically persecute the church. Over the course of the next 220 years, periods of intense persecution against the disciples of Christ came and went,

---

8. This as well as many other aspects of this prophecy are explained in much more detail in John Oakes, *Daniel, Prophet to the Nations* (Illumination Publishers, Spring, Texas, 2008).
9. Actually, the name October is not all that fortunate a name either, since it means literally the eighth month, while October is actually the tenth month! The Romans inserted July (named after Julius Caesar) and August (named after Augustus Caesar) in front of September in remembrance of two emperors who deserved the honor much more than Domitian.

but ultimately, the persecutions ceased, and the church outlasted the Roman Empire.

How did Daniel, in 553 BC, know about Domitian and his persecutions against the church at the end of the first century AD? How did he know about Domitian's blatant boasting and his attempts to change the calendar? How did he know that Domitian would replace the entire Roman legal system? How did he know about the three kings Domitian was to subdue? How did he know that the eleventh emperor of Rome would be the first systematic persecutor of the church? How did he know that the persecutions were to be only temporary, and that ultimately the saints were to triumph? Good question. Only one possible answer comes into my mind. Bear in mind that this prophecy passes all the tests described before. It definitely is a prophecy of the future and its fulfillment is certainly a matter of historical record. By the way, there are many other very specific details contained in this vision that were fulfilled in a dramatic way in history (please see my book on Daniel), but for the sake of space and time, we must move on to Daniel eight.

The second beastly vision of Daniel is found in chapter eight of the book. It fills in more details of what was, for Daniel, future history. Hopefully, the reader will review chapter eight of Daniel to get the context. This vision was received in the third year of Belshazzar, which was 551 BC. In it, Daniel witnessed two beasts—a ram and a goat. In this vision, the ram and the goat are the silver chest and bronze belly of Daniel 2. They also are the bear and the leopard of Daniel seven; the Medo/Persian and the Greek Empires.

In the vision, Daniel described the first of the two beasts.

> "I looked up, and there before me was a ram with two horns, standing beside the canal, and the horns were long. One of the horns was longer than the other but grew up later. I watched the ram as he charged toward the west and the north and the south. No animal could stand against him, and none could rescue from his power. He did as he pleased and became great" (Daniel 8:3,4).

For a person reading Daniel who is unacquainted with ancient history, this would certainly seem a strange vision. However, a little reading of the history of the sixth and fifth centuries BC will readily provide an interpretation of this vision. The ram represents the empire that destroyed the Babylonian Empire. Daniel described a ram with two horns. It just so happens that the empire which destroyed Babylon was an alliance of the more powerful Medes and the less powerful Persians that defeated Babylon. These are the two horns. The leader of the campaign against Babylon was the Persian general named Cyrus. Because of his extraordinary leadership, ultimately Persia became the dominant partner in the Medo/Persian Empire. This is certainly reminiscent of, "One of the horns was longer, but it grew up later." Under Cyrus, the Persians first defeated Babylon (to the west), then the great kingdom of Lydia, under King Croesus (to the north), and finally Egypt itself (to the South). Daniel said that the "ram charged toward the west and the north and the south. Would anyone like to wager on whether Daniel got this right by luck rather than by the inspiration of God?

Even more impressive in its detail of future history is Daniel's description of the goat.

> "As I was thinking about this, suddenly a goat with a prominent horn between his eyes came from the west, crossing the whole earth without touching the ground. He came toward the two-horned ram I had seen standing beside the canal and charged at him in great rage. I saw him attack the ram furiously, striking the ram and shattering his two horns. The ram was powerless to stand against him; the goat knocked him to the ground and trampled on him and none could rescue the ram from his power. The goat became very great, but at the height of his power, his large horn was broken off, and in its place four prominent horns grew up toward the four winds of heaven" (Daniel 8:5-8).

Again, without some background in history, this vision would probably seem bizarre. In the vision, the goat is Greece and the prominent horn is Alexander the Great. Just over two hundred years after the great victories of Cyrus, the Persian Empire had lost much of its strength, although it still retained almost all of its territory. Suddenly, in the year 334 BC, a brilliant and bold Macedonian general charged across the Dardanelles Straits from Greece into Asia. With a small army, Alexander raced across the entire Persian Empire, seemingly "without touching the ground." With his small but extremely disciplined army, he repeatedly routed the far larger armies of the Persians, "the two-horned ram." The Persian/Median Empire was completely destroyed by 331 BC. Its last emperor, Darius III, was killed in 330 BC.

Alexander conquered Egypt and all of Palestine. He continued into present-day Pakistan, and was beginning to threaten the entire Indian subcontinent, when he was forced to turn back, not because of a military defeat, but by a mutiny of his troops. Finally, "at the height of his power, his large horn was broken off." In 323 BC, Alexander died at the age of only 33 years. The accuracy of Daniel's vision in predicting the future is enough to challenge the skepticism of any critic.

Actually, there is more. In Daniel's vision, the large horn (Alexander) was replaced by "four prominent horns," which grew up "toward the four winds of heaven." What is the vision referring to? When Alexander died, he left only an infant as an heir. Almost immediately, fighting broke out between his generals for control of his vast empire. By the year 319 BC, the empire had been effectively split up between four powerful generals, each of which established a Greek dynasty. The four generals were Lysimachus in the north (Thrace and Asia Minor), Cassander in the west (Macedonia and Greece), Ptolemy in the south (Egypt and Palestine) and Antigonus in the east (from Syria to India). Does that sound like one very powerful horn being replaced by four prominent horns toward the four winds of heaven? But Daniel is not through.

> Out of one of them [one of the horns] came another horn, which started small, but grew in power to the south and to the east and toward the Beautiful Land. It grew until it reached the host of the heavens, and it threw some of the starry host down to the earth and trampled on them. It set itself up to be as great as the Prince of the host; it took away the daily sacrifice from him and the place of his sanctuary was brought low. Because of rebellion, the host of the saints and the daily sacrifice were given over to it. It prospered in everything it did, and truth was thrown to the ground (Daniel 8:9-12).

The reader will not be surprised to learn that every part of this vision was fulfilled in history, right down to the smallest detail. The fifth horn that came out of one of the four horns but started small was Seleucus. Seleucus was Ptolemy of Egypt's most powerful general. He was so successful in fighting against Antigonus that he was able to carve out a territory of his own in Mesopotamia. Ultimately, he established a dynasty that was a rival of the Ptolemies. Seleucus and his successors expanded to the south (conquering Syria and Palestine) and to the east (conquering Elam, Persia and Media). Eventually, Antiochus III, the great grandson of Seleucus, took Jerusalem from the Ptolemaic kingdom, taking the "Beautiful Land." This is exactly as foretold by Daniel. As one can see, the details of Daniel's prophecy were unfolded point-by-point.

Eventually, Antiochus III's son, the dreaded Antiochus IV Epiphanes, took the throne. He promulgated a policy of destroying the Jewish religion, beginning what may well have been the most intense persecution against Judaism in ancient times. Antiochus outlawed circumcision upon pain of death. He had a statue of himself placed in the temple. He committed what must have seemed the worst conceivable abomination to the Jews when he sacrificed a pig to a pagan god in the

Temple. He outlawed the daily sacrifice as well. This is what Daniel was referring to in his vision when he mentioned that the fifth horn would "set itself up to be as great as the Prince of the host," "take away daily sacrifice" and "throw truth to the ground." This was a pretty accurate description, considering that Daniel was writing in 551 BC concerning events that occurred in 167 BC.

If one reads on in chapter eight, he or she will see Daniel predicted that the persecution of Antiochus IV would only be temporary, lasting about 1,150 days, or just over three years. In fact, the desecration of the Temple in Jerusalem began in early December of 167 BC and ended on December 25, 164 BC, a period of almost 1,150 days. How did Daniel know the length of a period of persecution almost four hundred years before it happened? The rededication of the temple on December 25, 164 BC is still celebrated by Jews today in the feast of Chanukah. One can imagine the Jews who remained faithful to God during the horrible persecutions of Antiochus reading Daniel eight and counting the days until God brought judgment on Antiochus.

Probably the reader does not need more convincing that the Daniel is inspired, but there is more. Daniel chapter eleven will undoubtedly take home the record as the most specific and detailed prophecy in the whole Bible. In this chapter, one can find what seems like an almost endless description of a war between "the king of the North" and "the king of the South." The author can vividly remember reading this passage for the first time and saying to himself "what in the world is Daniel talking about?" Perhaps the reader has felt this way when reading Daniel chapter eleven. In order to change that way of thinking, all that is required is to read a history book about the time between the Old and New Testaments. Daniel chapter eleven is a point-by-point, king-by-king, almost year-by-year description of the endless wars between the Greek Ptolemaic Dynasty (the kings of the South) and the Seleucid Dynasty (the kings of the North). It would be beyond the scope of this book to go into all the details to show how Daniel chapter eleven is future history, but let one very short paragraph taken at random from my book on Daniel suffice. It describes just one incident in the war between the Ptolemies and the Seleucids. The section below is a paraphrase of Daniel 11:9-11, supplying the actual historical details that are available from the works of such ancient historians as Josephus.

> (v.9) Later, Antiochus III, sometimes known as Antiochus the Great, will take the throne in the Northern Kingdom. He will attack the Southern Kingdom in 221 BC, with some success, but will be forced to retreat by a Ptolemaic general, Theodosius. (v. 10) Undaunted, Antiochus III will return to the attack in 218-217 BC, taking the strongholds of Tyre, Gaza, and even Raphia, a fortress on the border of Egypt proper. (v. 11) However, this particular victory will be

short-lived, as Ptolemy IV Philopater will raise an army and visit a disastrous defeat on Antiochus III, retaking all the conquered territory.[10]

A comparison of this historical sketch to the vision given in Daniel 11: 9-11 will show how convincing a mark of inspiration God has provided in this passage.

One might wonder why God gave such a detailed vision of a series of wars that did not pertain to the Jews directly at all. Actually, they pertained very much to the Jews. Eventually, the wars between the Ptolemies and the Seleucids came to Jerusalem. In fact, these same wars ultimately led to the persecutions of Antiochus IV. These persecutions are described in even more vivid detail in Daniel 11:31-35 than they were in Daniel chapter eight. This incredible prophecy was given to provide encouragement to the Jews who were to undergo the horrendous persecutions of Antiochus IV. It shows that God will ultimately prove himself faithful to his people no matter how bad the situation may appear at the time. The Jews could read in Daniel about specifics of Antiochus' persecutions, but also about his ultimate judgment by God. "Some of the wise will stumble, so that they may be refined, purified and made spotless until the time of the end, for it will still come at the appointed time" (Daniel 11:35). Even today, anyone who reads the book of Daniel can take heart from this prophecy and its fulfillment as well.

NEW TESTAMENT PROPHECIES FULFILLED

By now the reader is convinced that messianic prophecies are not the only predictions that can be used to show that God inspired the Bible. We have seen a number of prophesies that were fulfilled hundreds of years after the prophet spoke, but before Jesus arrived on the scene. There are a smaller number of examples of New Testament prophecies that were fulfilled during New Testament times. Although the number of examples is smaller, they provide an interesting insight into biblical prophecy that is fulfilled within the lifetime of the original hearers. In this section, we will look at a few of them.

Prophecies both given and fulfilled in New Testament times may not provide quite as dramatic proof of the inspiration of the Bible to the modern-day reader as some of the examples above. This would be true because the predictions were not as far removed in time from the fulfillment of the prophecy. Because the original hearing of the

---

10. John Oakes, *Daniel, Prophet to the Nations,* (Illumination Publishers, Spring, Texas, 2008) p. 175.

message, the writing down of that prophecy and the fulfillment of the prophecy all occurred within a generation or two, the skeptic can argue (whether right or wrong) that the evidence was manipulated. However, these prophecies will help to complete the picture of how God worked both in Old Testament and in New Testament times through predictive prophecies.

It has already been claimed that the prophets in the Old Testament often made short-term predictive prophecies, which were fulfilled within their own lifetime. These predictions were primarily intended to provide evidence, not to us, but to the actual hearers, that the prophets were speaking for God. For this reason, they usually did not "make the cut" to get into the Old Testament. Fortunately, there are a number of examples of relatively short-term prophecies that "made the cut" and got into the New Testament. As the reader considers these, she or he should make the application to the Old Testament as well.

Go used these New Testament prophecies as evidence of the inspiration of the message concerning Jesus Christ primarily to increase the faith of the first and second century Christians. Please bear this in mind as you consider some very interesting New Testament prophecies.

PROPHECIES OF THE KINGDOM OF GOD

The Old Testament includes a number of prophecies about the coming of the Kingdom of God, or the church.[11] We have already seen two of them. Daniel 2:44,45 describes how God would establish a kingdom during the time of the Roman kings that would destroy and outlast all the earthly kingdoms. Daniel 7:18 includes the prophetic statement that the saints would possess the kingdom forever and ever. A list of Old Testament prophecies of the kingdom would include Isaiah 2:2-4, which describes the Kingdom of God as a mountain, much like Daniel two. One could mention Zechariah 13:1,2 and dozens of others as well.

In the Old Testament, the prophecies of the Kingdom speak of an event seemingly in the distant future. The case with the New Testament is quite different. For example, in Matthew 3:2, John the

---

11. If the definition of "the church" in the Bible is taken as the body of believers of Christ, then the church and "the Kingdom" are closely related but not exactly identical terms. The church represents the Kingdom of God on the earth. The coming of the Kingdom (as described both by Old Testament prophets and by John the Baptist and Jesus) and the beginning of the Church can both be viewed as occurring at the same time, on the day of Pentecost which followed the death of Jesus. The kingdom of God is a larger concept, as it would include the new heaven and the new earth (Revelation 21:1).

Visions of the Future

Baptist said, "Repent, for the kingdom of heaven is near." Here one gets the feeling that the Kingdom is in the very near future. Jesus said the same thing concerning the Kingdom (Matthew 4:17). He expanded on this theme when he said, "I tell you the truth, some who are standing here will not taste death before they see the kingdom of God" (Luke 9:27). Jesus predicted that some of his disciples would see the coming of the Kingdom, which had been prophesied for so many centuries, in their own lifetime. Other prophecies of the kingdom given by Jesus included his claim that the Kingdom of God would be a spiritual reality, rather than a physical kingdom with border, capital and so forth (John 18:36, Luke 17:20), and that the kingdom would be ushered in with a great show of power, beginning in Jerusalem: "...and repentance and forgiveness of sins will be preached in his name to all nations, beginning at Jerusalem...I am going to send you what my Father has promised; but stay in the city until you have been clothed with power from on high" (Luke 24:47-49). Both Jesus and John the Baptist prophesied an outpouring of the Spirit and of fire (Matthew 3:11, Acts 1:5). Jesus also prophesied that Peter would be his key to usher in the Kingdom of God (Matthew 16:19).

From the context of the New Testament, it would seem that the followers of Jesus were pretty much clueless about the meaning of his prophecies about the Kingdom of God until many of them were fulfilled in one dramatic incident on the feast day of Pentecost immediately following his resurrection. The events are related in Acts chapter two. As prophesied, a great outpouring of power from God occurred at Pentecost, as the apostles were enveloped in flames and a violent and unexplained rush of wind. They were able to speak to a crowd of onlookers from virtually every known nation "beginning in Jerusalem," just as described in a number of the Kingdom prophesies. Not only that, they spoke in the hearer's native languages. Of course, as Daniel had predicted, the Kingdom came in the time of the Roman kings. Besides, it still endures today in the form of faithful disciples of Jesus Christ ("but it will itself endure forever"). The Kingdom came within the lifetime of some of the disciples (but not all: Judas was dead) as Jesus had said. In addition to all this, it was Peter who stood up before the people, preaching the first public sermon about the Kingdom of God, fulfilling Jesus' prophecy that he would hold "the keys of the kingdom of heaven."

Imagine the followers of Jesus, when they considered with hindsight all these things. They could scan all the prophecies of the Kingdom, strung out throughout the Old Testament, and sprinkled through the teachings of Jesus. They could see how all these predictive prophecies came true in one event—the outpouring of the Spirit on the Day of Pentecost. Surely, their faith in the Old Testament scripture, as well as in the sayings of Jesus must have been greatly built up. Remember that for the earliest evangelists, the basic gospel sermon outline included describing how biblical prophecy of the Messiah (and the Kingdom) was fulfilled.

THE DESTRUCTION OF JERUSALEM

One of the most significant events in the history of God's people occurred in AD 70. Because it is not recorded in the Bible, many who study the scriptures are not aware of the event, never mind being cognizant of its significance. The event being referred to is the destruction of Jerusalem by the Roman armies under Vespasian and later, his son Titus. When Jesus was crucified and raised from the dead in about AD 30, he ushered in the New Covenant. At that point, as the Bible indicates, the Old Covenant had become null and void. Nevertheless, God allowed for the Jewish sacrificial system to continue for the next forty years, allowing a window of opportunity for those Jews who were willing to accept the message of Jesus Christ. After a forty-year grace period, an event occurred that had been prophesied by Daniel as well as by Jesus himself. The destruction of Jerusalem in AD 70 brought to an end once and for all the Mosaic sacrificial system.

Daniel prophesied the destruction of Jerusalem by the Roman armies over six hundred years before the event.

> "After sixty-two 'sevens,' the Anointed One will be cut off and will have nothing. The people of the ruler who will come will destroy the city and the sanctuary. The end will come like a flood: War will continue until the end, and desolations have been decreed. He will confirm a covenant with many for one 'seven,' but in the middle of that 'seven' he will put an end to sacrifice and offering. And one who causes desolation will place abominations on a wing of the temple until the end that is decreed is poured out on him" (Daniel 9:26,27)

The Jewish historian Josephus recorded the event being prophesied by Daniel in great detail.[12] Josephus, who was not a Christian, was an eyewitness to the destruction of Jerusalem by the Roman armies. In fact, he was actually an ally of Titus, the avowed enemy of the

---

12. Josephus, *The Jewish Wars*, (English translation by William Whiston, Kregel Publications, 1960).

Jews. The account of Josephus contains many graphic depictions of the two-year siege of Jerusalem. It describes the defection of many, including the Christian remnant, to the Romans. Josephus recounted rebellion and civil war within the city, pestilence, starvation and even cannibalism. Ultimately, the soldiers of Titus undermined the walls of Jerusalem, took the city and slaughtered tens of thousands of Jews. They burned the temple to the ground and totally leveled the entire wall of the city (with the exception of the tiny remnant now known as the wailing wall). Exactly as foreseen by Daniel, the Roman priests performed pagan rites on the site of the burned-out temple, placing "abominations on the wing of the temple," providing what for the Jews was a horrifying illustration of the fact that God had "put an end to sacrifice and offering."

How did Daniel know all this over six hundred years before it happened? In addition, Jesus prophesied about AD 29 concerning the destruction of Jerusalem, providing further details beyond those found in Daniel. Speaking to the Jews, Jesus said:

> "The days will come upon you when your enemies will build an embankment against you and encircle you and hem you in on every side. They will dash you to the ground, you and the children within your walls. They will not leave one stone on another because you did not recognize the time of God's coming to you" (Luke 19:43, 44).

Jesus said these words with tremendous anguish of heart and with tears. When Jesus prophesied about the event to his disciples, he provided more details concerning the destruction of Jerusalem under Titus. At least part of the purpose of the prophecy was to provide warning for the Christian church to flee Jerusalem before they were trapped and ultimately killed in the destruction of the city.

> "When you see Jerusalem surrounded by armies, you will know that its desolation is near. Then let those who are in Judea flee to the mountains, let those in the city get out, and let those in the country not enter the city. For this is the time of punishment in fulfillment of all that has been written [referring to Daniel 9:26,27]. How dreadful it will be in those days for pregnant women and nursing mothers! There will be great distress in the land and wrath against this people [referring to the Jews, not the Christians]. They will fall by the sword and will be taken as prisoners to all the nations. Jerusalem will be trampled on by the Gentiles until the times of the Gentiles are fulfilled" (Luke 21:20-24).[13]

---

13. Also see Matthew 24:15-25, Mark 13:2, and Mark 13:14-20.

In his book *The Jewish Wars*, Josephus described the fulfillment of this prophecy of Jesus in graphic and chilling detail. He described the ramp built by Titus, the anguish of the mothers, forced to sell or even to kill their children for food. He described the ultimate massacre and enslavement of the Jews who remained in the city until the end. Interestingly, Josephus does not record any Christians being harmed in the siege and destruction of Jerusalem, probably because they had already heeded the words of Jesus and fled the city. When it comes to specific prophecies being fulfilled, Jesus was just as reliable as any of the Old Testament prophets.

Another prophetic commentary on the destruction of Jerusalem is found in the book of Hebrews. In a letter that was most likely written around AD 60, the writer says, concerning the Old Covenant, "By calling this covenant "new," he has made the first one obsolete; and what is obsolete and aging will soon disappear" (Hebrews 8:13). The writer of Hebrews told his hearers that the Jewish system of sacrifice had run its course of usefulness. It had become obsolete. In AD 70 God allowed the Old Covenant to literally disappear.

Jesus' prophecy concerning Jerusalem had the desired effect. Thanks to his warning, when the Roman armies under Vespasian surrounded the city, the Christians took Jesus' advice and fled the city. There is no record of any disciples of Jesus being killed during this terrible event.

DOMITIAN

As Luke 21 and Matthew 24 parallel Daniel chapter nine, so Revelation 17:9-11 is parallel to Daniel 7:7-8. As we have already seen, Daniel described ten horns and an eleventh horn, which were the first ten emperors of Rome and the eleventh—Domitian. Revelation 17:9-11 is very similar, but perhaps the difference is the most interesting part.

> "This calls for a mind with wisdom. The seven heads are seven hills on which the woman sits. They are also seven kings. Five have fallen, one is, the other has yet to come; but when he does come, he must remain for a little while. The beast who once was, and now is not, is an eighth king. He belongs to the seven and is going to his destruction."

The book of Revelation contains a prophecy about Domitian. God was warning his people about the coming systematic persecutions from the Roman government. In this vision, the seven hills are Rome. Rome was set in a swampy valley of the Tiber River on seven hills. It has always been known as the city on seven hills. The seven kings in Revelation are the ten kings in Daniel. Three of the ten kings of Daniel's vision (Galba, Otho and Vitellius) ruled more or less simultaneously over the course of only about a year, and never completely consolidated their power. Apparently, for this reason, they were not included in the list in Revelation. That is why, where Daniel had eleven horns, Revelation has eight kings. The eighth king, "the beast who once was, and now is not," is Domitian, the persecutor of the church. Daniel predicted these events hundreds of years in advance. While the writings of John preceded the persecutions of Domitian and his successors by less than a generation, they nevertheless show the continuity of the New and the Old Testaments, as well as supporting the inspiration of the whole Bible.

Daniel and John agreed that the persecutions under Rome would be intense. They also agreed that the persecutions would be temporary, and that ultimately God would judge the persecutors: "He belongs to the seven and is going to his destruction." The primary purpose of the book of Revelation was to give comfort and support to those in the early church who were to undergo the great persecutions under the Romans. We also can be encouraged in our faith, because the events prophesied came to pass. In addition, the fulfillment of this prophecy makes it even clearer that ultimately, God's people will be vindicated.

There are other New Testament prophecies that were fulfilled in the first century AD (for example Acts 1:8, John 21:18, Acts 11:27,28 and Acts 21:10,11). All of these fulfilled prophecies can help one to understand why many of the early Christian teachers and their writings were accepted as inspired by God. We will look at one more example. The last New Testament prophecy we will consider is the most significant one Jesus made. This prophecy is so well known that it is often taken for granted.

> "The Christ will suffer and rise from the dead on the third day" (Luke 24:45).

> "Destroy this temple, and I will raise it again in three days" (John 2:19).

> He answered, "A wicked and adulterous generation asks for a miraculous sign! But none will be given it except the sign of the prophet Jonah. For as Jonah was three days and three nights in the belly of a huge fish, so the Son of Man will be three days and three nights in the heart of the earth" (Matthew 12:39,40).

Jesus prophesied that he would be killed, and that he would rise from the dead on the third day. This was a bold prophecy, to say the least. Has anyone other than an insane person ever had the nerve to predict that they would be raised from the dead? Jesus even said how long he would be in the grave! Surely, God has been among us.

CONCLUSION

One finds scattered throughout the Bible, from front to back, from Genesis to Revelation, predictive prophecies, the sum of which leave the honest person seeking after truth with only one reasonable conclusion. The Bible as a whole is the inspired word of God. We have seen people, places and events, generals, nations and wars. We have seen prophecies of the distant future and prophecies that were fulfilled just a few days later. We have seen the most amazing history books—ones about the future! So what is the conclusion of the matter? Let us look at one of the prophecies of Jesus that have not yet been fulfilled.

> "But the day of the Lord will come like a thief. The heavens will disappear with a roar; the elements will be destroyed by fire, and the earth and everything in it will be laid bare.
> "Since everything will be destroyed in this way, what kind of people ought you to be?" (2 Peter 3:10,11).

Given Jesus' track record on his prophecies coming true, it would appear that any sane person would give careful consideration to how they live their life. What about you?

For Today

1. The evidence for the inspiration of at least parts of the Bible seems beyond question. What are your remaining doubts and questions? What will you do to get answers to these questions?

2. It seems that the inspiration of Daniel is a settled issue because of the fulfilled prophecy found there. What effect does this have on your thinking about the inspiration of a book such as Job or Proverbs that has little or no predictive prophecy?

3. How do you think God chose the events for which he would prepare his people through prophecy and the events that he would allow to sneak up on them?

Challenge: Find one other predictive prophecy in the New Testament that has not yet been fulfilled and think about the implications of this prophecy for your life.

Chapter Six
A Remarkable Collection

> *If we would destroy the Christian religion, we must first of all destroy men's belief in the Bible.*
>
> *— Voltaire*

In this chapter we will investigate some of the most often-asked questions about the Bible. Where did it come from? Who decided what was going to be on the official list of accepted writings? How do we know if the Bible we read today is a reliable version of the original writings? Have any people or religious groups changed the Bible to reflect their own beliefs? Are all parts of the Bible equally reliable? Who wrote the books of the Bible, and how can I be sure about that? What about the different versions? If one can assume that the original writings are inspired, what about when we read translations?

These are questions that are bound to come up for any thinking person who reads the Bible regularly. Some would say asking questions such as these shows a lack of faith. "It says in 2 Timothy 3:16 that all scripture is inspired by God. For me that settles it. Why are you asking these annoying questions? Don't you trust God?" Unfortunately such an attitude will not make legitimate questions go away. In fact, buried questions have a habit of resurfacing at the most inopportune times, when our faith is at its weakest. A better approach would be to keep a good record of significant questions, and systematically, one by one, over a period of time, seek reasonable answers to these questions.

Many have claimed that the Old Testament contains a number of myths and legends that were created by Jewish writers in the two or three centuries before the time of Christ or soon thereafter. Others would claim that most of the New Testament was written well into the late second century AD by Christian apologists who were creating a Jesus very different from the historical person. They would claim that the gospels are not an eyewitness accounts at all. Another common claim is that the Catholic Church radically edited the original writings of the apostles in the period after the conversion of the Roman Empire in order to make it reflect Catholic doctrine. These people would claim that the doctrines found in the New Testament are very different from the original teachings of Jesus Christ. Still others will claim that there were additional gospels written by the apostles that were excluded by leaders in the early church because of their bias against certain teachings.

Do these claims have merit? What is the history of the authorship and of the collection of both the Old and the New Testament writings? How faithfully were the originals passed on? These questions will be answered in this chapter.

It may seem logical to consider the origin and history of the Old Testament before the New Testament for the obvious reason that it was written earlier. However, for several reasons, we will consider the evidence for the New Testament first. The New Testament was written over a shorter period of time. It will be considerably easier to trace the origin of the New Testament canon. Besides, the manuscript evidence and the different versions provide an easier evidence trail to follow with the New Testament.

Before considering the evidence for the origins of the New Testament, it will be helpful to define a few technical terms, some of which have already been used.

Manuscript

For the purposes of this discussion, a manuscript will be any ancient document that contains all or parts of either the New or the Old Testament. The word literally means handwritten. Manuscripts may be in the original language or they may be a translation from the original language. The manuscripts are the basic materials available that can be used to attempt to reconstruct the original biblical writings.

Canon

The canon of either the New or the Old Testament is the officially accepted list of books to be included in the scriptures. How the canon of the New Testament and of the Old Testament was arrived at is a very important question to be dealt with in this chapter.

Scroll

A long piece of material, usually leather, which contains a number of pages of writing in rows, arranged in columns, designed to be rolled up and stored. This was the principal form of manuscripts before the time of Christ (2 Timothy 4:13).

Codex

A long piece of either leather or papyrus, folded up in a format basically like a modern book. This was the most common form of manuscripts after about AD 200.

Papyrus

Papyrus is a reedy plant found mostly in the Nile delta. It was split open and rolled out. Horizontal and vertical layers were glued together to create a light and easy-to-use writing substrate. Unfortunately, papyrus is the least likely of the ancient writing materials to survive for long periods without disintegrating.

Vellum, Parchment

These are both specially prepared kinds of leather, which were commonly used as writing materials. Parchment was made of sheep or goatskins, while vellum was made of calf or antelope skins. When papyrus became scarce in the early centuries AD, vellum became the chief material for creating manuscripts.

Uncial

These are manuscripts that are written using all capital letters. The oldest Greek manuscripts are uncials.

Cursive

These are manuscripts that use both capital and small letters, similar to a modern style of writing. The later manuscripts in Greek are usually cursives.

THE NEW TESTAMENT TEXT

"All Scripture is inspired by God" (2 Timothy 3:16 NAS), but how do we know that the words we read in our Bibles are the same as those penned by the writers of Scripture? Over the years, many have attempted to undermine confidence in the Bible by claiming that what we read bears only a very slender relationship to the original writings. These same people will often claim that many of the books of the Bible were written a number of generations and even hundreds of years after the events recorded, casting doubt on their historical accuracy.

In the case of the New Testament, some scholars have claimed that most of it was written in the second half of the second century AD. Others have pointed out that there are "over two hundred thousand errors" in the manuscripts that we use to reconstruct the Greek New Testament text, implying that we can only guess at the original writings. Still others have claimed that the Catholic Church made substantial changes to the Bible, especially in the fourth and fifth centuries to remove unwanted teachings and to add statements that would support their own peculiar doctrines. What is the history of the New Testament text, and is there any validity to these claims? Let us examine these questions.

First, one must remember that the original books of the New Testament were written in Greek.[1] Producing an accurate New Testament begins with restoring the original Greek text. Do we have the original Greek text of the New Testament or at least a copy that is absolutely identical to it? The simple answer is no. The original letters of Paul, probably written on papyrus, have long since perished. The same can be said of the original gospel accounts. In order to give wider circulation of their teachings, the writings of the apostles were copied many times and widely circulated among the churches.

Therefore, the accuracy of our Greek text is dependent on how carefully the early Christians made copies. How can we be sure we have the original writings available to us? This question brings us to the manuscript evidence for the Greek New Testament.

The most famous English translation of the Bible is the King James Version. This translation was originally published in 1611. The group of scholars who produced the King James (or "Authorized") version relied heavily on the translation made by William Tyndale about eighty years before. The full Greek text of the New Testament was only made available to the Western world by the work of the Dutch scholar Erasmus. His Greek New Testament was published in 1516. When Erasmus composed his text, he had only about five Greek manuscripts available to him, none of them older than the ninth century AD. It was certainly conceivable at the time that these manuscripts were significantly different from the original.

The case today is very much different. Scholars now have nearly ten thousand Greek manuscripts to work from in their efforts to reconstruct the original Greek text. This is to be compared to less than ten manuscripts available to Tyndale and Erasmus. Besides, some of these manuscripts are several hundreds of years older than the oldest available to the first translators of the Greek text into English. Consider a list of some of the most important Greek New Testament manuscripts.

1. The Codex Vaticanus, or Codex B. The Codex Vaticanus is a vellum codex on 759 pages in uncial script. The manuscript has been dated to around AD 350. It contains the entire New Testament, except Hebrews 9:13-18, I and II Timothy, Titus and Revelation. It

---

1. Some have claimed that portions of the New Testament were originally written in Aramaic—the common language of Palestine at the time, and the language spoken by Jesus in his lifetime. In particular, many have claimed that all or part of Matthew was composed in Aramaic. It would be difficult to disprove such a claim, although the evidence to support it is slim. Even if it is valid, one can be sure that a Greek version of Matthew was in existence at about the same time, making the likelihood of the Greek version being significantly different from the Aramaic very small.

also contains all of the Old Testament in Greek except the first few chapters of Genesis and several Psalms. The manuscript has been kept in the Vatican since at least 1481.

2. The Codex Sinaiticus, or Codex Aleph. The Sinaiticus manuscript received its name because the biblical scholar Tischendorf discovered it at St. Catharine's Monastery on Mt. Sinai in 1844. It was found in a basket of old parchments that were about to be thrown into a fire. This manuscript is now in the British Library. Like the Vatican manuscript, it has been dated to around AD 350. It contains much of the Old Testament in Greek, but most significantly, it has the entire New Testament in Greek.

3. The Alexandrian Codex, or Codex A. This is a fifth-century codex, containing most of the Old Testament and all the New Testament except a few pages of Matthew, two from 1 John and three from 2 Corinthians. This manuscript was found in Alexandria in Egypt, but was given as a gift to the king of England in 1621. The manuscript is now located in the British Library.

4. The Washington Manuscript, or Codex W. This manuscript from the end of the fourth century contains the four gospels. It is especially significant, as it contains Mark 16:9-20, unlike the three manuscripts already mentioned. This manuscript is located in the Smithsonian Museum in Washington, D.C.

5. The Chester Beatty Papyri (P^{46}). This is a collection of a number of papyrus codex fragments, most of which are located in the Chester Beatty Museum in Dublin, Ireland. One of the papyri contains thirty leaves of the New Testament in Greek, which have been dated to the late second or early third century (i.e. around AD 200). Another includes 86 of 104 leaves of the letters of Paul from around from the early third century. The Chester Beatty collection is found both in Dublin, Ireland and Ann Arbor, Michigan.

6. The Bodmer Papyri. This is a group of manuscripts housed in the Bodmer Library of World Literature in Oxford, England. Included are a complete manuscript of Luke and John dated to 175-225 AD, as well as a manuscript of over half of the book of John, which has been dated as early as AD 150.

7. The John Rylands Fragment. This papyrus fragment contains only John 18:31-33 and 37,38, which would make it an insignificant find except that it has been dated to AD 130. This fragment was copied within fifty years of the death of the apostle John.

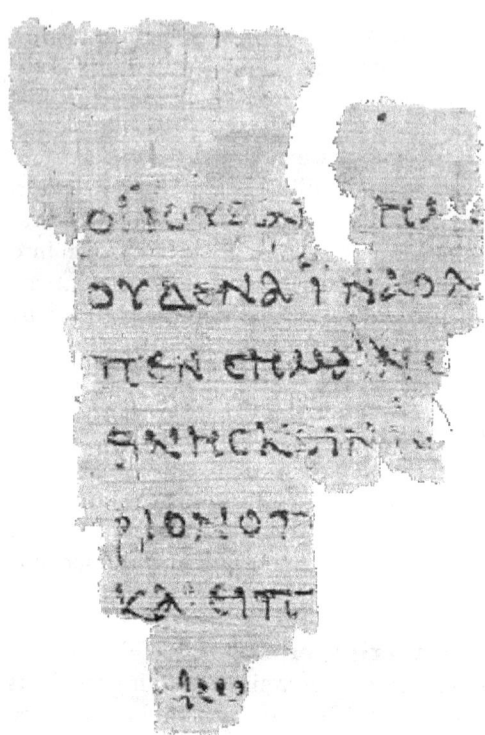
The Rylands Fragment
Courtesy John Rylands Library

Many other important ancient manuscripts could be mentioned as well. Some fragments of Mark found in Egypt very recently have been tentatively dated as early as around 45 AD. The situation with the Greek New Testament today is very different from what it was when the King James Version was translated. We have available entire manuscripts of the New Testament from less than three hundred years after the original writings. Besides this, we have manuscripts of large portions of the New Testament from one hundred fifty years after they were written, and even fragments that were copied only about fifty years after the original was written—during the lifetime of some who had seen the original documents. Scholars who seek to produce a Greek text as close to the original as possible have thousands of manuscripts to compare.

Besides, the manuscripts are not the only evidence supporting the text of the Greek New Testament. In addition, there exists a large body of letters written by the early church "fathers" such as Clement of Rome, Polycarp, Justin Martyr, Iranaeus and others. These early Christian writers quoted extensively from every part of the New Testament. The letters known as the Epistle of Barnabas, the Didache and the Letter of Clement have all been dated from around AD 100. These authors quote from Matthew, Mark, Luke, Acts, Romans, I Corinthians, Ephesians, Titus, Hebrews, I Peter and others. The early church father Ignatius was martyred in AD 115. In a set of letters he composed on his way to his execution in Rome, he quoted from nearly every New Testament book. Such evidence puts to rest any claims that these books were written in the second half of the second century AD, as some have claimed.

A Remarkable Collection

One could continue by mentioning the much more extensive writings of Justin Martyr from around AD 150, and those of Iranaeus, from near the end of the second century. The list could go on and on. Experts have claimed that using quotes from early Christian writers in the first three centuries, one could reconstruct virtually the entire text of the New Testament.

Being able to compare the oldest extant manuscripts with the quotes from the first two or three centuries allows scholars to reproduce the original New Testament text with even greater reliability. The relatively small number of passages in the New Testament about which there is some doubt (see below) can have their validity tested by examining the letters of the church fathers. The evidence for our Greek text of the New Testament is so strong that one can say with great confidence that we have a virtually exact copy of all the original Greek writings. It is worth quoting Sir Frederic Kenyon, one of the most noted scholars of the Greek text of the Bible.

> The interval then between the dates of original composition and the earliest extant evidence becomes so small as to be in fact negligible, and the last foundation for any doubt that the Scriptures have come down to us substantially as they were written has now been removed. Both the authenticity and the general integrity of the books of the New Testament may be regarded as finally established."[2]

As already mentioned, some have attempted to date some of the New Testament books to the second century. In general, this has been done in order to support a theory that many of the miraculous events recorded in its pages are later inventions. For example, F. C. Bauer, a German theologian from the nineteenth century, wrote a thesis in which he claimed that a number of the New Testament books were written after AD 160. Most likely he came up with such a late date, not because of any real evidence, but because of a philosophical presupposition against the miraculous. Nevertheless, in the nineteenth century such a conclusion, although very questionable, was at least still conceivable based on the available evidence. However, to quote from Neil Lightfoot:

---

2. Sir Frederic Kenyon, *The Bible and Archaeology*, 1940, pp. 288. Of course the case for Kenyon's statement has been made even stronger by evidence unearthed in the past sixty years.

...the amount of such evidence available in our own day is so much greater and more conclusive that a first-century date for most of the New Testament writing cannot reasonably be denied, no matter what our philosophical presuppositions may be."[3]

The exemplary evidence to support the text of the New Testament is made even more convincing when one compares it to the manuscripts available in support of some of the other significant writings of the ancient world. Those who have questioned the accuracy of the Biblical manuscripts are legion, yet few have raised significant questions concerning the authenticity of the ancient manuscripts available for such important works as Homer or Julius Caesar, Herodotus or Tacitus. The fact is that the manuscript evidence for these works is extremely thin when compared to nearly ten thousand manuscripts in the original language; both in terms of numbers and of age relative to when the originals were written.

For example, consider the most famous writing of Julius Caesar, *Gallic Wars*, with its famous "*Veni, Vidi, Vici*" (I came, I saw, I conquered). This important historical piece was written between 58 and 50 BC. The oldest available manuscript in Latin (the original language) was produced around AD 850—nine hundred years after the original was penned. This is to be compared to the New Testament, for which we have some evidence only fifty years after the original, and significant manuscript support only one hundred and fifty years after the original was composed. In all, there are only about ten ancient manuscripts of *Gallic Wars*, compared to about ten thousand in the case of the New Testament.

As further examples, consider the writings of Livy, along with those of Tacitus, the greatest of Roman historians. Livy lived from 59 BC to AD 17. Of his original 142 books, only thirty-five survive in any form at all in a total of only about 20 manuscripts. There is a fragment of Livy from the fourth century, but all the others are from hundreds of years later. In the case of Tacitus, who wrote for Roman emperors around AD 100, four and one-half of his fourteen *Histories* survive, while manuscripts of twelve of his sixteen *Annals* have been found. These are from a total of only two manuscripts, one from the ninth and one from the eleventh century. Yet, when Tacitus is quoted from, who questions the validity of these manuscripts?

The examples above are all Latin authors. What about ancient Greek writers? The Greek literature with the most manuscript evidence is the Iliad of Homer. This book was written around 800 BC.

---

3. Neil R. Lightfoot, *How We Got the Bible*, (Baker Books, Grand Rapids, Michigan, 1988), p. 15.

Over six hundred manuscripts have survived, including a fragment of the Iliad as old as 400 BC. However, the oldest complete manuscript to survive is from the thirteenth century—over two thousand years younger than the original. The two most important Greek historians were Herodotus and Thucydides. Both lived in the 400s BC. By an interesting coincidence, both historians' writings survive in eight manuscripts. Each has as his oldest surviving manuscript one from around AD 900, over 1,300 years after the original composition.

Author	Date	Oldest Copy	Interval	Copies
Aristophanes	400 BC	AD 900	1,300 years	45
Aristotle	340 BC	AD 1100	1,450 years	5
Demosthenes	300 BC	AD 1100	1,400 years	200
Julius Caesar	50 BC	AD 900	950 years	10
Herodotus	435 BC	AD 900	1,350 years	8
Homer	800 BC	AD 100	900 years	643
Plato	360 BC	AD 800	1,150 years	15
Sophocles	415 BC	AD 1000	1,400 years	7
Thucydides	410 BC	AD 900	1,300 years	8
Old Testament	1500 BC-500 BC	200 BC	200-400 years	5,000
New Testament	AD 50-90	AD 130	50 years	7,000

Other examples could be mentioned, but the point is made. Unquestionably, the New Testament is by a very wide margin the best attested of all ancient writings in the world. Few question the accuracy of the text of these other ancient writings, yet in every case they are supported by far fewer manuscripts, which are much farther removed from the original date of authorship.

One can concede that it is only reasonable to put the Bible under a closer scrutiny than these other books. This is only fair because, unlike Caesar, Tacitus and Herodotus, the writers of the Bible claim that it has authority over human lives. Nevertheless, the current Greek text of the New Testament will pass the most rigorous possible test of its accuracy as a representation of the original writings of the New Testament.

MANUSCRIPT ERRORS

Those who would question the integrity of the New Testament might interject at this point in the discussion to ask "But what about those two hundred thousand errors in the Greek manuscripts? How can you claim you have an accurate record of the original if it is riddled with errors?" This sounds convincing at first, but let us consider the nature of these hundreds of thousands of scribal mistakes.

First of all, this number is so large because there are so many manuscripts. Dividing two hundred thousand scribal errors by the well over five thousand manuscripts brings the number of mistakes into realistic perspective. And what is the nature of the differences between the available manuscripts? Do they reflect differences that draw into question the accuracy of our manuscripts compared with the original?

A page from a typical Greek uncial manuscript is pictured above. The text of an uncial contains all capital letters, with no spaces between the words, and with no punctuation. In this type of manuscript, if the end of a line was reached in the middle of a word, the copyist simply went to the next line, continuing with the rest of the word. For comparison, consider the passage below in uncial-like script.

NOTEVERYONEWHOSAYSTOMELORDLORDWILL
ENTERTHEKINGDOMOFHEAVENBUTONLYHEWH
ODOESTHEWILLOFMYFATHERWHOISINHEAVEN

With this type of script, it is easy to imagine even the most careful copyist making a minor mistake such as dropping off a letter, interposing two letters, repeating a line, or skipping a line. The vast majority of the supposed two hundred thousand mistakes in the Greek manuscripts are just such scribal slips of the pen. These errors are very easily detected and corrected by the scholars who study the Greek text of the New Testament. They have absolutely no effect on the integrity of the Greek New Testament.

Uncial Manuscript Example
Codex Sinaiticus

By taking into account the large number of manuscripts and by eliminating very easily corrected slips of the pen from the list, the 200,000 mistakes are reduced to a couple of hundred variations between the manuscripts. What is the nature of these variations? These would include such minor changes as a single rather insignificant word such as an article being added or dropped by a copyist. The copyist either as a subconscious error or intentionally in an attempt on the part of the copyist to "improve" the text may have made these changes.

There are also some examples in which it would appear that a copyist detected a difference between parallel accounts, for example in the gospels of Matthew and Mark, and attempted to smooth the differences by making Matthew and Mark say exactly the same thing. Textual critics use some basic rules when comparing different manuscripts. For example, if the Greek manuscripts exhibit two variant readings of a particular passage in Matthew, and if one of the two readings is identical to a parallel passage in Mark, scholars will lean toward using the reading of Matthew that is different from that in Mark. They do this on the assumption that a scribe had tried to make the two passages identical in an unfortunate but well-intentioned attempt to "improve" the text.

Bear in mind that in almost every case like this, the differences are so minor that they have no significant effect on the meaning of the scriptures. For example, in Matthew 11:19, two slightly different readings are found in the Greek manuscripts. Some end with the phrase, "But wisdom is proved right by her children." Others end with the phrase, "But wisdom is proved right by her actions." In this case, the oldest and most reliable manuscripts, the Vaticanus and Sinaiticus, have "actions," while most of the later manuscripts have "children." Despite the fact that a majority of manuscripts have the alternative reading, because the earliest manuscripts have "actions," most English translations use the word actions.

Whether one uses "actions" or "children" in Matthew 11:19, clearly this represents a very minor difference in the text of the New Testament. The saying of Jesus has the same meaning in either case. This minor difference is typical of the supposed errors in our New Testament.

When all the truly minor supposed mistakes in our received Greek New Testament are removed from consideration, the student of the Bible is left with only about a half dozen non-trivial variations in the Greek text. These would include the following examples.

1. John 7:53-8:11. The story of the woman caught in adultery. None of the earliest and most reliable versions include this passage.

It is probably a very early tradition of the primitive disciples that was later inserted into John. Almost certainly it is a genuine story, but it was not part of the original book of John. This passage is not particularly controversial because the story is so consistent with everything we know about Jesus.

2. Acts 8:37 and 1 John 5:7. These examples are listed together because the nature of the evidence is similar. In both cases, absolutely none of the earliest manuscripts include these passages. They are both rather transparent attempts by scribes to "improve" the text to support orthodox doctrine. They found their way into the King James Version because in 1611 only much later Greek manuscripts were available. None of the modern English translations include these passages, except in the marginal notes. These variations are not controversial because no scholars accept them as a part of the original New Testament text.

3. Mark 16:9-20. This is an account of Jesus' final words to his disciples. Virtually every Greek manuscript, including the Codex Alexandrinus, includes this passage. The problem with this is that the two exceptions are the Sinaiticus and the Vaticanus codices. These two are universally considered the most authoritative manuscripts. Besides, the oldest version of the Syriac translation of the New Testament also does not include Mark 16:9-20. In the final analysis, it is not an absolute certainty that this passage was in the original Gospel of Mark.

A couple of other similar but less significant examples could be mentioned, but that is it! Of the four examples listed above, only the last one is actually controversial. Of the 200,000 supposed mistakes in the Greek New Testament, we are left with only one significant passage that is truly controversial. Count them...one! Of course, if the reader would like to check out this claim more carefully for herself by looking into a resource that covers this topic more thoroughly, that would be a great idea.[4] Sir Frederic Kenyon, the world famous Biblical scholar and former director of the British Museum for twenty-one years, sums up the evidence nicely.

> The Christian can take the whole Bible in his hands and say without fear or hesitation that he holds in it the true word of God, handed down without essential loss from generation to generation throughout the centuries.

---

[4]. For example, Neil R. Lightfoot, *How We Got the Bible* (Baker Books, Grand Rapids, Michigan, 1988), F. F. Bruce, *The New Testament Documents, Are They Reliable?* (Eerdmans, Grand Rapids, Michigan, 1960), Bruce M. Metzger, *The Early Versions of the New Testament: Their Origin, Transmission and Limitations* (Oxford University Press, New York, 1977) and Sir Frederic Kenyon, *The Text of the Greek Bible* (Duckworth, London, 1975).

THE NEW TESTAMENT CANON

Before moving on to considering the Hebrew text of the Old Testament, a few significant questions regarding the text of the New Testament remain. How were the actual books contained in the New Testament chosen? How can we know these books are inspired? Were there any other writings that were inspired, but which were not included in the New Testament? These questions are all related. They all concern what is known as the canon of the New Testament. The word canon comes from the Greek word *kanon,* which springs from the Hebrew word *qaneh,* which means reed or cane. The implication of the word is a measuring stick, standard or ruler. In other words, the canon of scripture is the standard list of books accepted by the main body of believers. In the case of the Old Testament, this body would be the Jewish leaders in the centuries before the time of Christ, while in the New Testament, it would mean the leaders in the early church.

Some have made claims that church leaders in the fourth or fifth centuries AD chose the New Testament canon. These same people have claimed that such spurious works as the Gospel of Thomas (a second century Gnostic writing) were removed from the official list of scriptures at a late date. These attempts to cast doubt on the authenticity of the New Testament scriptures have one problem. They are not supported by the facts.

The fact is that the authority of the letters of Paul, of the Gospels and the book of Acts, as well as the other books of the New Testament, was established in the early second century by acclamation of the church. The church as a whole chose the New Testament books on the basis of the fact that these particular books had apostolic authority. The data is conclusive that by about AD 150 a more or less fixed list of accepted writings was already circulating amongst the churches throughout the Roman world. There were minor differences in some of the lists, but these were worked out by about AD 200.

Writing in the middle of the second century, Justin Martyr described the customs of the church in his time. The "memoirs of the apostles" and the "writings of the prophets" were read to the people on the first day of the week. Apparently, a more or less fixed list of apostolic writings ("the memoirs of the apostles") was already in existence at this time. For example, a small manuscript known as the Muratorian Fragment was found and published in the 1700s. It has been dated to the latter part of the second century, or around AD 180. It contains an early list of accepted scriptures. This fragmented list begins with Luke, but mentions it as the third gospel. The list mentions John, Acts, and all thirteen letters of Paul. In fact, all the letters in the New Testament are mentioned or implied except for Hebrews, James,

1 and 2 Peter and 1 John. In the third century, the Christian leader Origen recorded the accepted list of letters. His list was identical to our New Testament, although he mentioned that some questioned Hebrews, James, 1 and 2 John, and Jude.

One can see that the books of the New Testament were collected together gradually in the late first and early second centuries. In every case apostolic authority appears to have been the key factor determining whether or not they would be included in the canon. In some of the earliest lists, other books were included. Some mentioned the letters known as the Epistle of Barnabas and the Shepherd of Hermas. These are non-apostolic writings from around AD 100. The Muratorian Fragment specifically mentions that the Shepherd of Hermas could be read in public, but that it was not to be considered as part of the apostolic writings. One can see that other letters circulated, but that the dividing line between those that could be read for the encouragement of the church and those that were considered canonical was clearly based on apostolic authority. Even today it is not uncommon for excerpts from other spiritual books written by Christian authors (the modern equivalent of the Shepherd of Hermas) to be read during a sermon. Of course there is always a clear line drawn between such books and the Scripture.

As already mentioned, some have tried to claim certain apocryphal works such as the *Gospel of Thomas* and other lesser-known writings were excluded from the New Testament canon by church councils in the fourth and fifth centuries. The fact is that none of these works were ever accepted as being apostolic by the church as a whole. They may be controversial to some now, but they were not in the first centuries. In any case, by the time of the first major church council at Nicea in AD 325, the canon of the New Testament had been unchanged for over a hundred years. There is no way that the bishops who assembled at Nicea could have changed the canon of the New Testament even if they had wanted to.

This still leaves a couple of the questions raised above unanswered. How can we know all the books of the New Testament are inspired? What we can say from the evidence with regard to this question is that all the New Testament books were accepted by the church as a whole as having apostolic authority—in other words to be inspired—during a time when some who had known the apostles themselves were still alive. Whether or not the letters show the marks of inspiration is a separate matter from the subject of this chapter.

Were there any other inspired writings that did not make the cut to get into the Bible? The answer is probably yes. One can assume that Paul and the other apostles wrote other letters to encourage or admonish the churches. Surely, some of these letters contained inspired messages to disciples in the scattered churches. Why were these letters not saved? That would be a matter of speculation. Believers accept on faith that one way or another God caused those books he wanted in the Bible to find their way into the canon of accepted scriptures.

It is fun to speculate about such matters, but we will stick to what we know. In summary, one can conclude from the evidence that the text of the Greek New Testament available to us today is virtually an exact representation of the original writings. In addition, the evidence points to the fact that those books we have in our New Testament are there because, by the overwhelming consensus of the early church, they were accepted as having apostolic authority.

THE TEXT OF THE OLD TESTAMENT

To some extent, the evidence supporting the Old Testament text is similar to that of the New, but there are some major differences. The first and most obvious difference is that the Old Testament is substantially older. These writings had been passed down over a time span from about five hundred to well over one thousand years before the first words of the New Testament were put to papyrus. The second obvious difference is that the original language of the Old Testament was Hebrew.[5] We have already seen that the Sinai and the Vatican manuscripts include nearly complete copies of the Old Testament. These manuscripts do provide important corollary support to the Hebrew text, but their evidence is only indirect, because they are copies of a Greek translation of the Hebrew text. The history of the Old Testament text on the whole is the history of the Hebrew manuscripts.

We have already seen that the manuscript support for the Greek New Testament is astonishingly good. It is far stronger than that of any other ancient book. What is the case with the Hebrew Old Testament? To answer that question, one's first instinct might be to turn to the manuscripts and writings left behind by the early Christian movement. It turns out that this is not the most helpful place to start because the Old Testament of the Christian church was a Greek translation known as the Septuagint (more on that later). Even the writers of the New Testament, when quoting the Bible, used the Greek Septuagint translation rather than the Hebrew. For our oldest and most reliable Hebrew manuscripts we must rely on copies made by the Jews themselves.

Therefore, our study of the sources of the Old Testament turns to the history of the Jewish stewardship of their Hebrew Bible. Up until well into the twentieth century, the oldest Hebrew manuscripts were from the late ninth century onward. The oldest and most reliable Hebrew manuscripts until fairly recently were:

---

5. Actually, parts of Ezra (Ezra 4:8-6:18 and Ezra 7:12-26) and of Daniel (Daniel 2:4-7:28) are in Aramaic.

1. The Cairo Codex (*Codex Cairensis*). A codex of the former and latter prophets dated at AD 895.

2. The Leningrad Codex of the Prophets. This codex includes Isaiah, Jeremiah, Ezekiel and the twelve Minor Prophets. It is dated at AD 916.

3. The Leningrad Codex (Codex Babylonicus Petropalitanus). The Leningrad Codex is the oldest Hebrew copy of the entire Old Testament. It was copied in AD 1008.

All of these manuscripts are examples of what is known as the Masoretic Text. The Masoretes were a group of Jewish scribes who were active in Tiberias, a town on the Sea of Galilee from about AD 500-1000. They took their name from the Hebrew word *masorah*, which means authoritative traditions. These Jewish religious leaders took it upon themselves to compile and analyze the various somewhat different strands of Hebrew texts in existence at the time. By carefully justifying the different textual traditions, they created one authoritative version. It would appear that they did a very good job of producing an accurate text of the Hebrew Bible. However, they systematically destroyed all the variant readings of the Hebrew, which is unfortunate for those scholars who attempt to study the ancient text.

Another significant factor that reduced the number of available ancient manuscripts was the Jewish law that old and damaged copies of the Hebrew scripture were to be destroyed. The Jews had a ritual in which they performed a ceremonial burial of old or defective copies of the Scriptures. This helps explain why there are no copies of the Hebrew Bible from before the ninth century (with one exception to be mentioned below).

On the whole, though, the work of the Masoretes at preserving the Hebrew Scripture was positive. These scholars were absolutely fanatical about preserving the Bible. The Masoretes were meticulous to the extreme about maintaining the text as an exact copy. It would appear that they had an almost superstitious reverence for the actual letters themselves.

Before even starting to copy the scrolls or codices, the scribe was required by the Masoretes to go through an elaborate ceremony. In order to preserve the integrity of the text, the Masorete scribes counted all the letters in the Old Testament. They kept track of such arcane details as the middle verse of the Pentateuch (Leviticus 8:7). They also found the middle verse of the entire Hebrew Bible (Jeremiah 6:7). They were aware of the middle word of the whole Old Testament, as well as the middle word of each book. In addition, they kept record of the

A Remarkable Collection

middle letter and verse of each book. Taking it to the extreme, they also counted the number of times each Hebrew letter appeared in each book and counted the number of verses that contained all the letters of the Hebrew alphabet. All this was intended to produce exact copies of the Scriptures. Imagine doing all this letter and word counting, and using it to check every copy of the entire Old Testament. And they did not have word processors!

The evidence is that the Masoretes were only continuing a tradition passed down to them by earlier scribes. This almost unbelievable level of meticulousness on the part of the Jewish scribes has allowed the text of the Old Testament in Hebrew to come down to us with remarkable accuracy since before the time of Christ.

In their efforts at reproducing as close to an original Hebrew text as possible, scholars have a number of sources available besides the Masoretic text. A very significant help in reconstructing the Hebrew text is the Septuagint translation. This is an early translation of the Hebrew into Greek, which provides an independent comparison to the Masoretic text. The word Septuagint is Latin for seventy, after a tradition that it was seventy scholars in Alexandria, Egypt who accepted the task in around 250 BC to make a Greek translation of the Pentateuch. This translation was commissioned for the famous library in Alexandria. Over the decades following the translation of the Pentateuch, the entire Old Testament was translated into Greek, forming the Septuagint translation. Because the Septuagint and the Hebrew texts have a separate history, scholars are able to get an excellent snapshot of the content of the Hebrew text in around 200 BC. Often scholars make minor corrections to the Masoretic text using the Septuagint as can be seen by looking in the margins of most Bibles. The Septuagint translation was the Bible of the early church, which explains why there are so many good ancient manuscripts of this version.

Other translations that are helpful in reconstructing the original Hebrew writings include the Samaritan Pentateuch. This was a translation of the first five books of the Old Testament from the Hebrew into Aramaic. It was used by an ethnically mixed splinter group of Jews who later came to be know as the Samaritans. These are the same Samaritans as the woman at the well (John 4:1-43) and the "good Samaritan" (Luke 10:25-37). They only acknowledged the Pentateuch as being Scripture. The translation is particularly useful since it was made in around 400 BC, again providing an excellent parallel check to how the first five books appeared at this very early date. There are around 6,000 variations from the standard Masoretic text in the Samaritan Pentateuch, the great majority of which are grammatical differences and spelling changes of places and names.

Besides these, there are a number of other independent checks on the Hebrew text, which include the Syriac translation from around AD 100, as well as the Latin translation known as the Vulgate. Jerome, a Hebrew scholar of great reputation, made this excellent translation in AD 390-405. Also, a great number of quotes from the Hebrew are found in such Jewish commentaries as the Talmud (AD 200-500) and others.

The Talmud contains rules for copying the Hebrew Scriptures similar to those of the Masoretes. One list of the regulations from the Talmud is recorded below.

> A synagogue roll must be written on the skins of clean animals, prepared for the particular use of the synagogue by a Jew. These must be fastened together with strings taken from clean animals. Every skin must contain a certain number of columns, equal throughout the entire codex. The length of each column must not extend over less than forty-eight, or more than sixty lines; and the breadth must consist of thirty letters. The whole copy must be first lined; and if three words be written in it without a line, it is worthless. The ink should be black, neither red, green, nor any other color and be prepared according to a definite recipe. An authentic copy must be the exemplar, from which the transcriber ought not in the least deviate. No word or letter, not even a *yod* (a vowel mark), must be written from memory, the scribe not having looked at the codex before him.... Between every consonant the space of a hair or thread must intervene; between every word, the breadth of a narrow consonant; between every new section, the breadth of nine consonants; between every book, three lines. The fifth book of Moses must terminate exactly with a line, but the rest need not do so. Besides this, the copyist must sit in full Jewish dress, wash his whole body, not begin to write the name of God with a pen newly dipped in ink, and should a king address him while writing that name he must take no notice of him.... The rolls in which these regulations are not observed are condemned to be buried in the ground or burned; or they are banished to the schools, to be used as reading books.[6]

From this excerpt it is clear that the fanatical dedication of the Jewish scribes to producing accurate copies of the Scriptures began long before the work of the Masoretes. We owe a great debt of gratitude to the Talmudists (AD 200-500) and to the Sopherim before them (400 BC-AD 200) for preserving a Hebrew text of outstanding accuracy.

---

6. From Sir Frederic Kenyon, *Our Bible and the Ancient Manuscripts* (Harper and Brothers, New York, 1958) pp. 78-79.

A Remarkable Collection

THE DEAD SEA SCROLLS

Before 1947, despite all the evidence already presented, the oldest available Hebrew manuscripts of the Old Testament were made over one thousand three hundred years after the original. Clearly this is a very long gap, possibly allowing room for errors in transcription. This gap was closed considerably with the discovery of what is known as the Dead Sea Scrolls.

The story of the discovery of the Dead Sea Scrolls is now famous. In 1947, an Arab boy looking for a lost goat happened upon a cave in the hills above the Dead Sea. In the cave he discovered a trove of clay jars containing a number of very old parchment scrolls. He removed some of the scrolls from the jars. Ultimately, a few of these priceless scrolls ended up in a market place where a dealer recognized them for what they were. Members of the Qumran community had hidden these scrolls in the cave. The inhabitants of Qumran were from a Jewish sect known as the Essenes. The Essenes were an ascetic Jewish splinter group. They had moved to the remote desert hills east of Jerusalem where they could practice their communal religious lifestyle in relative peace. In a time of persecution, probably during the Roman/Jewish wars, they hid a number of their most valued manuscripts in a series of caves in the hills above their settlement.

Following the initial discovery, a careful search of the caves in the area revealed a large number of well-preserved scrolls. The scrolls had been hidden away some time around AD 70, but some of the manuscripts were as old as 250 BC. This discovery ultimately proved to be the most significant find in the history of biblical manuscripts. A number of the scrolls contain the writings of the Essenes themselves on religious topics ranging from end-time prophecies to rules for monastic living. Most significantly however, scattered among these writings were a number of fragments of Old Testament books, and even some complete books of the Old Testament in Hebrew.

The Dead Sea Scrolls include at least fragments of every Old Testament book except Esther. Included is a manuscript of the entire book of Isaiah, which has been dated to 100 BC or earlier. Imagine the delight of scholars of the Hebrew Bible to suddenly have available an entire copy of Isaiah one thousand years older than any that had been previously available. This copy of Isaiah could be compared to the Masoretic text, giving scholars the ability to measure how much the text had been changed through being copied over a thousand year period. Ultimately, in the 1952 translation of the Revised Standard Version of the Old Testament, only thirteen very minor changes were made to reflect the new discovery. That makes thirteen changes to the second longest book in the Old Testament over the course of one thousand years.

Also included in the Dead Sea Scrolls were two manuscripts of the books of Samuel. One of these is a copy of forty-seven out of an original fifty-seven pages of the book from the first century BC. The other is a partial manuscript of 1 and 2 Samuel from the third century BC. That is only about two hundred years after the last book of the Old Testament was completed. Another major find is a scroll containing forty of fifty-seven pages of the book of Exodus in a very old type of Hebrew script known as paleo-Hebrew. This manuscript is from just after 200 BC.

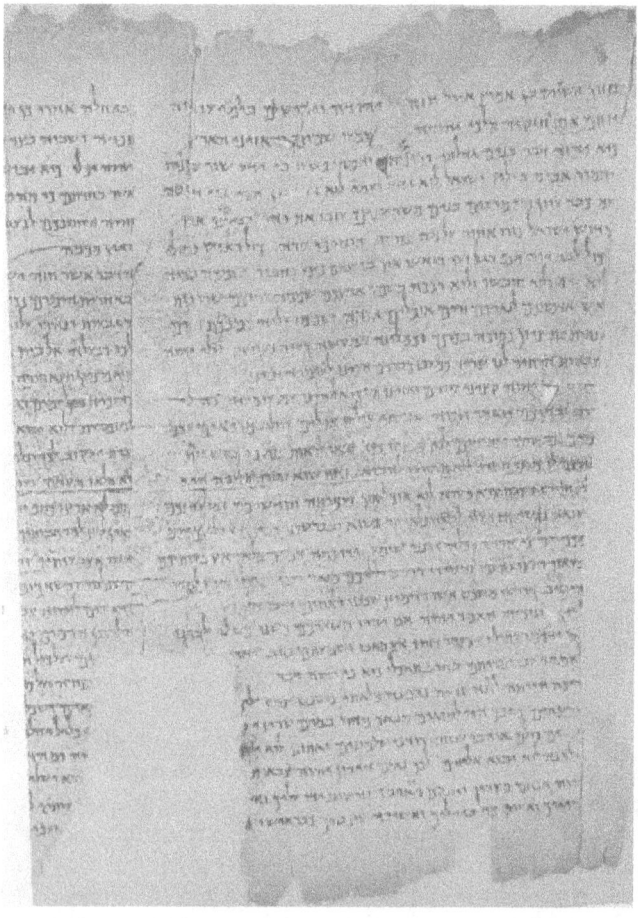

Isaiah Scroll Chapter 1:1-29
Courtesy Great Isaiah Scroll Directory - http://www.ao.net/~fmoeller/qumdir.htm

A Remarkable Collection

To get a feel for how significantly the discovery of the Dead Sea Scrolls moved the date of the earliest available manuscripts toward the time of the books having been written, consider the graph below.

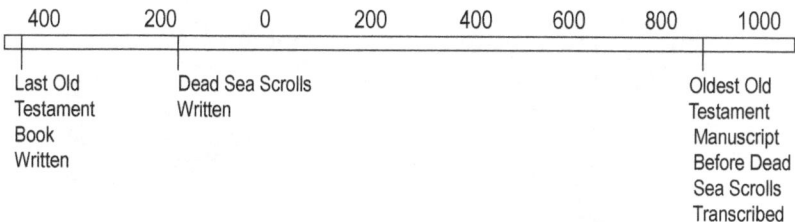

It is difficult to overestimate the significance of this remarkable find. The evidence of the Dead Sea Scrolls reveals that over a one thousand year span, a number of changes had crept into the Hebrew text. However, virtually all of these are minor changes in spelling, in word order or in grammatical usage. To quote the noted biblical scholar F. F. Bruce:

> The new evidence confirms what we already had good reason to believe—that the Jewish scribes of the early Christian centuries copied and recopied the text of the Hebrew Bible with utmost fidelity.[7]

The Dead Sea Scrolls reveal that over the course of a thousand years, the Old Testament was preserved with essential but not perfect accuracy. Do we have a nearly perfect copy of the original Old Testament writings? The simple answer is no. We know from the evidence of the Dead Sea Scrolls what we could have guessed without it. Over the many hundreds of years in which the Jewish scribes copied the Old Testament, a significant number of minor changes in spelling, word order and grammatical usage crept into the text.

In fact, the Hebrew script is particularly prone to minor copying errors. Some of the Hebrew letters are very similar. For example, the Hebrew letters *daleth* (ד) and *resh* (ר) are very difficult to distinguish. Similarly, the letters *he* (ה) and *heth* (ח) could easily be mistaken for one another. The fact that the Hebrew text, like the Greek, includes strings

---

7. F. F. Bruce, *Second Thoughts on the Dead Sea Scrolls* (Eerdman's Publishing Co., Grand Rapids Michigan, 1956) pp. 61-62.

Qumran Cave #4, Dead Sea, Israel
(Photograph by Rex Geissler, 1999)

of letters without large spaces between words, made it very difficult to produce perfect copies. Besides this, the original Hebrew writing was without vowels. This was an additional impediment to producing perfect copies, because in the spoken language, vowels give context to the consonants, making it less likely to make a copying mistake.

Another problem in producing a perfect copy of a Hebrew manuscript arose with the use of numbers. The Hebrew script used letters for numbers, similar to the use of Roman numerals. With words, a copier can use the context to help decide what letter is being used. For example, if one saw a manuscript with a line such as *the man ra# to the store*, with one obscured letter, they can easily decide that the missing letter is an "n", not a "t". In general, numbers do not offer such contextual clues. It is easy for 510 soldiers to become 500 or 51 or 5100. In general, one should be careful about assuming when numbers are found in the Old Testament, that they are exactly the same as written in the original.

All this having been said, it is important to bear in mind that in almost every case we are talking about are truly minor changes. The additional evidence from the Dead Sea Scrolls is that despite a significant number of changes in spelling and grammatical endings, the original meaning is preserved in almost every case. Whether the king of the Babylonians was Nebuchadnezzar (as in most Bibles) or Nebuchadrezzar (probably a more accurate spelling by looking at outside sources), has no impact on the meaning of the book of Daniel.

In summary, God chose the Jewish people to be the stewards of his written word. The wisdom of his choice was proven by the incredible devotion of the Jews to preserving the Old Testament Scriptures with amazing fidelity. Despite some changes in numbers, spelling and grammar, thanks to the Jewish scribes, we have the Old Testament essentially preserved as it was written well over two thousand years ago.

THE OLD TESTAMENT CANON

One last set of questions needs to be raised regarding the Old Testament as it was with the New Testament. How were the books now found in our Old Testaments chosen? What criteria were used? Are they all inspired? What about the Apocrypha?

One thing that can be said with absolute certainty is that the early Christian church had no part in choosing the Old Testament canon. The list of accepted scriptures was set long before Jesus Christ walked the earth. In the New Testament, Jesus himself quoted from nearly every Old Testament book. Yet, he never once quoted from such unaccepted writings as the Apocrypha.[8]

Jesus specifically referred to the Old Testament canon when he claimed that he had fulfilled all that was "written about me in the Law of Moses, the Prophets and the Psalms" (Luke 24:44). The divisions of the Hebrew Bible were the Law of Moses (the Pentateuch), the Prophets, and the Writings (or Psalms). Again, he referred to the entire Hebrew canon in the phrase "from the blood of righteous Abel to the blood of Zechariah son of Berekiah" (Matthew 23:35). Of course, the murder of Abel is found at the beginning of the Bible. The assassination of Zechariah son of Berekiah is found in 2 Chronicles 24: 20,21. The Jewish Bible has a different order than what is traditional in Christian editions. In the Bible of Jesus' day, 2 Chronicles was the last book. When Jesus used the phrase, from the blood of Abel to the blood of Zechariah, the Jews were aware that he meant from the beginning to the end of the Bible.

When and by whom was the canon of the Old Testament set? It has been said that a group of Jewish teachers gathered in the Palestinian city of Jamnia at the end of the first century to agree on a final list of accepted writings. The meeting at Jamnia did occur, but almost certainly all they did was confirm the canon that had already been set for at least two hundred years. Before the meeting at Jamnia even occurred, Josephus mentioned a list of the Old Testament scriptures:

> "We have not 10,000 books among us, disagreeing with and contradicting one another, but only twenty-two books which contain the records of all time, and are justly believed to be divine. Five of these are by Moses, and contain his laws and traditions of the origin of mankind until his death....From the death of Moses till the reign of Artaxerxes, king of Persia, who reigned after Xerxes, the prophets who succeeded Moses wrote down what happened in their times in thirteen books; and the remaining four books contain hymns to God and precepts for the conduct of human life."[9]

---

8. Although the New Testament writers do not quote from the Old Testament Apocrypha, they do allude to it. For example, Hebrews 11:37 mentions a man of faith who was sawn in two. This is probably an allusion to the martydom of Jeremiah which is mentioned in the Apocrypha. The fact that the New Testament writers allude to without quoting from the Apocrypha implies that they were well aware of these extra books, but did not consider them canonical.

9. Josephus, *Against Apion*, I. 8.

A Remarkable Collection

The five books referred to by Josephus are the Pentateuch. The thirteen historical/prophetic books may seem like a low number. That is because the Hebrew Bible at that time combined 1 and 2 Samuel into one book. Similarly, the pairs 1 and 2 Kings, 1 and 2 Chronicles, Ruth and Judges, Jeremiah and Lamentations, and Ezra and Nehemiah were each combined into one book. The supposed "minor prophets" (Hosea through Malachi) were combined to form one book known as "The Twelve." If the four "books containing hymns" of Josephus are the traditional Psalms, Proverbs, Ecclesiastes and Song of Solomon that make up the Hebrew "writings," then the list of Josephus is exactly the same as our canonical Old Testament.

Who chose the Old Testament books? The bottom line is that we do not have a detailed record of how these books were chosen. In a manner similar to New Testament, it would appear that the list of the Old Testament books was chosen gradually by acclamation of the Jewish teachers. Apparently, only the accepted books passed the mark as being inspired writings. In the end, the believer is left with the evidence of the books themselves, combined with faith that God had his hand in what ended up in his Bible. One of the main points of this book is to show overwhelming evidence that the books we do find in both our Old and New Testaments show marks of inspiration.

One of the best ways for students of the Bible to prove to themselves that the accepted canon of the Old Testament has the marks of inspiration is to pull out a Roman Catholic Bible (for example the New American Bible) and begin reading the apocryphal additions to the Old Testament. A quick reading of Tobit or of the additions to Daniel or of Judith will reveal the glaring difference between an inspired writing and the work of human ingenuity. It will be obvious to most why the Jewish community unanimously rejected these writings as not being inspired by Jehovah.[10] When one reads what is obviously religious fiction (Tobit and Judith for example) or historical books in which the author apologizes for his mistakes (2 Maccabees), it will bring out in stark contrast the quality of the inspired writings in the Old Testament.

This extremely brief discussion of the Old Testament canon has barely even begun to address the possible questions about specific books or parts of books and whether they belong in the list of inspired writings. Anyone who has read the Bible at all and does not have at least some questions about particular passages has not been paying

---

10. The Old Testament Apocrypha is dealt with in some detail in my book on Daniel. John Oakes, *Daniel, Prophet to the Nations*, (Illumination Publishers, Spring, Texas, 2008), pp. 224-234. This includes a discussion of how the Apocrypha slipped into the Roman Catholic Bible, as well as a brief overview of each of the books.

attention. What about such and such book? Isn't there even one that never mentions the name of God? What about this one story? It doesn't seem to fit the flow of the book. Am I to take this literally or not? How could God allow that to happen? Isn't there at least an appearance of contradiction between these two passages? It is in stubbornly seeking answers to such difficult questions that I personally have found some of my greatest conviction about the inspiration of the Bible. It has been through facing rather than avoiding asking the hard questions that I have become convinced that the Bible as a whole fits together in a way that can only be explained by accepting that it is ultimately the work of God himself. Let the adventure begin.

It would be helpful to summarize some of the conclusions of this chapter.

1. We have a Greek text of the New Testament that is almost an exact copy of the original writings.

2. Theories that all or parts of the New Testament were written well into the second century or that major changes were made to the New Testament during the third or fourth centuries are simply unsupportable from the evidence.

3. The New Testament canon was essentially fixed by AD 150 and has certainly remained unchanged since about AD 200.

4. The canon of the New Testament was set by general consensus of the first and second century Christian leaders based on apostolic authority.

5. It would be an overstatement to say that we have a Hebrew text of the Old Testament that is an almost exact copy of the original writings. Copying the rather difficult Hebrew script over many centuries allowed a number of changes in numbers, in spelling and in other minor details. Nevertheless, the evidence allows one to conclude that the received text of the Old Testament is remarkably close to that of the original writings.

6. The canon of the Old Testament was set by general consensus of the Jewish teachers perhaps as early as 400 BC, but almost certainly by 200 BC. The books were chosen because they had the marks of inspiration.

A Remarkable Collection

For Today

1. Assuming that you did not know it already, how does it affect you to learn that the story of the woman caught in adultery may not have been in the original version of John?

2. The evidence for Mark 16:9-20 is fairly solid, but not conclusive. Can you think of any important teaching that would be compromised if this passage were not included in the Bible? If a person is teaching the Bible to others, should they:

   a. Not use this passage.
   b. Use it but consistently mention that there is some question about it.
   c. Use it without comment?

3. Not much mention in this chapter was made of the fact that most of us obviously cannot read Greek or Hebrew. What is the significance, if any, of reading a translation rather than the original?

4. What would you say to someone who told you that the teaching of reincarnation was originally part of the New Testament, but that the Catholic Church expunged all references to reincarnation at the Council of Nicea?

Challenge: Begin keeping a written record of legitimate questions you have about specific passages, sections or whole books in the Bible. Begin to seek answers to those questions from your own study and/or from those you know who might be qualified to answer your questions.

Chapter Seven
Let the Stones Speak

The stones cry out,
Long silent through the ages,
Unfolding now, a written scroll,
God's truth in dusty pages.

—Anne Moore

"...So David triumphed over the Philistine with a sling and a stone; without a sword in his hand he struck down the Philistine and killed him." Many of us grew up hearing this story at a Sunday school class or on our parents' laps. Is this a quaint story, a fable with a religious message; or is this a faithful record of an actual event, part of the saga through which God brought the Son of David, Jesus Christ, to Israel? This is an absolutely key question at the very heart of Christianity. The Bible, far more than any other religious book, finds its fundamental message steeped in an historical context.[1]

If Moses did not really lead God's people out of Egypt, as described in the book of Numbers, then the Law of Moses is a man-made tradition. If David was not the anointed ruler of Israel, then Jesus, the Son of David, was a pretender to a false legacy. If the stories of Abraham, Isaac, Jacob and Joseph are just the creation of an imaginative and pious Jew in the second century BC, then Paul's statement in Romans 4:16,17 concerning Abraham, "He is the father of us all. As it is written: I have made you a father of many nations" becomes a meaningless statement.

Let us put it out there very clearly: if the events recorded in the Old Testament are just religious stories with little or no basis in fact, then both the Old and the New Testaments lose nearly all their meaning, and Christianity becomes a manmade religion. In that case, Christianity becomes what many religious philosophers claim it is—one of many paths to the same thing. Do not be deceived. This is the view of

---

1. The Book of Mormon is an exception to this claim. This book mentions a number of tribes and nations, as well as great cities, wars and even entire civilizations which supposedly existed somewhere in the New World. There is not a single shred of archaeological evidence to support any of the supposed history recorded in The Book of Mormon. One resource on this subject is http://www.irr.org/mit/bomarch1.html and references to be found at this site.

the vast majority of the intellectual elite, and believe it or not, even of many supposed Christian theologians today.

Did David kill a giant of a man named Goliath with a stone from his sling, and was this event a stepping stone to his eventually becoming king of Israel? These questions are no mere intellectual exercise. And there is no middle ground here. Either David killed Goliath or he did not. Fortunately, the discoveries of modern archaeologists shed considerable light on this question. Archaeologists have excavated the fortress at Gibeah. This was the chief fortress of Saul, the first king of Israel. This is the same Saul who, according to the Biblical account, tried to loan his armor to David for his battle with Goliath. The excavators at Gibeah found proof that slingshots were a primary part of the arsenal in Saul's army.[2] David did not use a child's toy to kill Goliath. In fact, given Goliath's far superior physical strength, David chose what was the most effective military weapon available to him in the arsenal of the king.

It was quite common for theologians in the nineteenth century to claim that King David was a fictional character, created by Jewish teachers in the post-exilic period to teach moral lessons to Hebrew children. Did the Jewish teachers in the second century BC know that the slingshot was a standard weapon of the army of Israel eight hundred years before? If King David is just a fictional character, then how is one to explain the discovery by Avraham Biran in 1993 of an inscription from the ninth century BC? This discovery, known as the Tel Dan inscription, refers both to King David himself and to the dynasty that it calls the House of David.

The Old Testament is absolutely full of historical details that could only have been known to authors who were recording actual events in their own lifetimes or soon thereafter. We will see many examples of this principle in the present chapter. The excavation of King Saul's palace, the evidence that slingshots were a standard part of the military arsenal of Israel in the eleventh century BC, and the discovery of a stone inscription mentioning the household of King David all lend historical credence to the story of David and Goliath.

Is there any actual physical evidence that David killed a huge soldier in the Philistine army? No. In fact, it is difficult to imagine what that physical evidence might be. The only conceivable direct evidence would be a carving in bas-relief representing the battle. The problem with this is that the Jews were prohibited from making carvings in human likeness by one of the Ten Commandments. Bear in mind that the book of 1 Samuel records events that occurred three thousand

---

2. Thus indirectly confirming the account in Judges 20:16 of seven hundred expert slingers in the army of Israel.

years ago. This is three hundred years before the founding of Rome, and over five hundred years before the great flowering of the Greek culture. The reign of King Saul followed by only about one hundred years the semi-mythical battle of Troy, as recorded in Homer's *Iliad*. To date, there is no direct physical evidence of the battle between David and his very tall adversary, but this is not surprising. What the evidence of archaeology tells us is that the events recorded in 1 Samuel are in good accord with both the historical and the cultural setting of tenth and eleventh century BC Palestine. The book of 1 Samuel has every appearance of being an accurate account of actual events.

This claim gains credence from a number of the other events recorded in 1 Samuel and the parallel account in 1 Chronicles that have been substantiated by archaeological discoveries. For example, 1 Samuel mentions that after King Saul was slain in battle, his armor was put in the temple of Ashtaroth (a Canaanite goddess) in the city of Beth Shan. This is found in 1 Samuel 31:10. In what has been described as a contradiction by Bible critics, 1 Chronicles records that King Saul's head was put into the temple of Dagon (a Philistine god) in the same city. This story is found in 1 Chronicles 10:10. Those who would try to prove that the Biblical accounts are a late fabrication have claimed that it is very unlikely that there would have been temples to both Ashtaroth and Dagon in the same city at the same time. They would claim that the accounts in 1 Samuel and 1 Chronicles are in historical conflict with one another.

Archaeological discoveries have proven the Bible critics wrong once again. Excavations at Beth Shan have revealed that there were indeed two separate temples in the city—one devoted to Dagon, the other devoted to the Ashtoreths. In fact, only a hallway separated the two temples. Those who would attack the historical reliability of the Old Testament will have to explain how the combined record of two separate authors could be in such complete accord with the archaeological evidence. What are the chances that someone writing an allegorical moralistic fable hundreds of years later could have known that there were temples to both gods in Beth Shan at the time of the death of King Saul?

A number of other archaeological finds that lend great credence to the Biblical accounts of the life of David could be cited, but first it will be helpful to back up and take a look at the big picture.

THE BIBLE AS HISTORY

The Bible is not a history book, but it is a book entirely immersed in history. This is especially true of the Old Testament. In fact, it is impossible to understand the New Testament message fully unless one sees the ministry of Jesus Christ and the gospel itself as the culmination of the drama that was worked out in the history of God's people as recorded in the Old Testament. The story of the Old Testament is the story of God preparing a people through whom to send the messiah. As stated above, this makes Judaism/Christianity unique among world religions. It is impossible to separate these religions from their history.

For anyone who is in doubt about the claim that the Old Testament is immersed in history, consider the first three chapters of Joshua. These three chapters alone contain the names of twenty-nine places, ten individual people and no less than sixteen "peoples" (the modern word "nation" does not really apply here). Each of the twenty-nine cities or other places either existed or they did not. One can search for these cities, and in fact a large proportion of the places mentioned in these three chapters have been identified and at least partially excavated. One gets the strong impression from reading the book of Joshua that in the fourteenth century BC, Canaan contained a large number of small walled cities. Again, this claim is verifiable. In addition, the sixteen "peoples" of these three chapters, such as the Hittites, the Hivites, the Jebusites and so forth are either real or imaginary. Either they were real ethnic/cultural groups at that time or they were not. Of course, Bible critics have in the past attacked all or nearly all the peoples listed in Joshua as mere inventions. Archaeological studies to date have confirmed the existence of nearly every group mentioned in these chapters. Canaan in the fourteenth century BC was ethnically a very diverse place.

Does anyone really care what the names of all these peoples and cities were? That is not the point. What is essential to the Bible believer is that the book of Joshua records God using Joshua to lead his people from the wilderness, across the Jordan River, into the Promised Land. Joshua, a living, breathing, historical figure, is a symbol of Jesus, who brings followers of Jesus from the wilderness of a sinful life, through the water (not of the Jordan river, but of baptism), into the promised land of salvation and a life in fellowship with God. If the story of Joshua is historical fiction, then the entire picture does not work. In Hebrews 4:8-11 the writer implies that what Joshua did physically is what Jesus does spiritually. If Joshua did not "save" Israel physically, then in what sense does Jesus save people spiritually?

For this reason, the question of the accuracy and reliability of the history recorded in both the Old and New Testaments is absolutely essential to the validity of the claims of Christianity. The goal of this chapter is to examine this question carefully.

It is not as if the writers of the Old Testament were professional historians. In fact, at the time much of the Old Testament was written, there was no such thing as a professional historian anywhere in the world. There was not a single author who was trained to write a carefully researched historical account. The methodology of careful historical documentation had not even been developed. If the Bible turns out to contain accurate and unbiased history, this would certainly reveal a powerful mark of inspiration.

It will be helpful to compare the Bible as history to the work of the greatest historians of the ancient world. Perhaps most appropriate is to compare it to the works of the Greek writer Herodotus. Herodotus lived from about 480-425 BC. The Bible was recorded over about a one thousand year span, beginning somewhere around 1400 BC,[3] ending with the writing of Malachi, in approximately 440 BC. Therefore, the last of the Old Testament biblical writers was a contemporary of Herodotus, the "father of history."

Clearly, there were many chroniclers in the ancient world before Herodotus. Since the beginnings of humankind, oral histories had been passed down. These oral histories, of course, were extremely susceptible to distortions, exaggerations, and downright fabrications. Herodotus is considered by many historians to be the first true, systematic historian. He took pains to travel throughout the known world looking for primary sources. Besides, Herodotus was a great writer of prose. Many consider him not only the first, but also the greatest historian of the ancient world. The question is, in terms of accuracy and reliability, how does Herodotus compare to the Old Testament as history?

Remember, this is a key question in the overall case for the inspiration of the Bible. If the Bible contains bogus or highly distorted historical accounts, as some critics claim, then the statement of Paul in 2 Timothy 3:16 that, "All Scripture is inspired by God," is simply not correct. Jesus himself often referred to events recorded in the Old Testament as if they were factual events. There is no getting around this question, so it must be faced. Therefore, it is helpful to ask the question, how does the Bible as history compare to Herodotus?

There is much to be commended in the writings of Herodotus. As already stated, he took great pains to find primary sources. He studied inscriptions and where possible interviewed eyewitnesses or those who had known eyewitnesses to events. He traveled from Greece to Italy, Asia Minor, Southern Russia, Palestine, Babylon, Susa (the capital of

---

3. The book of Genesis was probably put together in its final form somewhere around the time of Moses, but parts of it may have been in existence in written or oral form for hundreds of years before that time. Also, it is very difficult to date the writing of the book of Job. Its context is from the patriarchal period of biblical history, suggesting that it may have been recorded hundreds of years before the date of 1400 BC mentioned above.

Persia), and to Egypt and other parts of Northern Africa. His attention to detail and the clarity of his writing style serve even today as a model for historians. However, despite his painstaking efforts, the histories of Herodotus are far inferior to those found in the Old Testament in terms of accuracy and reliability. This is a big claim, but consider some of the evidence.

Although Herodotus did do a lot of his own research, he accepted into his histories much of what is clearly local myth and fable. He did this, not so much because he could not tell the difference between fact and myth, but more likely to liven up his writings. Herodotus was not unwilling to include a fable if it served as a useful illustration of one of the themes of his histories. One finds his writings laced with the phrase "It is said," or "I was told," as Herodotus recorded local legends that even he obviously did not take at face value. In fact, Herodotus often said in his histories, "But I did not believe a word of it." Can you imagine a phrase like that in the Bible?

For example, Herodotus described the founding of the Oracle of Zeus at Dodona: "Two black doves, long ago, flew from Thebes in Egypt (over a thousand miles away). One arrived on an oak at Dodona and spoke (in Greek?) with a human voice, telling all there that in that place would be founded an oracle of Zeus." Here Herodotus included in his histories what is obviously a local fable.

Herodotus also chronicled the campaigns of the Persian King Cambysses in Egypt. He described the Ethiopians, who "manacled their prisoners with gold chains, lived to be a hundred and twenty, drank water from a spring which smelled like violets, used bows which no one but themselves could bend,..." and the like. According to Herodotus, the entire army of Cambysses, a quarter of a million men, was lost in a sandstorm in the desert and never seen again. Herodotus described ants "as big as foxes" in India as well as flying snakes in Arabia. According to the Father of History, the female flying snakes bit off the heads of the males after mating. Herodotus also passed on the reports of a tribe of one-eyed Scythians and griffins who guarded their gold. In the words of one historian:

> Thus we have in Herodotus' account, mixed up with first-hand reporting of the greatest value and interest, a number of contemporary folk-tales and local legends which, though not history in the strict sense, are yet assuredly a part of history, as representing what the common man believed about his past.[4]

---

4. Aubrey de Selincourt, *The World of Herodotus*, (Little, Brown and Company, Boston, 1962) p. 218.

Does the Bible, like the Histories of Herodotus, contain folktales, local legends and stories that represent "what the common man believed about his past?" The emphatic answer is no. As we will see clearly, the Bible is free of such clutter in its history.

The histories of Herodotus contain not only fables, but also obvious inaccuracies. He had Solon, the great Athenian statesman, visiting Croesus, king of Lydia, well after Solon was dead. He described the armies of the Persian King Xerxes as he crossed the Dardanelles Straits. According to Herodotus, the army was composed of two and one-half million soldiers. In addition, he mentioned two and one-half million camp workers of all sorts, besides an innumerable group of other hangers-on. This would be an army with a total of well over five million people. No wonder Herodotus described this army as literally drinking the rivers of Greece dry! No one can believe these numbers. Despite the claims of its critics, we will see that the Old Testament simply does not contain this type of blatant errors.

One could list hundreds of examples of blatant inaccuracies, as well as of obvious myths and legends from the writings of Herodotus. However, his contemporaries criticized Herodotus, not for these problems, but for his obvious bias toward his friends the Athenians. The principle subject of his histories was the struggle of the Greeks to repel the attacks of the Persians under Darius and Xerxes, and the subsequent civil wars between Athens and her allies and the Spartans and their allies. In these events, Herodotus is persistently favorable to the Athenian version of the events. To quote the historian Aubrey de Selincourt:

> However, it is not for this sort of innocent falsification of fact that the Father of History came to be known as the Father of Lies. It was for a much more characteristically human reason, namely, that the tone of Herodotus' book is strongly pro-Athenian, and the enemies of Athens, very naturally, resented what they considered this absurd prejudice and did what they could to discredit the author of it.[5]

In calling Herodotus the "Father of Lies" his critics were being unfair to him. Despite his obvious bias, Herodotus generally did not fabricate lies to make Athens look good. To be fair to Herodotus, he probably wrote a more fair-minded history than anyone before him (with the exception, of course, of the biblical writers). Nevertheless, he was guilty of blatant bias in favor of his friends. Can the same be said

---

5. ibid. p 41.

for the history recorded in the Bible? Did the Biblical writers record a version of events that ignored the failings of Israel and exaggerated the failings of her enemies? Does the history recorded in the Old Testament paint a rosy picture of God's people and especially of the leaders of the Israelites?

Anyone who has read even a little bit of the Old Testament will find that question very easy to answer. The Old Testament is brutally honest about the failings of both the people of Israel and their leaders. This is absolutely unique among ancient writings. Virtually all the chronicles left behind by ancient cultures mention only their victories. If they refer to the defeats of their kings or their armies at all, they are referred to in a very indirect way. The Old Testament is a striking exception to this rule. The many defeats and humiliations of the people of Israel are described in as much detail as the great victories.

In the inscriptions left behind by such leaders as the pharaohs of Egypt or the Emperors of Assyria, the leaders are praised for their wisdom and strength. These rulers seem almost godlike in their perfection. Anyone reading these accounts can be sure that these are highly biased records. To quote a well-known archaeologist:

> The peoples of the ancient Near East kept historical records to impress their gods and also potential enemies, and therefore rarely, if ever, mentioned defeats or catastrophes. Records of disasters would not enhance the reputation of the Egyptians in the eyes of their gods, nor make their enemies more afraid of their military might.[6]

In the Bible, the greatest heroes are presented "warts and all." King David is a hero, but also an adulterer and a poor father. Jacob is a man of great faith, but he is also a jealous deceiver. Abraham, Gideon, Solomon and Hezekiah are all Bible heroes, but they all are seen to have sins and character weaknesses. To an extent far greater than any other ancient history, the Bible authors were not afraid to reveal the unflattering faults of its central characters. Again, the Old Testament shows its history to be far superior to that of Herodotus, the "Father of History."

One is forced to ask how it could be that the history recorded in the Old Testament, written by dozens of authors over a thousand year period, could be singularly superior in both its accuracy and lack of bias to all the histories of contemporary peoples. Even the father of history cannot hold a candle to the Old Testament. To put it simply, the Old Testament is the greatest, the most accurate, the most reliable, the most unbiased historical account we have from the ancient world. How could this be? Could this be a sign of inspiration?

---

6. Charles Ailing, *Egypt and Bible History from Earliest Times to 1000 B.C.* (Baker Books, Grand Rapids, Michigan, 1981), p. 103).

Actually, the rather strong claims for accuracy and lack of bias for the Old Testament made in the previous paragraph have not yet been proven, at least not in this book. Perhaps the author has gotten ahead of himself. It is required to present a detailed case for the accuracy of the Bible as history. Let the story of David and Goliath serve as an opening example. It is time to start with Genesis and continue through to Revelation, investigating the Bible as history.

HISTORY AND THE OLD TESTAMENT

The purpose of this section, then, is to present evidence relating to the accuracy and reliability of the Old Testament as an historical document. Actually, the examples used will not start with Genesis chapter one. The accounts contained in Genesis chapters one through ten, including the creation and fall of man, the story of Cain and Abel, and the account of the flood are from a period of prehistory. It is difficult or impossible to even assign dates to these events, despite attempts by some to do so. Our study of the Old Testament as history will begin with Abraham. Before doing a more detailed study, it will be useful to keep a few points in mind as one looks at the Old Testament.

1. From the time of Abraham to the time Israel left Egypt under Moses, the people of God are described in the Bible as a relatively insignificant tribe. For the simple reason that the people of God had very little impact on historical events, it would be expected that archaeologists would not find records of actual people and events described in the Old Testament from this period. As much as you or I might hate to admit it, we will probably not be remembered by historians a thousand years from now. In looking at this section of the Bible what will be required is to show that the language, the traditions, the culture, the religious background and so forth found in the biblical accounts are in agreement with what is known from archaeological evidence of the same time and place as the events recorded in Genesis.

2. From the time of King David on (about 1050 BC), there should be increasing actual historical and archaeological evidence supporting Biblical accounts, because at this point, Israel became a formidable power.

3. The cultural, historical and religious background for Genesis chapters 11-38 (Abraham through Jacob) should be that of Mesopotamia somewhere between 2050 and 1800 BC. Anything found in this part of Genesis that is clearly from outside this culture and time frame would be an anachronism.

4. The cultural/historical/religious background of Genesis 39 through Deuteronomy (Joseph through Moses) should be that of Egypt from around 1800 to 1400 BC.

5. The cultural/historical/religious background of Joshua through 2 Chronicles (Joshua through the destruction of Jerusalem in 586 BC) should be that of Palestine after about 1010 BC.

Included below is a table that supplies time periods for the important phases in the history of Israel. For the earlier periods, the years are only approximate. For the later periods, dates become fairly exact because comparison to historical records and astronomical events can be made. In addition, a table relating the dominant political power in Palestine over the same time period is supplied. This will provide helpful context to the archaeological evidence to be presented.

IMPORTANT PERIODS IN THE HISTORY OF ISRAEL

Period in the History of Israel	Dates
The Patriarchs Abraham, Isaac, Jacob and Joseph	2050-1800 BC
Moses and Joshua The Exodus and the Conquest	1450-1400 BC
The Period of the Judges Deborah, Jephthah, Gideon and Samuel	1400-1050 BC
The United Kingdom Saul, David, Solomon and Rehoboam	1050-931 BC
The Northern Kingdom (Samaria) Destruction and captivity under Assyria	931-722 BC
The Southern Kingdom (Judah) Destruction and captivity under Babylon	931-586 BC
Defeat and destruction of Jerusalem The period of the exile in Babylon	605-536 BC
Return of the captives, rebuilding of the temple and of Jerusalem	536-440 BC
The period "between the Testaments":	440-6 BC

THE PATRIARCHAL PERIOD

We will begin, then, with the time of Abraham. In the Bible, Abraham is the father of Israel, both spiritually and by descent.

> Therefore, the promise comes by faith, so that it may be by grace and may be guaranteed to all Abraham's offspring—not only to those who are of the law but also to those who are of the faith of Abraham. He is the father of us all. As it is written, "I have made you the father of many nations" (Romans 4:16,17).

Abraham is an extremely important figure in the history of Israel. However, he was a fairly minor player on the stage of world history. Therefore, one would not expect to find much in the way of direct physical evidence of Abraham and his clan. What is expected is that if the account of Abraham and his descendents, Ishmael, Isaac, Jacob and Esau is accurate, then Genesis 11-38 should reflect what is known of the history, the culture and the religious atmosphere of Mesopotamia in around 1800 BC.

DOMINANT POWERS DURING THE HISTORY OF ISRAEL

Dominant Power	Dates
Hittites and the Egyptians	2000-900 BC
Assyria	900-606 BC
Babylon	605-539 BC
Persia	538-331 BC
Alexander and the Greek Dynasties	330-63 BC
Rome	After 63 BC

First of all, the Bible records that Abraham was born in the city of Ur. The remains of the city of Ur are located in southern Iraq, in Mesopotamia. Ur was one of the leading cities in the Babylonian period, around 2000 BC. Sir Leonard Wooley and others have excavated it. Ur was a large city with prosperous trade industries. This was definitely not the case twelve hundred or more years later when Bible critics contend the story of Abraham was made up. How did these people know of Ur? Genesis chapter eleven records Abraham's father Terah moving his family to Haran. One gets the impression that Haran was a smaller city, more on the outskirts of Babylonian culture. This is exactly the case.

The ruins of Haran have also been excavated. It was a smaller, but still significant city in the Northwest of Mesopotamia. The city was abandoned around 1800 BC, not long after the biblical account has Abraham living there. It is extremely unlikely that someone making up a story of Abraham hundreds of years later would have had him living in a city that had not even been heard of for hundreds of years.

Harran Ruins in Mesopotamian Plain Near Sanli Urfa, Turkey
(Photograph by Rex Geissler)

Another example of archaeological evidence that parallels Genesis is in the names of places and people. In 1975 a storeroom in the ancient city of Ebla was uncovered, which contained 17,000 clay tablets. Ebla was a powerful city in what is now Syria, in the region between Mesopotamia and Palestine. The peak of importance for Ebla was around 2500-2000 BC. On these tablets, a number of names are recorded. Included among these typical names of the period are Isaac, Jacob and Abraham, as well as the names of Abraham's father, grandfather and great grandfather, Terah, Nahor and Serug. These names are also known from other sources in Northwest Mesopotamia in both Babylonian and Old Assyrian texts. Interestingly, the names of the patriarchs are rare or unknown in extant material from later centuries. To understand the importance of this evidence, imagine reading a letter whose author supposedly wrote it in the U.S. during the year 1900, referring to people named Tabitha or Courtney. One would know right away that the letter was a fake. Similarly, if one were reading a letter between friends in the 1990s containing names such as Harold, Rutherford or Gertrude, one would know a serious mistake was made. As expected, the names of the patriarchs fit the historical and cultural context of Mesopotamia around 2000 BC.

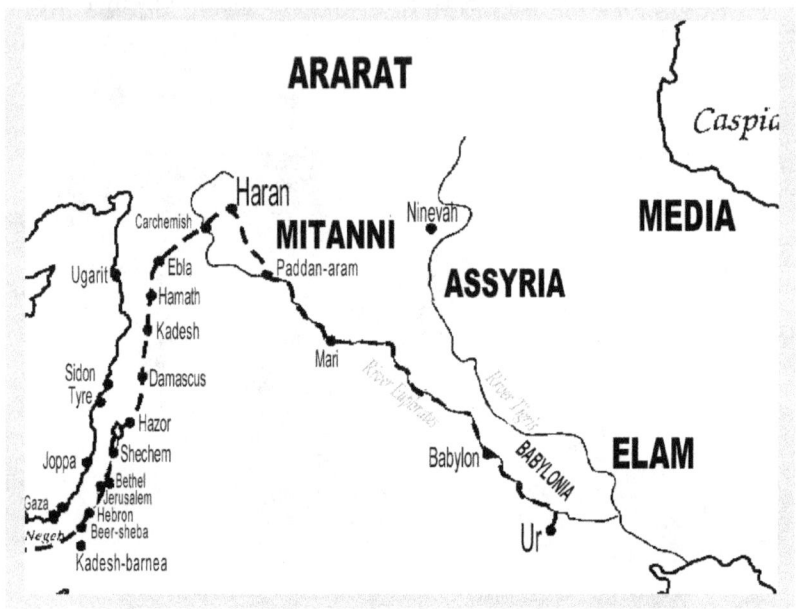

Near East Map showing an Ur at the bottom right, Haran at the top left, and Hebron at the bottom left.

It is not just the names of Abraham's relatives that fit the correct context as described in Genesis. For example, Genesis 14 mentions a coalition of kings who fought against Abraham and his allies. Among them is Kedorlaomer, king of Elam. At first, it may seem unlikely that Kedorlaomer would be involved in a campaign in Palestine, as Elam is very far from Palestine (in present-day southwestern Iran). Yet, the name Kedorlaomer has been found in ancient Elamite inscriptions. Could someone making up a story hundreds of years later have known that Kedorlaomer was the name of a ruler in Elam?

The names of peoples mentioned in the Bible in the patriarchal period agree with historical records as well. For example, the Hittites figure prominently in the text of Genesis 11-38. These people are mentioned forty-seven times in the Bible. They are described as a dominant political, cultural and economic influence in Palestine during this time. One can find in Genesis 23 a description of Abraham buying land from the Hittites for burying his wife Sarah. As late as the time of King David, the Hittites were still described as a major world power. David was reported as selling chariots from Egypt to the Hittites.

As recently as the late nineteenth century, many scholars doubted the very existence of these people known as the Hittites, despite the fact that they figure so prominently in the Bible. Many considered the Hittites, Horites, Jebusites, Amorites and so forth as simply historical fiction. That was until 1906 when the German archaeologist Hugo Winkler began excavating the site of the ancient city of Hattusha in present-day Turkey. He excavated five large temples, as well as a citadel. Ten thousand clay tablets containing what is now known to be the Hittite language were also discovered. A great number of other cities that were once part of the great Hittite Empire have since been excavated. The Hittites were the dominant power in the Near East, along with Egypt and Assyria, for well over a thousand years. It is now possible to earn a college degree in Hittite studies. So much for the Bible being an historical fantasy.

It is not only the Hittites who were unknown outside the Bible until fairly recently. Excavations and inscriptions have confirmed the presence in Palestine of the Horites, the Jebusites and a number of other nations listed in the book of Genesis.

Another place name provides very suggestive support for the Biblical account. The oldest known reference to the ancient city of Beersheba is found in an inscription in the Egyptian city of Karnak. In this ancient inscription, Beersheba is referred to as "the fortified town of Abram." It just so happens that the Bible describes Abraham founding the city of Beersheba (Genesis 21). Is there any chance this could be coincidence?

Possibly the most famous biblical place names from the period of the patriarchs are Sodom and Gomorrah. The story of the degradation and of the ultimate destruction of these cities by "fire and brimstone" is found in Genesis 18 and 19. Of course, many intellectuals consider the story of God bringing down fire from heaven to be pure fantasy. One important Bible scholar has called it a "purely mythical tale." What does archaeology have to say about this story?

Actually, Genesis describes Sodom and Gomorrah as members of a league of five cities in the plain surrounding what is now known as the Dead Sea. The five-city league included Sodom, Gomorrah, Admah, Zeboiim, and Zoar (Genesis 14:2). Sodom was the leading city in the league. The Bible describes a fairly well-watered and fertile land in a region that is now desolate wasteland. The biblical description of climate in the Dead Sea area is corroborated by archaeological studies of such evidence as seeds and pollen, which have revealed that four thousand years ago, the Dead Sea region was much wetter than it is now. The Dead Sea was about twice its present size, and was not nearly as salty as it is today.

There are half a dozen wadis (canyons with seasonal streams) in the area, which lead into the Dead Sea. In five of those wadis, the ruins of ancient cities have been discovered. Mysteriously (to those who do not accept the Bible as history, anyway) all five cities were abandoned and never reoccupied some time around 2000 BC. The largest of these is almost certainly the ancient Sodom. Archaeologists found this city to be surrounded by walls twenty-three feet thick! A layer of ashes covers the entire city, as much as seven feet deep. This, of course, is very suggestive of the biblical account, but towns being burned in the ancient world are not exactly a unique event. Perhaps more interestingly, a graveyard that is located a considerable distance from the city was also burned at the same time as the city. It is not the usual practice for conquering armies to burn down a graveyard some distance from a city. In fact, the grave structures discovered there had been burned from the outside in, suggesting burning material was dropped on them. This would be even more unusual.

All five of the "cities of the plain" were burned to the ground at about the same time, as evidenced by surprisingly deep ash deposits on the top of the ruins of each of the cities. Is it fair to call the biblical description of a massive, catastrophic event occurring to these cities a "purely mythical tale?"

As a side note, all five of the cities mentioned in Genesis 14 were found mentioned together, in the same order, on one of the tablets from the city of Ebla. This find is somewhat controversial because of arguments about the spelling of the names. Nevertheless, the tablets of Ebla do add further credence to the biblical account of the five cities on the plain of the Dead Sea.

A number of other events described in Genesis 11-38 fit uniquely into the cultural setting of Mesopotamia or Palestine two millennia before Christ, but not into a later period. For example, the Old Testament seems to describe two different laws of inheritance. In Genesis 49, Jacob gave *equal* portions to his twelve sons from his inheritance, while Moses stated that the first son should inherit a *double* portion of his father's inheritance (Deuteronomy 21:17). Critics have claimed that the difference in rules of inheritance represents an historical mistake by the author or authors of the Pentateuch.

Beni-Hasan Egyptian Tomb Painting Reproduction
Painting reproduction showing Semitic peoples coming to Egypt for food.
(Courtesy of the Egyptian Museum in Cairo)

A study of other law codes from the relevant periods will explain the difference. For example, the Babylonian code of Lipit-Ishtar, from about 2000 BC (a period just before the time of Jacob) states that each son receives an equal inheritance. The famous Code of Hammurabi, also from Babylon, from the eighteenth century BC (just after Jacob), also legislates equal portions for the children of the first wife, but lesser portions for children of additional wives. Law codes from the cities of Mari and Nuzi, in a timeframe closer to the time of Moses, both state that the first son will receive a double portion of the inheritance, as does Moses in Deuteronomy. Again, the biblical text from the patriarchal period reflects the social context of Mesopotamia in the period between 1800 and 2000 BC, providing further evidence that this is an accurate historical account.

Another interesting example that supports the claim that the accounts of the patriarchs are accurate history is found in Genesis 31. This is the record of Jacob taking his wives, his children and all his possessions and escaping from under the control of his father-in-law, Laban. When they snuck away, Jacob's wife Rachel stole the family idols from her father, Laban. Oddly enough, it seemed that Laban was as concerned with the idols being stolen as all the other possessions combined, including his daughters! When Laban finally caught up with Jacob and his followers, his first interest appeared to be in getting back the family idols. This behavior might seem odd until one considers a passage found in one of the Nuzi tablets from about the same timeframe. The Nuzi tablets include an account of a son-in-law who had possession of the family idols, or teraphim, having the legal right to lay claim to his father-in-law's possessions. This would explain why Laban was so concerned about the family idols. Not only does the account in the Nuzi tablets help to illumine the biblical text, it also proves that the biblical accounts of the patriarchal period reflect the culture of Mesopotamia in the timeframe when the events occurred.

A further example is found in the Nuzi tablets. One of these tablets stipulates that a barren wife must provide a slave girl to her husband in order to produce an heir. This would help explain the actions of Sara in Genesis 16:1-2, when she brought Hagar to Abraham to bear him a son. The Code of Hammurabi required that the father must keep the child of a slave as an heir, which might help to explain why Sarah was so determined to drive Hagar away from Abraham.

Literally dozens of other examples could be mentioned of historical, cultural or religious details found in Genesis that are in remarkable agreement with the findings of archaeologists.[7] Let us

---

7. For example, Randall Price, *The Stones Cry Out,* (Harvest House Publishers, Eugene, Oregon, 1997), pp. 89-107; and Josh McDowell, *More Evidence That Demands a Verdict,* (Here's Life Publishers, San Bernardino, California, 1975), pp 328-332.

consider one more. The well-known Egyptologist K. A. Kitchen has studied the price of slaves in Egypt from inscriptions found there over a period from 2400 to 400 BC.[8] Due to a steady inflation, the price of slaves went up dramatically over the centuries. Kitchen's studies have revealed that the average price of a slave in the eighteenth century BC was about twenty shekels. It just so happens that the account in Genesis 37:28 has Joseph being sold some time in the late nineteenth or early eighteenth century BC for twenty shekels. A couple of hundred years in either direction, and the price of slaves was much different. Aside from invoking some sort of very good luck, how can one explain the accuracy of the price of a slave in this account, unless one concedes that the story in Genesis is genuine history?

And speaking of Joseph, what about the account of his rise from slavery to become the Egyptian equivalent of prime minister? According to Genesis, he was put in control of all the grain supplies of the great empire. Skeptics have claimed that a Canaanite would never rise to such a height of power in the highly nationalistic Egyptian hierarchy. Egyptian records from the second millennium BC mention an official Yanhamu. Yanhamu is a Semitic name. This foreigner rose to become "fanbearer to the king," which implies one of his closest counselors. In fact, Yanhamu is described as being in charge of issuing supplies from the Egyptian granary. His name is found in correspondence from several locations in Syria and Palestine. The career of Yanhamu confirms the possibility of a Semitic foreigner such as Joseph rising to become prime minister in charge of the granary of Egypt.

THE EXODUS AND THE CONQUEST

We will now shift forward a few hundred years to the time of the exodus of the Israelites from Egypt, their sojourn in the wilderness and their entrance into and (partial) conquest of Canaan. This is obviously a crucial part of the history of God's people. The Jewish feast of the Passover reminded God's people of the fact that God "passed over" their sons when the destroying angel took the lives of the firstborn of Egypt. Jesus is called the Passover lamb in the New Testament because his sacrifice saves souls today in a way analogous to the blood of the Passover lamb. The Old Testament Law was given to Moses during this time. If the Law of Moses was not given by God, but was simply a collection of manmade laws, then whole portions of New Testament doctrine cease to make sense. The exodus of God's people from bondage in Egypt is used often in the New Testament as an historical

---

8. Kenneth A. Kitchen, "The Patriarchal Age: Myth or History?" *Biblical Archaeology Review*, 21:2 (March/April, 1995), pp. 48-57.

pre-figure for salvation from sin. If this event never occurred, then the meaning of many New Testament passages is lost. "These things happened to them as examples and were written down as warnings for us, on whom the fulfillment of the ages has come" (1 Corinthians 10:11).

A very reasonable question, then, is did Moses really lead a very large contingent of Hebrew-speaking Israelites out of slavery in Egypt? Or should we believe the Jewish humanist Rabbi, Sherwin Wine, who said that the story of the Exodus was "created by priest scribes in Jerusalem" from "a series of old legends and distorted memories which had no relationship to history."[9] Did these people, in fact, stay in the region of Sinai for a number of years? Did they later defeat a number of armies east of the River Jordan, subsequently cross the Jordan en masse, and conquer large portions of Palestine under the leadership of Joshua? What light does history and archaeology shed on this question?

A little background in Egyptian history can be helpful here. Some time probably in the eighteenth century BC, a group of outsiders known as the Hyskos began to infiltrate into Egypt, especially in the northern parts of the empire. The origin of the Hyskos is still somewhat of a mystery, but many believe they were from the islands of the Mediterranean such as Crete. Eventually, the Hyskos defeated the native dynasty in Egypt. It may very well have been one of the Hyskos pharaohs who allowed Joseph and his family to immigrate into Egypt. This might help to explain why the Pharaoh was willing to allow an outsider such as Joseph to wield such power in Egypt, as the Hyskos were outsiders themselves.

In the 1400s BC, a native dynasty was reestablished. This is the most likely time frame for the exodus.[10] It may explain why the Egyptian pharaohs seemed to suddenly turn on the Israelites, using them as slaves in their great construction projects. Foreign, Semitic-speaking people were suddenly of suspicious loyalty. According to the book of Exodus, God used this hardening of attitude of the Egyptian dynasty to bring his people out of Egypt, into the Promised Land.

What is the evidence for the presence of the Israelites in Egypt, of the subsequent exodus from slavery, the wandering in the wilderness and finally the conquest of Canaan? Despite their large numbers, the Hebrews left very little evidence of their presence behind in Egypt. Although they were involved in building massive monuments for Pharaoh, presumably, they lived in very humble dwellings. However,

---

9. Charles E. Sellier and Brian Russell, *Ancient Secrets of the Bible,* (Dell Publishing, New York, 1994), pp. 179-180.

10. Some, including some conservative scholars, prefer about 1270 BC as the date or Israel entering Palestine. It is the author's opinion that the date cannot be ruled out, but that it is not as well supported by the evidence.

their entry into Canaan did not go without notice. Evidence of this is found in what are known as the Tel el-Amarna tablets.

Tel el-Armana Tablet Letter,
Louvre Museum, Paris, France
Photograph by Rex Geissler, 2000

The Tel el-Amarna tablets were discovered in the ruins of the Egyptian city el-Amarna. This was the capital city of Pharaoh Akhnaton, ruler of Egypt from 1387 to 1366 BC. The tablets are letters from local officials in Palestine and Syria, describing the situation in their provinces, requesting supplies and so forth. The letters in general describe a state of near anarchy in the outlying reaches of the Egyptian realms.

Most interestingly, the Amarna letters appear to mention events recorded in the book of Joshua. A number of the letters mention cities falling to an invading group. Specifically, they mention the fall of Gezer, Ashkelon and Lachish. All three of these cities are mentioned in the list of conquered cities in Joshua. This is quite significant, because the book of Joshua clearly implies that not all the cities of Canaan were conquered. Megiddo and Jerusalem were notable holdouts. These cities are not mentioned in the el-Amarna letters as being conquered. One of the letters found at el-Amarna is from a certain Abdi-Hiba, governor of Jebus (later known as Jerusalem). The letter is addressed to Akhnaton, which implies it was written somewhere between 1387 and 1366 BC. This fits well with an approximate date of the exodus of 1420 BC (and therefore a date of entering the Promised Land of 1380 BC). In the letter, Abdi-Hiba pleaded for military aid from Pharaoh Akhnaton.

> "The Habiru plunder all lands of the king. If archers are here this year, then the lands of the king, the lord, will remain; but if the archers are not here, then the lands of the king, my lord, are lost'"

Could the Habiru (or Apiru) of this letter be the armies of the Hebrews, conquering large parts of Canaan from the native dynasties, as described in Joshua? Some archaeologists have denied this contention. Many do so because they like to date the conquest to some time around 1270 BC. The obvious similarity of the spelling, combined with the good correspondence with the list of conquered cities makes the identification of the Habiru of the Tel el-Amarna letters with the Hebrews in the Bible seem possible. At some point, archaeologists will have to consider the possibility that the Old Testament is the most accurate and useful primary source of historical information we have for the ancient Near East.

The book of Deuteronomy mentions that Moses wrote down a number of laws he was given from Jehovah. Many have claimed that the whole idea of Moses writing at all would be an anachronism. They have contended that there is no way that an impoverished and semi-nomadic Semitic tribe such as the Hebrews could even possess a written language as early as 1400 BC. The Ebla tablets belie this claim. These tablets, as mentioned previously, contain a written Semitic language as early as 2500 BC. Besides this, archaeologists have discovered inscriptions from the Egyptian mines in the Sinai dating from around 1800 BC. These inscriptions are in a Semitic language as well.

Further evidence for the historical nature of the exodus accounts was found in the Iron Age ruins of Deir Alla in present-day Jordan. A number of written fragments on shards of clay were found in this excavation and dated to the eighth century BC. Included is a historical reference to a prophet and seer known as Balaam. This is probably the Balaam of Numbers 22-24. Balaam is the one who refused to prophesy against the Israelites when they sought to pass through the territory of Moab, on the way to Canaan. Here we have external historical confirmation of an important biblical figure in the time of the conquest of the Promised Land.

The book of Joshua records the actual conquest of Canaan. It is important to note how Joshua describes the conquest. First, although Israel is described as overtaking significant territory, the conquest was far from complete. "Very much of the land remain[ed] to be possessed" (Joshua 13:1) at the end of Joshua's life. Two very important cities that Joshua did not conquer were Beth-Shean and Megiddo. In agreement with this fact, archaeologists studying the sites of Megiddo and Beth-Shean have discovered significant Egyptian influence well past the time of Joshua. Both cities show strong Israelite influence only after the time of Solomon. Not surprisingly, this is when the book of 1 Samuel describes Israel finally conquering these cities.

In addition, only three cities are specifically described in Joshua as being completely destroyed by fire. These three were Jericho, Ai and Hazor. Some Bible critics have pointed to the fact that only a few cities in Palestine show signs of massive destruction during the mid-1300s BC as evidence against the conquest under Joshua. In fact, this evidence actually strongly supports the biblical account. The two large cities in Palestine that show signs of massive destruction by fire in the fourteenth century BC are Jericho and Hazor—the very same cities mentioned in Joshua!

Important excavations at Jericho this century include those of John Garstang in the 1940s, by Kathleen Kenyon in the 1950s, and later by Bryant Woods. Garstang found a massive layer of destruction in the Bronze Age, followed by an extended period during which the city was abandoned. This, of course, would accord with the biblical account. Kenyon initially dated the layer of destruction to 1550 BC, but the further work of Wood confirms a date for the destruction of Jericho by fire at around 1400 BC—in reasonable agreement with the Tel el-Amarna letters. A charcoal sample was analyzed by carbon-14 dating to 1400 plus or minus forty years. A summary of what was discovered by Woods follows:[11]

1. The city was strongly fortified in the Late Bronze I period, the time of the Conquest according to the biblical chronology (Joshua 2: 5,7,15).

2. The city was massively destroyed by fire (Joshua 6:24).

3. The fortification walls collapsed at the time the city was destroyed, possibly by earthquake activity (Joshua 6:20).

4. The destruction occurred at harvest time, in the spring, as indicated by the large quantities of grain stored in the city (Joshua 2: 6, 3:15, 5:10).

5. The siege of Jericho was short, as the grain stored in the city was not consumed (Joshua 6:15,20).

6. Contrary to what was customary, the grain was not plundered, in accordance to the command given to Joshua (Joshua 6:17,18).

The location of Ai remains controversial, making it difficult to confirm its fate, but the city of Hazor, the third of the cities described as being completely destroyed by fire in Joshua (Joshua 11:11-13), has been excavated. The work at this city was begun by Yigael Yadin, and continued by Amnon Ben-Tor. Ben-Tor has stated concerning Hazor:[12]

---

11. As summarized in Randall Price, *The Stones Cry Out* (Harvest HousePublishers, Eugene, Oregon, 1997), pp. 152, 153.
12. Quoted from an interview with Amnon Ben-Tor by Tom McCall, Institute of Archaeology, The Hebrew University of Jerusalem, November 1996.

There is evidence of a massive destruction. I once called it the mother of all destructions. In Hazor, wherever you come down to the end of the Canaanite strata, you come upon this destruction. It is an unbelievable destruction...it left behind a thick debris of ashes. There was a terrible fire in the palace. So much so, that the bricks vitrified and some of the clay vessels melted. Some stones exploded because of the fire.

Ben-Tor identifies this destruction with the campaign of Joshua, as it fits the timeframe of the conquest.

In addition to these discoveries, an interesting inscription has been found on what is known as the Stele of Merneptah. On this stele is inscribed a record of a campaign of the pharaoh Merneptah in 1230 BC. This inscription mentions the incursions of the Philistines, as well as the presence of Israelites already in Canaan. This is the earliest known inscription that specifically mentions the nation of Israel.

Stele of Merneptah
Courtesy Egyptian Museum
Cairo, Egypt

As one comes closer to the modern age, the actual physical evidence in support of the biblical accounts becomes more substantial. We have seen that to be true for the time of the conquest. This trend will continue as we consider evidence from the time of the Jewish monarchy.

THE UNITED AND THE DIVIDED KINGDOMS

The kingdom period in the history of Israel began with the accession of King Saul to the throne in around 1040 BC. According to the account in 1 Samuel, the Israelites begged Samuel, the last of the judges, to appoint a king over them. Saul was really more of a figurehead than an effective ruler of the Israelites. He was unable to unite the twelve tribes, to form any real standing army or a centralized government. It was only when Saul was killed in battle and eventually David took the throne shortly before 1000 BC that the kingdom of Israel became a reality. It was at this point that the Hebrew people for the first time evolved into a true formidable power. For this reason, it is also at this point that one would logically expect to see significant archaeological and historical evidences that reflect specific events recorded in the Bible. A person making such a search will not be disappointed.

As mentioned above, many Bible critics have claimed that the stories of David's rise to power, of his victories over the Philistines, of his great wealth and so forth, are merely religious stories with a moral teaching. A century ago, it would have been difficult to disprove such a claim with solid evidence. Archaeological evidence that supports the biblical accounts in the early period of the kingdom has already been mentioned in the introduction to this chapter. This would include:

1. Slingshots discovered at King Saul's palace in Gibeah, which confirms that slingshots were standard weapons in Israel's arsenal at that time

2. The Tel Dan Inscription, a ninth-century BC inscription that mentions King David and the House of David

3. Twin temples to Ashtoreth and Dagon in Beth Shan, which confirms details of 1 Samuel 31:10 and 1 Chronicles 10:10

From the time of David on, there is mounting archaeological evidence in support of the accuracy of the Bible as history. This is a very extensive list. Included below are a few of the most significant archaeological finds from the time of the Kings. Also included are a few discoveries from the time immediately following the destruction of Jerusalem in 586 BC, including the return from exile to Jerusalem under the Persian emperors Cyrus and Darius I.

- **The Ebla Tablets**, already mentioned, include a record of the tribute the king of Mari gave to Ebla after a military defeat. The tribute included 11,000 pounds of silver and 880 pounds of gold. What makes this finding important is that it relates to the seemingly huge amounts of gold mentioned in such passages as 1 Kings 10:14 and 2 Chronicles 9:13. These scriptures report the annual tribute from the entire empire of Solomon, including over ten tons of gold. Some have scoffed at this amount of gold coming into the treasury of Solomon. The record from Ebla of almost half a ton of gold as tribute from one city makes the size of the annual tribute of the entire empire of Solomon seem quite reasonable.

Ebla Tablet

- **The Sheshonq (Shishak) Inscription**, a 920 BC inscription was found in a temple at Karnak in Egypt that records details of

Pharaoh Sheshong's raid against Rehoboam. This raid is also recorded in 1 Kings 14:25-28.

- **The Moabite Stone**, an inscription of Mesha, king of Moab from about 850 BC found in Dibon, the capital of Moab. On this stele, Mesha boasts of his exploits against Israel. This inscription specifically mentions "the House of Omri" (1 Kings 16:28), and "the son of Ahab."

Moabite Stone of King Mesha
Louvre Museum, Paris, France

- **The Black Obelisk of Shalmanezer III.** This is a carving in bas-relief from 840 BC that was found in Nineveh at the palace of Shalmanezer III, emperor of Assyria. It depicts Israeli leaders paying tribute to Shalmanezer. One scene on the obelisk shows King Jehu of Israel bowing before Shalmanezer as he brings his tribute. This is the first known portrait of an Israeli king.[12] The Bible does not record Jehu's journey to Nineveh, but it does record that Israel at this time began to pay tribute to Shalmanezer (2 Kings 17:3-6).

---

12. One factor to bear in mind in studying the archaeology of Israel is that very few statues or images of people or animals are found in ancient Israel. Presumably this reflects the command of God not to carve any "graven images." The fact that Israel was more or less faithful in obeying this command explains the relative rarity of such finds in Palestine.

Stele of Shalmanezer
Louvre Museum, Paris, France

Stele of Shalmanezer with King Jehu Bowing
Courtesy of British Museum, London England

- **The Tel Dan Inscription.** This inscription from about 820 BC was already discussed because it mentions the House of David. In this inscription, Hazael, King of Aram, also boasts, "I killed Jehoram, son of Ahab, King of Israel, and I killed Ahaziah, son of Jehoram, king of the House of David." It is interesting that 2 Kings 8:28,29 records Jehoram being injured in battle against Hazael, but later actually slain by Jehu. Presumably the Arameans knew he was injured and mistakenly assumed when he died soon thereafter that he had died of his wounds.

Tel Dan Inscription

Siloam Stone Inscription
Courtesy of Israel Museum, Jerusalem, Israel

• **The Siloam Stone Inscription.** This inscription was discovered in a manmade underground tunnel beneath the old city of Jerusalem. Carved into the rock is a description of how this amazing tunnel was dug through 1500 feet of solid rock, connecting the spring of Gihon, outside the walls, to the Pool of Siloam inside the city of Jerusalem. The inscription was made the same year the tunnel was completed, in 701 BC, at a time when Hezekiah was fortifying Jerusalem against Sennacherib's attacks. This is specifically mentioned in 2 Chronicles 32: 2-4, 30 and 2 Kings 20:20. The fact that a winding, 1500-foot tunnel was dug from both ends and met within a few feet in the middle is a marvel of human accomplishment. Again, a very specific account recorded in the Old Testament has been confirmed by archaeological discovery.

• **The Sennacherib Cylinder.** This "cylinder" is actually in the shape of a prism. It is also known as the Taylor prism. It was found in Nineveh. Events recorded on the prism imply that it was carved in 686 BC. It reports the attack and siege of Jerusalem by Sennacherib. These events are related in detail in 2 Kings 18:17-19:37. The writer of 2 Kings states that Jerusalem was put under siege by Sennacherib's army. After preparing the defenses of the city, King Hezekiah prayed to God for deliverance. As described in 2 Kings, that night the army of Sennacherib was slain by an angel of God, and Sennacherib retreated back to Assyria. The account of the siege as recorded on the Sennacherib cylinder is as follows:

Sennacherib Cylinder or
Taylor Prism
Courtesy of British Museum, London England

As to Hezekiah, the Jew, he did not submit to my yoke. I laid siege to 46 of his strong cities, walled forts, and to the countless small villages in their vicinity. I drove out of them 200,150 people, young and old, male and female, horses, mules, donkeys, camels, big and small cattle beyond counting and considered [them] booty. Himself I made a prisoner in Jerusalem, his royal residence, like a bird in a cage.[14]

Surely if Sennacherib had actually defeated and captured Hezekiah, it would have been mentioned on the cylinder. Apparently, both 2 Kings and those scribes who recorded Sennacherib's accomplishments agree that he put siege to Jerusalem, but that he left Canaan without overcoming Jerusalem.

Of course, the chroniclers of Sennacherib as usual for the ancients, did not mention the miraculous destruction of his troops, as described in the Bible in 2 Kings.

---

14. J. B. Pritchard, *Ancient Near East Texts*, (Princeton University Press, 1969)

- **The Silver Scroll.** This is a tiny silver scroll, which was discovered in 1979 in Jerusalem. It has been dated to the seventh century BC. It contains an inscription of Numbers 6:24-26. This is the oldest known quote from the Bible.

- **The Babylonian Chronicles.** These are tablets written in cuneiform script that were discovered in Babylon. They include an account from the Babylonian perspective of the capture of Jerusalem in 597 BC. The events are also described in 2 Kings 24:10-17 and in 2 Chronicles 36:5-7. An excerpt from the Babylonian Chronicles follows.

> [In] the seventh year, the month of Kislev, the king of Babylonia mustered his forces and marched to Syria. He camped against the city of Judah (Jerusalem) and on the second day of the month of Adar he took the city and captured the king. He appointed a king of his own choice there, took its heavy tribute and brought them to Babylon.

Silver Scroll
Courtesy of Israel Museum, Jerusalem, Israel

This account is in perfect accord with the biblical record. The king who was captured was Jehoiachin. The puppet king left in his place by Nebuchadnezzar was Zedekiah. It is also interesting to note that W. F. Albright discovered in Babylon a royal archive that includes Jehoiachin and his five sons on a list of those receiving rations from the royal court. This is dramatic proof of the accuracy of the biblical account of Jehoiachin as recorded in 2 Kings 25:30: "Day by day the king gave Jehoiachin a regular allowance as long as he lived."

Babylonian Chronicles
Courtesy of British Museum, London England

Seal of King Hezekiah Replica

- **The Seal of Gemariah**. A clay button used for sealing letters was found in a layer of Jerusalem that corresponds to its destruction in 586 BC. This seal is marked, "Gemariah, son of Shaphan." Surely this is the seal of the same Gemariah who is mentioned in Jeremiah 36:10-12, 25-26. He was one of those who advised King Jehoiakim not to burn the scroll that Jeremiah had sent to the king. Another seal has been discovered in Jerusalem that is inscribed "Baruch, son of Neriah, the scribe." This is almost certainly the seal of Baruch, who was the personal scribe of Jeremiah (Jeremiah 36:26). In fact, this seal has a fingerprint hardened into it, which may very well be the actual fingerprint of Jeremiah's personal scribe. Does the book of Jeremiah sound like a fabrication?

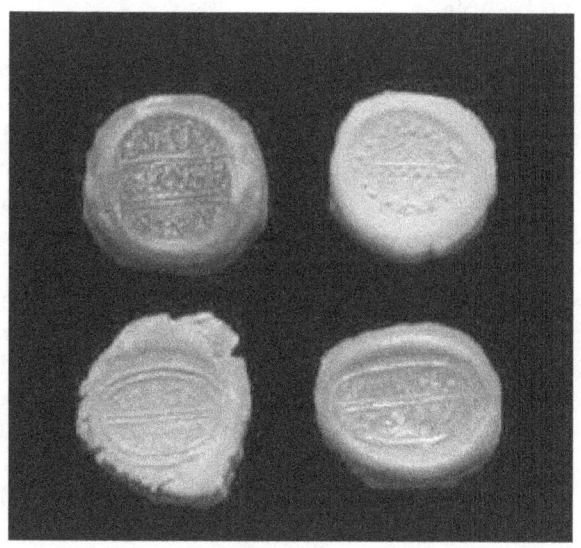

- **The Lachish Letters.** The biblical account of the final destruction of Jerusalem is confirmed in great detail thanks to a set of letters that were found in the city of Lachish. These letters were recovered from a room near the city gate. Lachish was the last city other than Jerusalem to hold out against the onslaught of Nebuchadnezzar when he came to avenge the rebellion of King Zedekiah. A total of six letters were discovered. The text of the letters is a plea to the armies in Jerusalem to come to the aid of Lachish as Nebuchadnezzar bore down on the city.  One poignant letter records the light at the top of the neighboring city of Azekah going out as Nebuchadnezzar's army destroyed it. Unfortunately for its inhabitants, soon after this letter was written, Lachish was overrun, along with Jerusalem itself. These tragic events occurred in 586 BC, and are recorded in Jeremiah 52:1-28. Jeremiah 34:6,7 specifically mentions the attack of Nebuchadnezzar on Azekah and Lachish.

- **Inscription from the Ziggurat in Ur.** The inscription has been found from one of the four corners of the ziggurat (a pyramid-like temple) in Ur. Nabonidus, the last emperor of Babylon, commissioned this inscription. The inscription specifically mentions Belshazzar, the son of Nabonidus, as his firstborn son. Belshazzar is referred to in the inscription in a way that implies he was royalty. Historians interpret this to mean that Belshazzar ruled as co-regent with Nabonidus. The reason this inscription is important to the accuracy of the Old Testament is that in Daniel, the last king of Babylon appears to be Belshazzar (Daniel 5). In the past, this has caused some to question the reliability of the book of Daniel, because before this inscription was found at Ur, there was no record anywhere outside the Bible of Belshazzar even existing, never mind his reigning as king in Babylon. Critics claimed that the Belshazzar of Daniel chapter five was just part of a Jewish legend. Since the discovery at the Ziggurat in Ur, the critics have moved on to more fertile ground. This is a familiar pattern. At some point they should simply admit that whenever an historical detail found in the Bible is not confirmed by outside sources, it is best to at least give the accuracy of the Bible the benefit of the doubt.

Ziggurat in Ur, Mesopotamia

- **The Cyrus Cylinder**. This is a record of one of the edicts of King Cyrus of Persia from 535 BC. The edict is strongly reminiscent of that recorded in Ezra 1:2-4, in which Cyrus decreed that the Israelites could return to Jerusalem from captivity to rebuild the temple. A quote from the cylinder of Cyrus follows.

> ...I returned to [these] sacred cities on the other side of the Tigris, the sanctuaries of which have been in ruins for a long time, the images which [used] to live therein and established for them permanent sanctuaries. I [also] gathered all their [former] inhabitants and returned [to them] their habitations. Furthermore, I resettled upon the command of Marduk the great lord, all the gods of Sumer and Akkad whom Nabonidus has brought into Babylon to the anger of the lord of the gods, unharmed, in their [former] chapels, the places which made them happy. May all the gods whom I have resettled in their sacred cities ask daily Bel and Nebo for long life for me and may they recommend me...to Marduk, my lord, may they say thus: Cyrus, the king who worships you and Cambyses, his son...all of them I settled in a peaceful place.

Cyrus Cylinder
Courtesy of British Museum, London, England

Again, many had claimed before this inscription was found that the whole idea of Cyrus allowing a conquered people to return to their native homeland, as described in detail in Ezra, was not credible. The Cyrus cylinder helps to make the biblical claim very credible.

The Behistun Inscription, Iran
Courtesy of Jona Lendering

- **The Behistun Inscription.** The last archaeological find we will mention in connection with the Old Testament is a huge inscription that was discovered on the side of a cliff along a caravan route in what is now southern Iran. Large figures of Persian soldiers and what is obviously a king along with his attendants are carved into the cliff face three hundred feet above the base. From a distance it would appear that the surface of the cliff behind the statues is smooth. It was the very brave archaeologist Sir Henry Rawlinson who finally scaled the cliff to inspect the carvings. In fact, what appears to be a smooth cliff-face contains a lengthy inscription in a cuneiform script. The inscription is actually in three languages: Old Persian, Babylonian and Elamite. It turned out to be the Rosetta Stone[15] of Mesopotamian languages.

When translated, the inscription included the introductory statement, "I am Darius, great King, King of Kings, the King of Persia." This is the same Darius who allowed the Jews to rebuild the temple in Jerusalem. His decree is found in Ezra 6:1-12. The inscription includes the following:

> I settled the people in their place, the people of Persia, and Media, and the other provinces. I restored that which had been taken away, as it was in the days of old. This did I by the grace of Ahuramazda.

Ahuramazda is the god of Zoroastrianism—a religion that still survives in Iran. This letter is in the same spirit as that found in Ezra, in which Darius decreed that the Jews should return to Jerusalem and rebuild their temple, using funds from the royal Persian treasury.

In summary, with the passage of time, the evidence in support of the accuracy of the Old Testament as history has mounted. Time and time again, members of the academic establishment have claimed that details in the Old Testament were in error or were simply fables, only to be forced into retreat in the face of undeniable evidence that the Bible was correct. More and more, the weight of evidence supports belief that the Old Testament is such an accurate historical record that it could only be explained by the providence of God. It is the most useful, most reliable, most accurate primary historical source from the ancient world. Those who claim that the Old Testament is a late fabrication do so, not so much because the evidence supports such a position, but because they are predisposed not to accept the miraculous events recorded on its pages.

---

15. The Rosetta Stone is a famous inscription which was found in Egypt in 1799 by French troops. It contains parallel passages in Greek, Heiroglyphic and Demotic (a later Egyptian script) which, when translated by Thomas Young, led to archaeologists being able to read the inscriptions found in ancient Egyptian tombs.

THE NEW TESTAMENT

It should not come as a surprise that many have attempted to undercut the authority of the New Testament based on supposed historical inaccuracies as well. Acceptance of the gospel accounts and the book of Acts as accurate history would imply that Jesus was who he said he was—the Son of God. In the eighteenth century, skeptics would claim that Jesus was not a real person at all. When evidence made that claim untenable, some retreated to conceding that Jesus was a real person, but claiming that the New Testament was a production of pious believers in the mid-second century AD. This allowed them to claim that most of the specific events described in the gospels and Acts were fictionalized accounts. As we will see, archaeological discoveries in the twentieth century have made that view simply not believable, even for the hardened skeptic.

The New Testament books with the most historical content are Luke and Acts. This is not a coincidence, as Luke, a companion of Paul on his missionary journeys, wrote both books. In his own words, Luke said:

> Therefore since I myself have carefully investigated everything from the beginning, it seemed good also to me to write an orderly account for you, most excellent Theophilus, so that you may know the certainty of the things you have been taught (Luke 1:3,4).

There is hardly a single historical detail in Luke or Acts that has not been challenged for its accuracy by one skeptic or another. Luke's writings hold up just fine to the criticism. For example, consider Luke 2:1-3.

> In those days, Caesar Augustus issued a decree that a census should be taken of the entire Roman world. (This was the first census that took place while Quirinius was governor of Syria.) And everyone went to his own town to register.

This is followed by the account of Mary and Joseph traveling to Bethlehem. Critics have claimed that Caesar Augustus never issued such a decree. They have also claimed that there was no way people would have been required to travel long distances to their home district for such a census in any case. To top it off, critics said that Quirinius was not governor of Syria at the time in question.

On all three points, archaeological discoveries have proven Luke to be accurate. More recent archaeological discoveries have proven that Augustus did in fact decree censuses every fourteen years. The first census was in 23-22 BC. The second was in 9-8 BC. Being in the far reaches of the empire, the census may not have reached Palestine until 7 or 6 BC, the latter being a probable date for the birth of Jesus.[16]

As to the need for Mary and Joseph to travel to Bethlehem from Galilee, a papyrus has been found in Egypt.[17] On it is written: "Because of the approaching census it is necessary that all those residing for any cause away from their homes should at once prepare to return to their own governments in order that they may complete the family registration of the enrollment and that the tilled lands may retain those belonging to them." This papyrus provides astounding confirmation of Luke's account of the birth of Jesus. Or perhaps it would be more accurate to say that the more reliable source (the New Testament) confirms the accuracy of the less reliable source (the papyrus found in Egypt).

As far as Quirinius is concerned, again historians doubted Luke because it was known from the writings of Josephus that Quirinius was governor in Syria after AD 6, which is definitely too late for the birth of Jesus Christ. This argument was eliminated when an inscription was found in Antioch ascribing to Quirinius the governorship of Syria in 7 BC. Apparently, Quirinius had two tours of duty in Syria, one from 12 to 6 BC as governor, the other after AD 6 as an imperial legate.

Being the careful historian that he was, Luke dated the beginning of John the Baptist's ministry as follows:

> In the fifteenth year of the reign of Tiberius Caesar—when Pontius Pilate was governor of Judea, Herod tetrarch of Galilee, his brother Philip tetrarch of Iturea and Traconitis, and Lysanias tetrarch of Abilene—during the high priesthood of Annas and Caiaphas, the word of God came to John son of Zechariah in the desert (Luke 3:1-3).

Many critics considered the governorship of Pilate a mistake because it was unconfirmed by any outside source. Unconfirmed, that is, until 1961 when an inscription was found in his capital at Caesarea Maritima. The inscription gives Pilate's title as "Pontius Pilate, Prefect of Judea." In addition, Luke has Herod ruling as tetrarch, rather than king. Roman records confirm that tetrarch is the correct title for this relative of King Herod the Great. The position of Lysanias was

---

16. As mentioned in a previous chapter, Jesus was probably born around 5 or 6 BC.
17. John Elder, *Prophets, Idols, and Diggers,* (Bobbs Merrill Co., New Youk, 1960), p. 159,160 and Joseph P. Free, *Archaeology and Bible History,* (Scripture Press, Wheaton, Illinois), p 285.

questioned at one time as well. Apparently, there was a Lysanias who ruled in the area, but who was killed in 36 BC. Again, Luke was criticized for making an error. This false charge was cleared up when an inscription was found in Abila, near Damascus, which reads, "Freedman of Lysanias the Tetrarch." This inscription has been dated to between AD 14 and 29. It would appear that there were two important personages named Lysanias. The one who ruled at the right time and place to confirm Luke's information was the second of the two.

Pilate Inscription Replica at Caesarea Maritima, Israel
(Photograph by Rex Geissler)

In fact, Luke named thirty-two countries, fifty-four cities and nine islands without error. He specifically said that Lystra and Derbe were in Lycaonia and that Iconium was not (Acts 14:6). Cicero, the great Latin debater, stated that Iconium was in Lycaonia, causing some to claim that Luke had made another mistake. Sorry, Cicero, but an inscription found by Sir William Ramsay in 1910 confirmed that Iconium was in Phrygia, not Lycaonia. Cicero may be excused for his mistake, as he was not an historian, but Luke proves to be an historian of the first rank.

In listing important personages, Luke appears to be a perfectionist of the highest order. He tied his accounts down with so many person and place names, it is almost as if he was daring his readers to check out the accuracy of his sources. The Romans used a very confusing array of names for its local rulers, from tetrarch to proconsul, governor, imperial legate, politarch and so forth. In every case that the titles used by Luke can be compared to other sources, Luke is correct. He has the Thessalonian magistrates in Acts 17:6,9 called politarchs, a term not known from any classical literature (except, of course, from one of its greatest historians—Luke). Yet, an inscription was found in Thessalonica that labels its leaders as politarchs. Luke has Gallio reigning as proconsul of Achaia (Acts 20:2). An inscription was found at Delphi in Greece that confirmed that Gallio reigned as proconsul of Achaia beginning in AD 51. Luke called the leader of Cyprus the proconsul Sergius Paullus (Acts 13:7). Cyprus was changed to an imperial province after 22 BC, at which time its leaders were no longer imperial legates, but proconsuls. Luke has the leaders of Ephesus described accurately as asiarchs (Acts 19:31), while the magistrates of Philippi are praetors (Acts 16:20,35). Actually, the correct technical title for the leaders of Philippi was duumvirs, but Cicero himself sarcastically commented about some duumvirs that "these men wished to be called praetors." Luke has the leader of the island of Malta a rather curious "the first man of the island." Latin inscriptions on the island, as well, confirm this title. The list could go on.[18]

There are an almost unlimited number of examples in which Luke got a detail of custom or place correct. The theatre in Ephesus at which the riotous mob met in Acts 19 has been excavated. An inscription from AD 103 was found in both Greek and Latin that describes how a Roman official named C. Vivius Salutaris presented silver images of Artemis and other statues to be set onto pedestals at each meeting of the citizen body in the theatre. These must be the same silver images whose manufacture was threatened by the Ephesians who were putting their faith in Jesus Christ. Fear of the local businessmen losing income led to the riot in Ephesus (Acts 19:23-41). Apparently, the church in Ephesus was not influential enough to completely put an end to this idolatrous worship.

Luke prominently mentions the high priest Caiaphas. He was the one who prepared the plot to have Jesus arrested and executed. From other records, we know that Caiaphas ruled as high priest from AD 18-36. The actual remains of Caiaphas were discovered in November 1990. At that time, workers were building a water park in what is known as the Peace Forest in Jerusalem. While digging at the site, they came upon a collapsed roof under which were found twelve very ornate ossuaries. On one of these was inscribed, "Caiaphas, Joseph, son of Caiaphas." Although the Bible simply calls him Caiaphas, Josephus identified him as "Joseph who was called Caiaphas of the high priesthood."

Sir William Ramsay is considered by many to be one of the greatest archaeologists of all time. He began his career as a skeptic

---

18. F. F. Bruce, *The New Testament Documents, Are They Reliable,* (Eerdmans, Grand Rapids, Michigan, 1983) pp. 82-86.

who held firmly to the belief that Luke was written in the second half of the second century AD, and that it was therefore a very unreliable document. It was in doing research to provide support for this belief that he was confronted with the undeniable fact that the books of Luke and Acts are accurate history. To quote Ramsay:

> I found myself brought into contact with the Book of Acts as an authority for the topography, antiquities, and society of Asia Minor. It was gradually borne upon me that in various details the narrative showed marvelous truth. In fact, beginning with a fixed idea that the work was essentially a second century composition, and never relying on its evidence as trustworthy for first century conditions, I gradually came to find it a useful ally in some obscure and difficult investigations.[19]

Another statement of Ramsay, the former skeptic, follows:

> Luke is a historian of the first rank; not merely are his statements of fact trustworthy; he is possessed of the true historic sense; he fixes his mind on the idea and plan that rules in the evolution of history, and proportions the scale of his treatment to the importance of each incident. He seizes the important and critical events and shows their true nature at greater length, while he touches lightly or omits entirely much that was valueless for his purpose. In short, this author should be placed along with the very greatest of historians.[20]

If Luke is an historian of the first rank, then how can some continue to doubt the historical accuracy of the New Testament? All the evidence points to the conclusion that those who question the accuracy of the New Testament do so, not because the facts point in that direction. Those who continue to question the accuracy of the gospel accounts do so principally because they are philosophically opposed to the implications of the New Testament. If Luke is an accurate historical account, then Jesus worked great miracles. If Luke produced a carefully researched account of actual events, then Jesus is the Son of God. There are many who are simply unwilling to accept

---

19. Sir William Ramsay, *St. Paul, the Traveler and the Roman Citizen*, (Hodder and Stoughton, 1920).
20. Sir William Ramsay, *The Bearing of Recent Discovery on the Trustworthiness of the New Testament*, (Hodder and Stoughton, 1915).

this truth. Wishful thinking has a very limited effect on the truth. Jesus the miracle-worker will not go away. Beginning with Voltaire, and following through with his successors for over two hundred years, a pattern emerges. Those who, for whatever reason, begin with the assumption that the miraculous events recorded in the Bible cannot be true simply must attack the integrity of the Bible. Again and again, facts prove the skeptic wrong in his or her assumption. At some point, the open-minded investigator will begin to give the Bible the benefit of the doubt. For those willing to accept it, the words of 2 Timothy 3:16 ring true: "All Scripture is inspired by God…"

For Today

1. Are there any historical details in the Bible that you have found particularly difficult to accept as true? Has this chapter had any effect on your feelings about them? How might you do research to investigate this question?

2. Why do you think that many who strongly attack the Bible as a collection of myth and legend generally accept the Greek historian Herodotus as a great historian?

Chapter Eight
Science and the Bible: Mortal Enemies?

> *The Bible was written to show us
> how to go to heaven, not how the heavens go.*
> *– Galileo Galilei*

> *Whence is it that nature does
> nothing in vain; and whence
> arises all that order and beauty
> which we see in the world?*
> *– Isaac Newton*

The Bible, A Book Written by an Ignorant People in an Ignorant Age. This is the title of a book a scientist friend of mine set out to write as a young and zealous atheist. The friend is John Clayton. John was raised by parents who were avowed atheists. In the process of writing the book, he became convinced that it was his own ignorance of the Bible that was on trial. Ultimately, John reached the conclusion, through comparing historical and scientific evidence to what is written in the Bible, that it is truly inspired by God. The evidence turned a zealous atheist into a zealous believer. He has spent the past thirty-five years giving lectures on science and the Bible throughout the United States.[1]

The Bible clearly is not a science book, but it certainly does include content that is relevant to the questions that scientists ask. What is the history of the earth? What is the history of the universe? What about life? What is the origin of mankind? What about the forces that determine the weather? These are questions that the ancients thought about, and which the Bible does address to some extent.

Did an ignorant people write the Bible in an ignorant age? That would be putting it a bit strongly, but the fact is that at the time the Bible was written, especially the Old Testament, people were in general quite ignorant of the laws of nature that have been discovered through modern science. There were no telescopes or microscopes available. People were not performing controlled scientific experiments to determine the age of the earth. Knowledge of how the human body works

---

[1]. www.doesgodexist.org

Science and the Bible: Mortal Enemies?

was virtually nonexistent. From the modern perspective, yes, the writers of the Old Testament were scientifically ignorant. The question, then, is whether the relatively small portion of the Old Testament that does relate to scientific questions reflects the scientific ignorance of the age in which it is written, or whether it reflects a supernatural knowledge of the laws of nature.

The question of science and religion—let us put it more plainly—the debate between certain religious persons and the atheistic scientific community has raged unabated since the publication of Darwin's *Origin of Species* in 1859. It is not the intent of this chapter to deal with all these questions. The scientific arguments for a creator, the laws of thermodynamics, a detailed discussion of the theory of evolution and so forth are very important, but they are outside the range of the current discussion. For a fuller treatment of these issues see my book *Is There a God?*[2] The subject of this chapter is the specific content in the Old Testament that relates to scientific questions. Do these passages show signs of scientific ignorance or of inspiration? In case there is any doubt in the mind of the reader about the lack of scientific insight of the ancient Jews, consider a passage from a Hebrew writing from around the time of the New Testament.[3]

> The flood was produced by a union of the male waters, which are above the firmament, and the female waters issuing from the earth. The upper waters rushed through the space left when God removed two stars out of the constellation Pleiades. Afterward, to put a stop to the flood, God had to transfer two stars from the constellation of the Bear to the constellation of the Pleiades. That is why the Bear runs after the Pleiades. She wants her children back, but they will be restored to her only in the future world.

Well, I guess that explains why the constellation Bear runs after the Pleiades. The scientific validity of male and female waters is a bit questionable, to say the least. Is anyone prepared to defend the view that two stars were moved at some point in the past from the Bear to the Pleiades? This myth is typical, not only of the writings of the Jews, but of myths that can be found from all the ancient cultures of the Near East. If the Bible was simply a book written by an ignorant people

---

2. John Oakes, *Is There a God*, (Illumination Publishers, Spring, Texas, 2008). Significant portions of the present chapter reflect material found in this book.
3. Lewis Ginsberg, *The Legends of the Jews*, (Jewish Publication Society of America, Philadelphia, 1956), p. 76.

in an ignorant age, or if it simply was written without the inspiration of God, myths like these would undoubtedly have crept into it. The scriptures of such world religions as Shinto, Hinduism, Jain and Buddhism certainly do contain such myths. The reader is invited to search the Bible for examples of the same sort of thing. Despite the false claims of its critics, one will simply not find such myths in the Bible. The reader may be saying to him or herself, "What about the Genesis creation myth?" That will be a good place to start.

CREATION

Without a doubt, the greatest amount of controversy surrounding questions of science and the Bible has revolved around the creation accounts found in Genesis chapters one and two. Genesis one describes the famous seven "days" of creation. Scientists and philosophers have railed against this "myth." Many, finding parallels with the Babylonian Gilgamesh epic, have claimed that the Genesis myth was borrowed and adapted from the contemporary mythology of the Hebrews' Mesopotamian neighbors. Let us consider carefully this most controversial of Bible passages.

A logical place to start is by actually reading Genesis chapter one. The first five verses will be quoted here. It is hoped that the reader will pull out a Bible and read the whole chapter.

> In the beginning God created the heavens and the earth. Now the earth was formless and empty, darkness was over the surface of the deep, and the Spirit of God was hovering over the waters. And God said, "Let there be light," and there was light. God saw that the light was good, and he separated the light from the darkness. God called the light "day," and the darkness he called "night." And there was evening, and there was morning—the first day.... God saw all that he had made, and it was very good. And there was evening, and there was morning—the sixth day (Genesis 1:1-5,31).

A reasonable first question to ask is, what is the overall message of Genesis chapter one? The message seems to be that God is the creator of all things in the heavens and on the earth. It also seems clear that according to Genesis chapter one, the culmination and the purpose of God's plan was the creation of mankind. What is the outline of Genesis chapter one? A possible bare-bones outline would be as follows:

1. God existed before the creation of the universe.

2. God created the universe out of nothing.
3. After creating the universe, including the stars and the earth, God created every kind of life.
4. Last of all, God created human beings.

It would be fair to ask at what point there is direct conflict between this outline and current scientific knowledge. Science cannot demonstrate the existence of God through experiment, but science can certainly be used to show that there was a creator.[4] In fact, the cosmological model now accepted by most scientists describes the creation of the entire universe *out of nothing*. This model is known as the big bang theory. The idea that the universe has always existed—that it was not created—has been more or less discredited because it does not agree with the evidence or with the laws of thermodynamics. This defunct idea is known as the Steady State model.

According to the predominant theory of cosmologists, the entire universe was created out of nothing from what is known as a singularity. By this widely accepted model, the initial "stuff" of the big bang was created at a very high temperature—trillions of degrees. The temperature was so high that all the energy existed in the form of light rather than particles with mass. According to the big bang model, the creator said, "Let there be light," and there was light.

Following the brief outline of Genesis chapter one above, after creating the universe, the stars and the earth, God created the various forms of life. Of course, many scientists believe that life came about by some sort of natural, random event. According to the atheist philosopher Thomas Huxley:

> We are as much a product of blind forces as is the falling of a stone to earth, or the ebb and flow of the tides. We have just happened, and man was made flesh by a long series of singularly beneficial accidents.

---

4. The author apologizes for not developing this claim thoroughly at this point because it is outside the scope of this book. For those interested, a few helpful references which demonstrate that both the universe and life require a creator are:

    1. Douglas Jacoby, *Genesis, Science and History,* (DPI, Billerica, Massachusetts, 2004). 2005), especially chapters 3, 4 and 10.

    1. John M. Oakes, *Is There a God?,* (Illumination Publishers, Spring, Texas, 2008), especially chapters 3, 4 and 10.

    2. Michael Denton, *Nature's Destiny,* (The Free Press, 1998).

    3. Gerald L. Schroeder, *The Science of God,* (Broadway Books, New York, 1997).

    4. Hugh Ross, *The Creator and the Cosmos,* (Navpress, Colorado Springs, Colorado, 1995)

    5. Henri Blocher, *In the Beginning,* (Inter-Varsity Press, Leicester, England, 1984).

This is the standard line of many scientists. However, those outside of science would do well to understand where this statement comes from. This is the statement of a person who began his investigation of nature by assuming that there is a "natural" explanation for everything that can be observed in nature. God is disallowed by definition from the very beginning as a force that might affect nature. The standard approach of the atheist is to begin by assuming that there is not now, nor has there ever been anything that might be described as a supernatural event. Those who start with the atheistic assumption are sure to come back around by circular reasoning to conclude that life was not created.

Despite the confident claims of circular-reasoning scientists, the fact remains that according to well-known and understood laws of nature, life must have been created. Many PhD theses have been written along with a multitude of books on the subject, but the fact remains that no plausible model for the creation of life by a natural process has yet been produced.

The same laws of thermodynamics, which completely preclude an eternal universe, rule out the possibility that an object of such irreducible complexity as a living thing could be created by random chance. Never mind the fact that the laws of nature themselves have every sign of having been designed in order to allow for the existence of life,[5] the laws of thermodynamics and of probability do not allow for a single working piece of DNA to be created by chance out of an inanimate primeval soup. One could go on to mention the impossibility that the proteins needed to allow for DNA to reproduce itself could be created at random at the same time and place as the DNA. The list of impossible coincidences required to create even the simplest life form could be continued until they fill an entire book. The more we learn about the biochemistry of life, the clearer it becomes that a living thing is a marvelously complex machine. Suffice it to say that despite the confident claims of many self-deceived scientists, life was created.

Last of all, according to Genesis chapter one (and last of all according to scientists as well!), man appeared on earth. Where is the myth and scientific blunder so far in Genesis one? But the devil, they

---

5. This idea is known as the anthropic principle. Physicists have pointed out that if the size of the force of gravity were either larger or smaller than it actually is by only one part in 10^{60} then stable galaxies, stars and planets would never have formed. Similarly if the other fundamental forces of nature, the electromagnetic force, the nuclear strong force or the nuclear weak force were different by a very small fraction, then stars would never have formed and stable molecules would not be possible. There are dozens of examples of parameters in our universe which are "fined tuned" to the correct value which is required so that advanced life forms can exist in the universe. This long list of amazing coincidences is the underpinning of the anthropic principle. It serves as dramatic evidence that the universe has an intelligent creator.

Science and the Bible: Mortal Enemies?

say, is in the details. What about the details of Genesis chapter one? In looking at the first chapter of Genesis, one should bear in mind that the creation account is obviously not a scientific treatise. The original Hebrew audience of Genesis did not even have words for such scientific concepts as species, DNA, genetics, chemical elements or energy. Of necessity, then, the creation account paints in the broadest of terms a process whose details would have escaped the original readers. Lest we feel too superior to the ancient Hebrews, it is probably safe to say that if God were to describe to us today in detail exactly how he created the universe and all the life on earth, he would go way over the head of even our most brilliant scientists!

The approach that will be used is to paraphrase Genesis chapter one, interjecting current scientific knowledge. This paraphrased version of the Genesis creation account will be written from the point of view of an observer at the surface of the earth (Genesis 1:1). This "observer" would first note that the sun, as it was formed, began to produce light through the process of nuclear fusion. The early atmosphere of the earth was so thick that the sun itself, as well as the moon and stars were invisible from the surface. When the earth formed, it was already spinning, so when the sun began to produce light, even though it was not visible from the surface, there were periods of light and darkness (Genesis 1:3). Later, as the earth "evolved," a separate atmosphere and ocean emerged (Genesis 1:6-8). Next, as the planet continued to cool and the crust thickened, lighter rocks, mostly silicates such as quartz and granite rose up above the lower-lying basalt, creating the first dry land (Genesis 1:9,10). Once the chemistry of the earth's atmosphere had evolved sufficiently, God created various life forms—gymnosperms (non fruit-bearing plants) before angiosperms (fruit-bearing plants) (Genesis 1:11-13). As the early plant and other life that God had created proliferated, they absorbed sufficient amounts of carbon dioxide and other gases, allowing the earth to cool to the point that the thick veil of clouds finally parted, allowing an observer on the surface of the planet to observe the sun, moon and stars for the first time (Genesis 1:15-19). Next, God created many different species of higher life forms, such as fish, amphibians, reptiles, birds and mammals; first in the water, then on the land (Genesis 1:20-25). Last of all, God produced his finest creation, man, *homo sapiens* (Genesis 1:26-28).

Where are the scientific blunders here? Is this a myth or is it a simplified account of God's creation of the earth and all the life on the earth? The supposed Genesis "myth" has a remarkable affinity with what is known from scientific investigation. How is one to explain this fact?

It is helpful to compare the Genesis creation account with the creation stories of other peoples. Most relevant is the Babylonian creation story, because some have claimed that Genesis chapter one was borrowed and adapted from the Babylonian Gilgamesh epic. The Babylonian creation myth involved gods emerging from a divine swamp that had existed forever. These gods came out of the swamp in male and female pairs. As the younger gods appeared, they did battle with the older gods. In one battle, Marduk, the son of Ea (the earth god) attacked and killed the first goddess of all, Tiamat. He caught her in a net and crushed her skull. As the divine blood of Tiamat spilled to earth, the blood and mud mixture formed the first humans.

It is possible to detect some similarity between the Genesis creation account and the Gilgamesh epic/myth. However, the clear difference between the two is that the Genesis creation account is consistent with scientific knowledge, while the Babylonian creation myth is clearly that—a myth. Who borrowed from whom?

Ancient Egyptian religion included a creation story as well. The Egyptian myth included belief that in the beginning the universe was filled with a primordial ocean called the Nun. The waters of the Nun were stagnant. Out of the limitless flood rose up the primeval hill. This hill eventually grew into the entire earth. The priests of the great cult centers in Egypt each claimed that their city was the point out of which the landmass of the earth originated. Some believe that the pyramids are intended as representations of the primeval hill.

It would be possible to continue with the creation myths of the Japanese Shinto religion, of Hindu scripture, of the Popul Vuh, the ancient Mayan creation myth, or with those of the Iroquois or other Native American groups and so forth.[6] Most ancient cultures had a creation myth. From the modern perspective, it is difficult to take these myths seriously in view of what we know from science. The radical exception to this rule is Genesis chapter one. Rather than showing signs that the Bible is a collection of fables and myths, Genesis chapter one shows signs that the Bible is inspired by the same God who created the world and everything in it.

A couple of objections could be raised at this point. First, some would point out that the book of Genesis seems to imply that creation took place just a few thousand years ago, over six twenty-four hour periods. After all, each of the six days ends with a phrase such as, "And there was evening, and there was morning—the first day." From this perspective it may seem impossible that scientific knowledge and Genesis one can agree. Even the most basic background in science would lead one to believe that the earth is very old.

---

6. Daniel G. Brinton, *The Myths of the New World*, (Genealogical Publishing Company, Baltimore, Maryland, 1994). John Oakes, *Is There a God?* (Illumination Publishers, Spring, Texas, 2006), pp. 88-89.

Science and the Bible: Mortal Enemies?

In answer to this point, let it be said that six twenty-four hour days of creation is certainly a reasonable interpretation of Genesis 1. In fact, if it were not for what we know from science, it would at least appear to be the most obvious interpretation. However, one should bear in mind that the Hebrew word used for day here is *yom*. In the Old Testament, this word is variously translated "day," "time," "forever," "age," "continuously," "today," "life" and "perpetually," depending on the context. In fact, long before the scientific revolution, many of both Christian and Jewish theologians took a nonliteral-day interpretation of Genesis chapter one. For example, one could mention the Jewish theologian Philo, as well as the early Christian authors Justin Martyr, Irenaeus, Hippolytus, Clement of Alexandria, Origen, Lactantius, Eusebius and Augustine. This incomplete list proves that the idea of taking the six "days" of creation to be ages rather than literal twenty-four hour periods is not necessarily a child of science. Careful Bible study can lead to the same conclusion.

Could an all-powerful, all-knowing God create the universe in six twenty-four hour periods, with an "appearance of age," with the light from distant galaxies already in transit, with dinosaur and trilobite fossils already in the ground? The answer is yes, it certainly seems reasonable that the same God who is powerful enough to create the universe could also create it with an appearance of age. Jesus created wine ready to drink and fish ready to eat. A better question is this: did he? All we can say for sure is that *what we know from scientific investigation is in dramatic agreement with the creation outline found in Genesis chapter one.*

The second point some would raise with regard to creation in Genesis actually has to do with chapter two. Some would claim that Genesis 2:4-25 is a second, contradictory creation story by a different author from chapter one. Whether the first and second chapters had different authors is, of course, difficult to prove one way or another. In either case, whether by two authors or one, there is no contradiction between these two accounts. Genesis chapter one is a description of the creation of the earth and everything on it. Genesis chapter two, beginning in verse seven, is a description of the creation of the first people. Unless someone can point out a specific contradiction between the two accounts, the criticism is not helpful. Having listened to such arguments, I have found myself shrugging my shoulders. What contradiction?

In summary, despite its lack of scientific detail and technical language, the creation account in Genesis is in striking agreement with what we know from science. When compared to the creation stories of other ancient cultures, the one found in Genesis has every mark of being inspired by the creator.

RATTLESNAKE FAT, ANYONE? MEDICAL EVIDENCE

Of the different fields of science, it is the area of medical knowledge that the Bible touches on the most. At first, this may seem surprising. However, if one thinks about it, knowledge about astronomy, chemistry, physics or biology may have been of some philosophical interest to the Jews, but medical knowledge was of very practical use. The survival of God's people was at stake. How did God communicate medical knowledge to Israel?

The Jews often referred to the first five books of the Old Testament as "the Law." The third book of the Law is Leviticus. This book contains the largest portion of the legal code in the Old Testament. A number of regulations can be found in Leviticus that are related to health and diet issues. A few examples will now be examined closely

Before doing this, however, it will be useful to consider the nature of medical knowledge in cultures immediately surrounding Israel in the time frame of the writing of Leviticus. If the Bible were simply a book written according to human wisdom, then its allusions to medical questions would reflect the level of insight or ignorance of the dominant cultures in the Near East at the time in which it was written. On the other hand, if God inspired the Bible, one would expect it to show insight that reflects that inspiration, even when it touches on medical knowledge.

Of the cultures surrounding ancient Israel, the Egyptians are considered by many to have been the most advanced in medical knowledge. Through trial and error, the Egyptian culture may very well have gained some useful knowledge about how to treat certain illnesses. However, if one looks at the written records of Egyptian medical science, some of the prescriptions in them would result in deadly consequences. A quote from the famous Ebers Papyrus, a medical text written about 1550 BC, prescribes:

> To prevent the hair from turning gray, anoint it with the blood of a black calf which has been boiled in oil, or with the fat of a rattlesnake.

Or concerning hair loss:

> When it falls out, one remedy is to apply a mixture of six fats, namely those of the horse, the hippopotamus, the crocodile, the cat, the snake, and the ibex.[7]

---

7. S. E. Massengill, *A Sketch of Medicine and Pharmacy* (S. E. Massengill Co., Bristol Tennessee, 1943), p. 16.

Science and the Bible: Mortal Enemies?

Other prescriptions from the Ebers Papyrus include such dubious drugs as dust-of-a-statue, shell-of-a-beetle, head-of-the-electric eel, guts-of-the-goose, tail-of-a-mouse, fat-of-the-hippopotamus, hair-of-a-cat, eyes-of-a-pig, toes-of-a-dog, and semen-of-a-man.[8] These medicines seem humorous to the modern reader, but the consequences of this medical and scientific ignorance was surely devastating to the people of that day. These examples are brought up not so much to reveal the ignorance of the Egyptians at that time, but to provide a background against which one may compare the writings of the Old Testament: writings which come from approximately the same time period as those of the Ebers Papyrus. Lest we in the modern world become too proud of ourselves, it is worth remembering that medical knowledge in the Western world two hundred years ago had barely progressed beyond that found in the Ebers Papyrus. As late as the mid nineteenth century, the typical doctor's bag contained mostly worthless remedies and extremely harmful toxins. What, then, was the state of medical knowledge found in the Old Testament? In looking at Old Testament health laws, the author acknowledges significant contributions in this area from a book by S. I. McMillen, M.D.[9]

Through most of its recorded history, the Jewish nation as a whole has been noted for its medical expertise. At least part of the reason for this fact may be discovered from a look at some Bible passages that gave the Jews an advantage in medical science. To the extent that they followed the "prescriptions" in the Old Testament, the Jews were automatically way ahead of their time. However, to show how advanced in areas of medicine the Israelites were in and of themselves, apart from the revelation of the Old Testament, consider an excerpt from a Jewish book of medical knowledge from a time roughly contemporary to the writing of the New Testament.[10]

> "Whatever God created has value." Even the animals and the insects that seem useless and noxious at first sight have a vocation to fulfill. The snail trailing a moist streak after it as it crawls, and so using up its vitality serves as a remedy for boils. The sting of a hornet is healed by the housefly, crushed and applied to the wound. The gnat, feeble creature, taking in food but never secreting it, is a specific against the poison of a viper, and this venomous reptile itself cures eruptions, while the lizard is the antidote to the scorpion.

---

8. C. P. Bryan, *The Ebers Papyrus*, (D. Appleton, New York, 1931).
9. S. I. McMillen, M.D., *None of these Diseases*, (Power Books, Old Tappan, New Jersey, 1984).
10. Lewis Ginsberg, *The Legends of the Jews*, (Jewish Publication Society of America, Philadelphia, 1956), p. 23.

Would anyone like to try one of these prescriptions? Also, note the scientific error regarding the digestive system of gnats. It seems reasonable to agree with the writer "everything God created has value," but most people would presumably not be eager to try out these prescriptions. This passage is typical of the writings of the Jews of the age as well as those of the Egyptians and other cultures at the time. However, it is in complete and remarkable contrast to what can be found in the Bible, as will be shown. Why? Is it because the Old Testament writers were lucky? Could it be because the Jewish doctors were using the scientific method to carefully examine their medical practices? Or could it be a sign that the Bible is no ordinary book, but rather the inspired Word of God? As the following sections are presented, the readers should judge for themselves.

Please note that no one is claiming that all the medical knowledge of the ancients, be they Egyptian, Chinese, Indian, Greek, Native American or any other is mere superstition. Through trial and error methods, some of the most ancient cultures evolved medical folklore that is of some value. However, this folklore inevitably contains a large proportion of remedies that are about as effective as using rattlesnake fat to prevent premature grayness.

As mentioned before, this section will focus primarily on the book of Leviticus, the book of Law received by Moses from God at a time contemporary to the writing of the Ebers Papyrus. Moses himself was born in Egypt. Anyone who would claim that the Bible represents the understanding of a scientifically ignorant ancient Hebrew culture should consider comparison of Leviticus to the Ebers Papyrus.

To begin, consider a remarkable claim made by God through Moses to the nation of Israel while they were wandering in the wilderness for forty years, as recorded in Exodus 15:26.

> If you listen carefully to the voice of the Lord your God and do what is right in his eyes, if you pay attention to his commands and keep all his decrees, I will not bring on you any of the diseases I brought on the Egyptians, for I am the Lord who heals you.

Here God was claiming that if the nation of Israel would obey his decrees, they would avoid all kinds of diseases. History bears out the ramifications of this claim. The Jews have always been a relatively small nation, yet they have survived repeated invasions and even attempts at extermination. Time and again the Assyrians, the Babylonians, the Greeks and the Romans as well as others have attacked and scattered the Hebrew people. Although scattered, the Jews have somehow always managed to recover and to grow in number. One factor in the

Science and the Bible: Mortal Enemies?

resilience of the Jews was their health practices as inspired by the Old Testament laws.

For example, consider Leviticus chapter eleven. A summary of this section is given here, rather than a detailed quote. In this chapter, God tells his people that pigs, rabbits, rodents, crustaceans, lizards, and all carnivores are "unclean"—in other words not acceptable to be eaten. On the other hand, fish with scales, cows, sheep, goats and certain non-carnivorous birds are "clean." It just so happens that all the animals on the unclean list are relatively dangerous to eat unless very thoroughly cooked. Pork is the type of meat that is most famous for being considered "unclean" by the Jews. Pork is also famous for causing trichinosis. On the other hand, beef, fish and lamb are relatively safe. All of these types of meat, if handled properly, may be eaten safely even when uncooked (although certain safety precautions are highly recommended). Could this correspondence between what Leviticus calls clean and what is in fact relatively safe be mere coincidence?

How did Moses know which types of meat were relatively safe? Did he learn it from the Egyptians? Certainly not, for they often ate many of the unclean meats, especially pork. Did he run some controlled scientific experiments—giving pork to some Israelites and sheep to others, and keeping careful record of how many got sick? That seems extremely unlikely. The nation of Israel at the time was relatively ignorant scientifically, but the Law contained in the Bible reflects a different level of knowledge. It is therefore not at all unreasonable to think that the ultimate author of the Law, God, was protecting his people from "the diseases I brought on the Egyptians."

Next, consider Leviticus chapters 13 and 14. Here one finds very specific laws regarding several different types of infectious skin diseases, including leprosy. Specific instructions are given to quarantine the subjects with certain skin diseases for a set period of time, to burn their clothing and even to destroy the pottery implements off which they had eaten.

Throughout time, the spread of leprosy has been blamed on such causes as heredity, the eating of certain foods, or even on the alignment of the planets. These false ideas naturally led to an inability to stop the spread of the disease. Finally, after thousands of years of human suffering, leprosy was brought under control in the Western world in the Middle Ages.

> Leadership was taken by the church, as the physicians had nothing to offer. The church took as its guiding principle the concept of contagion as embodied in the Old Testament... This idea and its practical consequences are defined with great clarity in the book of Leviticus...Once the

condition of leprosy was established, the patient was to be segregated and excluded from the community. Following the precepts laid down in Leviticus the church undertook the task of combating leprosy...it accomplished the first great feat...in methodical eradication of disease."[11]

The incredible devastation that has been caused by leprosy throughout Europe, Africa and Asia could have been largely avoided if medical practitioners had simply heeded the command in Leviticus 13: 46: "As long as he has the infection he remains unclean. He must live alone; he must live outside the camp." In fact, once quarantine was initiated, leprosy was dramatically reduced in Western Europe. Does anyone believe Moses made this up because he was a brilliant doctor, or because of the great medical knowledge he had acquired in Egypt? Even if someone was a skeptic who believed that the book of Leviticus was written by a group of Jewish priests at around 500 BC rather than by Moses at around 1400 BC, how could they explain the discovery of quarantine by these priests over two thousand years before its general application in Europe?

In 1873, Dr. Armauer Hansen identified the bacterium that causes leprosy, proving once and for all that it is indeed an infectious disease (medical science refers to leprosy as Hansen's disease). Today, if caught early, it is entirely curable. Fortunately, antibiotics can now control leprosy, so that there is no longer a need to quarantine lepers. However, from the time of the writing of the Old Testament, right up until the 1940s, God's prescription was the most effective way to prevent the spread of this disease.

> Three years later, the Norwegian Leprosy Act was passed. This law ordered lepers to live in precautionary isolation away from their families. In 1856, there were 2858 lepers living in Norway. By the turn of the century, only 577 lepers were left; and that number plummeted to 69. By 1930 the spectacular discoveries of science allowed Norway to control this disease, but the precautions had been written down by Moses almost 3,500 years earlier.[12]

Next, consider another law found in Numbers chapter nineteen. It would be helpful to read the chapter before continuing. Here one finds

---

11. George Rosen, *History of Public Health* (MD Publications, New York, 1958), pp. 62-63.
12. S. I. McMillen, MD, *None of These Diseases,* (Power Books, 1984), p 22.

the command from God that anyone who touches the body of a dead person is to be considered unclean for seven days. In addition, they are to be considered unclean until several very precisely specified hand and body washings have been completed. Even the person who aided in the cleansing was required to wash himself.

In Numbers 19, God specifically prescribed washing the entire body with water containing ash and hyssop. The ashes in combination with the oil of the hyssop plant made a kind of soap. It just so happens that the hyssop plant, a type of marjoram that grows in the Middle East, contains in its oil about 50% carvacrol, an organic compound almost identical to the commonly used antifungal and antibacterial compound thymol. Therefore, ash and hyssop work both as soap and as a natural antibiotic. God commanded the Jews that after touching a dead body they were to wash with an effective antibiotic soap. Does it seem reasonable to believe that this was just luck on Moses' part?

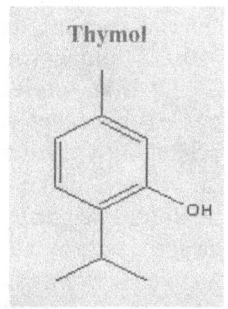

It is extremely interesting to note that the stringent practice of hand washing between the touching of patients or after touching dead bodies was only introduced to "modern" medicine by the work of Ignaz Semmelweis in the 1840s and 1850s.[13] Semmelweis worked at that time in a hospital in Vienna at which one in six of the maternity patients died in the hospital. No wonder women preferred to have their children at home! These depressing statistics were typical numbers for hospitals at that time. Semmelweis noted that a standard practice for the doctors in hospitals was to perform autopsies on the patients who had died the previous day before immediately proceeding to examine their still-healthy patients. Today, of course, one cringes to hear of this practice, but it should be noted that the concept of infectious disease, commonly known as the germ theory, was not introduced to the world or proved by modern science until the nineteenth century by the work of Oliver Wendell Holmes, Pasteur, Lister and Semmelweis. Semmelweis ordered that all doctors performing autopsies must wash their hands thoroughly before working with live patients. The death rate in the hospital dropped to one third what it had been. If only doctors had heeded the commands of Moses concerning washing after the touching of dead bodies before this date!

Semmelweis eventually noted that even the touching of a maternity patient after touching another live patient could result in infection, so he further ordered hand cleansing between obstetrical

---

13. The parallel work of Boston author and amateur scientist Oliver Wendell Holmes deserves credit as well.

examinations. The mortality rate went down to 1% (from an initial 16% mortality rate). Semmelweis could have referred to Leviticus chapter 12 at this point where women who give birth are proclaimed to be "unclean" for seven days. It is now known, of course, that the nature of childbirth, which opens the circulatory system of the mother to outside infection, makes it a particularly dangerous practice for doctors to move from one maternity patient to another without a very thorough washing of the hands. This remains true for several days after childbirth. The Bible prescribes seven days. Fortunately, thanks to modern science, obstetricians do not need to wait seven days between examinations. Nevertheless, one can see that if medical practitioners had obeyed the practice described in the Law of Moses, millions of unnecessary deaths would have been prevented.

It is an interesting side note that the medical establishment did not easily accept the work of Semmelweis, to say the least. He was ridiculed by many of his peers in the medical community. Eventually, he was persecuted so strongly that he was fired from the hospital where he did his original work. Even after publishing convincing proof of the effectiveness of hand washing, his conclusions were rejected by most of his peers. Eventually, Semmelweis was committed to a mental institution where, ironically, he died of a blood infection.

Semmelweis was not the only proponent of germ theory to be persecuted. Louis Pasteur, the great French chemist, proposed the existence of viruses to explain such infectious diseases as smallpox and rabies. Despite major successes in curing diseases such as rabies, his virus theory was vigorously opposed. One of his opponents, the fellow French scientist Guerin, even challenged him to a duel.

But there is more! For example, consider Leviticus 17:13,14.

> Any Israelite or any alien living among you who hunts any animal or bird that may be eaten must drain out the blood and cover it with earth, because the life of every creature is its blood. That is why I have said to the Israelites, "You must not eat the blood of any creature, because the life of every creature is its blood; anyone who eats it must be cut off."

Quite apart from the obvious health dangers in eating blood unless it is very thoroughly cooked, one finds an interesting statement here. "The life of every creature is its blood." The function of blood in carrying life-giving oxygen as well as all the other nutrients to the cells of the body was not discovered until the nineteenth century. Indeed, "bad blood" was one of the chief (incorrect) diagnoses of medical science for all kinds of symptoms until well into the nineteenth century. The

Science and the Bible: Mortal Enemies?

red and white stripes of the barber's pole represent a common practice of barbers from the Middle Ages right up to the 1800s: bloodletting! When someone had an infection or some other medical problem, a very common treatment was to attach leeches to suck out the bad blood from the patient. A study of the record of the medical treatment leading up to the death of George Washington shows an unusually large number of bloodlettings, prompting some to suggest that he may have actually died primarily from a loss of blood.

The medical/scientific fact is that blood is the carrier of an assortment of "white blood cells," the body's chief means of protection against all kinds of disease. Bloodletting never helped anyone to get well. If only medical practitioners had taken the opportunity to read the Bible on this subject: "The life of every creature is its blood." God was trying to protect his people so that they would not be overcome by "any of the diseases I brought on the Egyptians" (Exodus 15:26).

Possibly the best single piece of medical advice in the Law is found in Deuteronomy 23:12,13. In this scripture the Israelites were commanded to designate a place outside the camp to relieve themselves. They were specifically commanded to dig a hole and bury their excrement. This is an unpleasant topic, but the unpleasant fact is that even as we enter the twenty-first century, the leading cause of death worldwide among young children is a laundry list of diseases brought on by drinking unsanitary water. It has been estimated that in both the American Civil War and in World War I, more soldiers were killed from cholera, dysentery and the like than from wounds in battle. Of course, under the conditions of war, following the advice in Deuteronomy 23 is very difficult, but most of these deaths, as well as millions of deaths a year even now, could be avoided if people would carefully and methodically apply the command in Deuteronomy 23:12,13. The advice given to Moses may seem extremely obvious to us, but this was not common practice even for the most advanced civilizations of Moses' day. Almost without exception, from the great cities to the smallest village, allowing open sewage in the streets was common practice.

Consider circumcision. This practice was actually instituted a few hundred years before the time of Moses, during the lifetime of Abraham. In Genesis 17:12 one can read:

> For the generations to come every male among you who is eight days old must be circumcised, including those born in your household or bought with money from a foreigner—those who are not your offspring.

There are two points to be made here. First, it is commanded to circumcise all males. Second it is commanded to circumcise all these males on the eighth day. Circumcision is a painful process! Why would God have had his people go through this? From a theological point of view, God established circumcision as a mark of the covenant he was making with his people. It just so happens that there are interesting medical implications to this command as well.

Consider circumcision itself. Whether to circumcise or not is a matter of some debate even among the scientific community today. Because of the level of daily hygiene, the need for this somewhat radical procedure has been reduced dramatically in the United States. However, in a culture such as that of Israel over three thousand years ago, personal hygiene was certainly not up to the level available to most people today. In Old Testament times, people went extended periods without bathing. The warm, damp area behind the male foreskin is an excellent breeding ground for all kinds of bacteria and fungi. In our culture, with a much greater opportunity to care for hygiene, this does not present nearly so great a danger for the spread of disease. Consider, however, the advantage to God's people in this practice, both for preventing the spread of sexually transmitted diseases and for preventing any of a number of common infections. God could have commanded his people to take a bath every day, but this would have been impractical, especially as they wandered in the desert for forty years.

Did God institute circumcision of males for these health reasons, or did he have in mind only the theological implications? That would be hard to say since it is never specifically referred to in the Bible as beneficial to health. Whatever the case, there is clearly a pattern developing here. When the Jews followed the commands of the Bible, they were protected from all kinds of diseases. Could this be just coincidence? Or is the Bible the inspired Word of God?

It is interesting to note that circumcision is much safer if, as commanded by God in the Old Testament, it is performed on infants. In our modern culture, when older boys are circumcised, typically due to inability to retract the foreskin, the operation requires either general anesthesia, with its attendant risk of death, or a local anesthetic, which has been known to cause permanent impotence. On the other hand, circumcision of an infant is a simple and safe procedure. Within the first three weeks of birth, circumcision causes pain, of course, but the symptoms disappear almost immediately after surgery. On the other hand, adults experience pain for at least a week.

This leads to the next point. Why circumcision on the eighth day? While circumcision of a male child on the second or third day in a hospital setting is now virtually completely safe, for the Israelites this

Science and the Bible: Mortal Enemies?

was not necessarily the case. It has been noted by pediatricians that the risk of hemorrhage for children increases dramatically from about the second to the sixth or seventh day of life. After this point, the risk drops dramatically. Again, under proper care in a hospital, circumcision between the second and sixth day of life is quite unlikely to lead to major permanent harm. However, in the conditions of surgery prevalent in the times of the Old Testament, the implications are significant.

The reasons for this effect are now well known. Upon birth, the level of vitamin K in a baby is similar to that of its mother. However, the human body does not produce its own supply of this essential vitamin, necessary to the production of the protein compounds used by the body to cause blood clotting. Instead, bacteria present in the intestines supply vitamin K to the body. Infants are born without the required bacteria in their intestines. It takes a few days for the bacteria to build up to the point that a safe level of vitamin K is reestablished. Studies show that this level is reached by about the eighth day. Today, because of research on vitamin K levels, doctors give shots of the vitamin to newborns. Without these shots, the most preferred day for performing a safe and relatively less painful circumcision is somewhere between the eighth to tenth day of life, according to medical science.

One of the clotting proteins produced through the agency of vitamin K is prothrombin. The concentration of this essential compound drops dramatically in the first day or two of a newborn's life, making any sort of cut unusually dangerous. Once an infant's body begins to produce vitamin K, the prothrombin begins to rebound. It actually peaks out at approximately 110% of its normal level on about the eighth day.

Abraham's Experiment

Day Circumcised	Number of Hebrew Boys	Number of Deaths
1	823	4
3	759	6
5	693	8
7	855	3
9	770	2
11	698	4

Abraham clearly did not have access to these data, nor any way to generate it. Why did he tell the people of Israel to circumcise on the eighth day? Perhaps he did a carefully controlled, double blind experiment to determine the optimal day for circumcision of male children, as illustrated on the graph on the previous page. This seems very unlikely! How about a more reasonable explanation, which is that God told Abraham when to circumcise the male childen. Even if someone was a dyed-in-the-wool skeptic who will not even admit that Abraham ever existed, how could they explain that this is in the Bible? Presumably, the skeptic would claim that it is just luck or coincidence. How many coincidences will need to be pointed out before some are convinced that the same God who created life in the first place inspired this book?

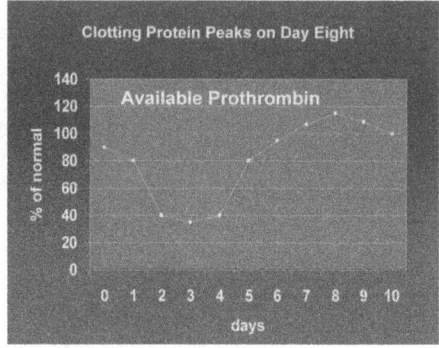

As another example (if another is needed), one can find in Leviticus 18 laws against incest. Specifically, the Jews were commanded not to marry or to have sexual relationships with blood relations. This would include aunts, uncles and cousins. Incest was a common practice of the day, continuing right up to modern times. Again, God may have had reasons of his own, but it just so happens that children born from a union between close blood relatives have shown a much higher incidence of genetic disease. Moses did not say why to avoid this type of behavior, but for the Jews who followed these decrees, much disease and heartache was avoided.

A brief trip through the Bible will reveal an almost innumerable list of commands that lead to our emotional as well as physical well-being. For example, one discovers in Leviticus 7:22-25:

> Do not eat any of the fat of cattle, sheep or goats....Anyone who eats the fat of an animal from which an offering by fire may be made to the Lord must be cut off from his people.

It would be interesting to think about how much lower the rate of arteriosclerosis and death due to heart disease was among the Israelites who obeyed this decree. The discovery of the direct correlation between animal fat consumption and death due to coronary heart disease is a recent one, but God provided protection to his people from this, the greatest killer in the Western world.

In Proverbs 23:20 is written: "Do not join those who drink too much wine or gorge themselves on meat." Both admonitions are good health advice, as has been well documented. Note that the Bible does not forbid consumption of either meat or wine in moderation. Meat in moderation can be an important part of a healthy diet. It would seem that the medical jury is still out on whether wine in moderation is harmful, or possibly even beneficial to health, but clearly much wine is extremely injurious to both mental and physical health.

Most of the commands above are unique to the Bible, providing an overwhelming weight of evidence for its inspiration. God's commandments concerning sexual relationships, although not unique to the Bible, provide still more evidence of the wisdom and practical nature of this great book in bringing health and happiness to anyone who will follow it. God specifically forbids homosexuality (1 Corinthians 6: 9,10, Leviticus 18:22 and Romans 1:26,27), prostitution (1 Corinthians 6: 9,10), adultery (Proverbs 5) and indeed any kind of sex outside of marriage (Galatians 5:19).

There is a pervasive belief in our "modern" society that open attitudes about sexual lifestyles are a good thing. The media plays down the significant minority in America who still accept the biblical teaching that sex outside of marriage is wrong. The prevailing attitude in our culture is that sexual experience before marriage, preferably with more than one partner, is a good thing—leading ultimately to greater sexual fulfillment. History, however, will prove that the opinion of the majority does not equal truth. Trust is an essential key to a healthy marriage relationship. There is a huge benefit to be reaped for those with enough self-control to delay sexual gratification until a commitment to a lifelong relationship has been sealed. If only people would listen to God's commands in this area! The emotional benefits (let alone the spiritual benefits) to human lives would be incalculable.

Obedience to the Biblical teaching in this area would yield benefits to our physical well-being as well as to our emotional health. Sexual promiscuity is certainly nothing new. Homosexual and heterosexual prostitution was at the heart of a great number of ancient religions. The list of sexually transmitted diseases, including gonorrhea, syphilis, hepatitis and AIDS seems to be always growing. These diseases would be wiped out in short order if people only had the wisdom and self-control to obey God's will. The amount of death and destruction wrought by a refusal to follow God's commands is difficult to fathom.

In conclusion, God was not playing the part of a cosmic politician—promising much but delivering little—when he promised

Israel that if they would obey his commands he would not bring on them any of the diseases of the surrounding peoples. However, God's principal interest was not in the physical health of his people. He was much more interested in their spiritual well-being. For a person who is willing to consider the Bible as their spiritual PDR (physician's desk reference), God has left many marks of inspiration, not the least of which are the commandments relevant to medical science.

BIOLOGY, CHEMISTRY AND PHYSICS

Although the greatest number of references in the Bible relevant to science is related to medicine, there are also a number of statements in the Bible of interest to geologists, biologists, astrophysicists and others. These will be considered in this section.

It has already been shown that the scientific sophistication of other cultures contemporary to the Hebrews was primitive to say the least. The picture from Greek mythology of Atlas holding up the sky, while interesting to contemplate, cannot be taken seriously as being "scientific." Such myths were prevalent even among the Greeks, considered almost universally to be the most advanced of ancient cultures in scientific learning. This backdrop of relative scientific ignorance is the environment in which both the New and Old Testaments were written.

Consider for example a passage in the Old Testament that might be of interest to a biologist. In Genesis 16:4 one can read concerning Abraham that, "He slept with Hagar and she conceived." Probably for the majority of Bible readers, this scripture and the scientific implications would slip right on by. Here the Bible is claiming that conception occurred in Hagar after sexual relationship with Abraham. A possible response would be "no kidding," but it just so happens that it was not generally accepted until the nineteenth century that conception occurs in this manner.

The first modern scientist to propose that both male and female have seed was William Harvey, chief surgeon to King James I of England. In fact, the human sperm was not discovered until the work of Robert Hooke, using a microscope, in the 1660s. The theory that the male sperm and the female egg are required for conception was not generally recognized by medical science until the nineteenth century. It is an interesting exercise to look at old medical textbooks from the eighteenth century replete with neat diagrams showing how men deposited the already conceived baby into the nice warm female nursery. In the Qur'an the scripture of Islam, one can read that man deposits the baby in the womb (Sura 16:4, Sura 22:5, Sura 23:14). Because man wrote the Qur'an, it reflects the knowledge of man. The Bible gets it right again.

Science and the Bible: Mortal Enemies?

What about cosmology? In Job 26:7 it is stated that "He spreads out the northern skies over empty space; he suspends the earth over nothing." Given that Job was written some time before 1000 BC, this is an extraordinary statement. Here one finds the Bible proclaiming that the earth is freely moving in space, not attached to anything else. Simple observation of physical events in the world would cause one to believe that everything falls downward. Not surprisingly, using simple human reasoning, the ancients pictured the earth either as a flat plate-like object resting on some larger object or as being the literal center of the universe, with the sun, moon, planets and stars somehow joined to the earth and circling it once a day. This second idea, called geocentrism, was the dominant theory of intellectuals up until the modern era. Popular religion generally held to flat earth ideas. However, the biblical book of Job gets it right.[14] The earth is suspended on nothing. As late as AD 1600 the theologian Bruno was burned at the stake for holding to a belief that the earth is suspended on nothing and that it moves freely through space. In fact, it moves through the universe under the influence of the force of gravity, primarily from the sun. Job 26:7 shows surprising insight for a scientifically ignorant people!

Did anyone else come up with this idea in so ancient a time? There is no record of this idea being proposed as early as 1000 BC. Actually, a few hundred years after the writing of Job, some Greek astronomers, Anaxagorus and Aristarchus among them, did reach the conclusion that the earth moves. However, the great mass of people as well as the supposedly wise men throughout history have held to ideas such as that contained in the Sutras, part of the scripture of the Hindu religion. Here we find the statement that the earth is on the back of four elephants on top of a turtle, encircled by a serpent, swimming in a sea of milk. Did God inspire the Sutras? What about the Vedas the Upanishads, or the other Hindu scriptures? These questions deserve thought, but it should be noted that each of these contain elements as scientifically suspect as the elephant/turtle/milk story.

Another common misconception of the ancients was that the sky is basically like a bowl, with all the stars moving at the same distance from the earth across the circumference of this bowl. The scriptures of the Jain religion (a belief system native to India) go a bit further to

---

14. In analyzing Job 26:7, the reader should bear in mind other passages in the book such as Job 9:6, in which an earthquake is metaphorically described as God making the earth's "pillars tremble." Job is a book of poetry, written in a dramatic style. It is not a systematic treatise on cosmology. The careful Bible student should use poetic writings such as Job and Psalms with caution in attempting to prove scientific points. Nevertheless, Job 26:7 is in striking agreement with our present knowledge of cosmology.

describe different levels of the heavens, with different celestial objects revolving at different distances from the earth. Obviously, none of these ideas bear any resemblance to the facts about the universe. The reason is that they are of human origin.

Concerning the stars, one can read in Jeremiah 33:22: "I will make the descendants of David...as countless as the stars of the sky..." Here the Bible is stating that the stars cannot be counted. Again, this may seem like an obvious point, but the number of stars in the sky was the subject of debate in the Near East in Jeremiah's time (about 550 BC). Greek philosophers speculated and debated about the total number of stars. Democritus, one of the Greek philosophers, is the first person known to have proposed that the Milky Way is actually unresolved stars, and that therefore there are an inconceivable number of stars in the universe. Actually he was the second, counting Jeremiah.

About the earth itself, one can read in the Bible in Isaiah 40:22 that the earth is round (the Hebrew word can also be translated "sphere"). Most who thought about such things at the time of the writing of Isaiah (about 750 BC), believed the earth was flat. In about 525 BC, the Greek mathematician Pythagoras (famous for the Pythagorean theorem) was the first person known to have claimed that the earth is a sphere. The first, that is, if one is to ignore Isaiah! In about 150 BC, Erastosthenes, a Greek living in Alexandria, measured the circumference of the earth indirectly. He was accurate to within about eight percent.

By the way, to clear up a common misconception, although the uneducated people of Columbus' day may have believed in a flat earth, the majority of intellectuals in the fifteenth century believed, along with Pythagoras and Erastosthenes, that the earth was spherical. Columbus did not have to convince Queen Isabella that the earth was round—he just had to convince her that the voyage was a good financial investment. However, Isaiah, writing two thousand years before Columbus, was ahead of his time. Is it unreasonable to conclude that his writing was inspired by God?

The point is not so much that Isaiah beat Pythagoras, but that the Bible, to the extent that it reflects scientific knowledge, appears to get it right every time. By contrast, consider the Qur'an, written in the twenty years or so before the death of Mohammed in the year AD 632. Mohammed claimed to be a prophet of God. If the claim were true, then it would be reasonable to expect that the Qur'an would be accurate to the extent that it can be compared to scientific knowledge. In the Qur'an it is written that the sun and stars revolve around the earth (Sura 21:33). This would be in agreement with the Greek concept of the universe prevalent in Mohammed's time: the geocentric theory. The only problem is that it is wrong. The reason the sun and stars appear to circle the earth is that the earth is spinning on its axis. This should cause one to question the scientific accuracy of the Muslim scripture.

But there is more. For example, the Qur'an records a piece of the sky falling and killing someone (Sura 34:9, Sura 52:44). In Sura 15:18 it is stated that shooting stars provide protection from evil spirits. In Sura 12, one can read about the eleven planets. The Qur'an has King David making an iron coat of mail (Sura 34:11) before such a thing was ever invented. There are other examples that could be given, but the point is that the Bible does not contain these kinds of mistakes.

To the ancients, rain itself was a mystery. Where does the rain come from? Why is it that the rivers continually flow into the sea but the sea does not ever overflow? It would be interesting to explore some of the fables and myths produced by ancient cultures to explain this phenomenon. The Greeks invoked the gods to explain the phenomenon. In Amos 5:8, it is stated that it is God "who calls for the waters of the sea and pours them out over the face of the land." Also, in Job 36:27 is found the statement that God "draws up the drops of water, which distill as rain to the streams." In other words, the Bible describes a cycle that begins with water evaporating from the surface of the earth, condensing, and distilling back to the earth as rain, only to evaporate and return to the earth again. The correct explanation of this process, called the hydrological cycle, gained general acceptance by the scientific community only in the nineteenth century. The Bible has it right again, three thousand years before man, in his own power, was able to answer the question. Skeptics would claim that the Bible is a book written by scientifically ignorant people in a scientifically ignorant age. To their surprise, the Bible gets it right again.

Another example worth mentioning is found in Genesis chapter six. Here God told to Noah the dimensions of the ark he was to build. The ark was to be 300 cubits long by fifty cubits wide by thirty cubits high. It just so happens that the thirty to five to three ratio of length to width to height for the construction of large ships has been found from long experience of oceangoing nations to be the ideal dimensions for large cargo-carrying ships. In modern times, engineering principles have been used to show that an approximately thirty to five to three ratio of length to width to depth creates ideal dimensions for a balance of large volume, stability and speed in the building of great ships of commerce. It is not clear that the ark needed to be built for speed, but large volume and stability were definitely important issues. Historically, the Hebrew nation was never an oceangoing people. This was especially true in the early part of their history. By contrast, the "ark" in the Mesopotamian Gilgamesh Epic was cubical. That would not be a good idea in a storm! How, then, did the writer of Genesis get the ideal dimensions for a large ship right? Could it be that God had a hand in providing this knowledge?

Some who would attack the Bible have tried to find passages that reveal its scientific errors—similar to those quoted above from the scriptures of other major world religions. Most of the skeptics' examples fall into one of two categories.

1. Simple misinterpretation of a Biblical passage—most commonly because the scripture is poetic.

2. Misconstruing what is clearly described as a miracle as a scientific mistake.

As an example of a supposed biblical scientific error that is simply a misinterpreted poetical passage, consider Isaiah 11:6-9. In this scripture, it is written that "the wolf will lie down with the lamb, the leopard will lie down with the goat" and "the infant will play near the hole of the cobra." Some have scoffed at this passage as describing an impossible situation. However, a careful study will show that this is a poetic and prophetic reference to the future kingdom of God. In God's kingdom, all kinds of people who would never have come together because of deep-rooted class, ethnic or nationalistic hatred will join hands in God's family. It is not a prediction that cobras will suddenly make good pets. The claim that Isaiah 11:6-9 is a scientific blunder shows a lack of understanding of the context and meaning of the scripture.

As an example of the second type, skeptics have referred to the parting of the Red Sea as an example of a biblical scientific "mistake." There probably is no natural explanation for the Red Sea spontaneously parting (despite efforts of some to find one). However, this event is unquestionably described as a supernatural miracle, not a natural event. By definition, a miracle is an event that defies natural explanation. The Bible writers never attempt to portray the parting of the Red Sea as being the result of a natural phenomenon. The parting of the Red Sea is only a scientific "mistake" if one uses circular reasoning by assuming *a priori* that miracles have never occurred.

In summary, many people claim that the Bible, and especially the Old Testament, is a collection of myths and fables that are the imaginative musings of a scientifically ignorant people. They would claim that the list of scientific mistakes in the Bible proves that it is a human creation. In response to this claim, one can reasonably ask, which fables? Where are all these examples of mistakes that hold up to careful scrutiny? When the writings of the Bible are compared to examples from ancient Jewish writers as well as to the scriptures of other religions, one finds a contrast so striking as to be unexplainable. Unexplainable, that is, unless one allows for the possibility of the inspiration of the Bible.

Science and the Bible: Mortal Enemies?

This book, which the skeptic would claim is the product of ignorance, is laced with accurate claims of a scientific nature, which should cause any open-minded person to question the validity of the atheistic/humanistic attacks on the Bible. Go ahead. Be skeptical. Good idea. Do not assume anything to be true unless the evidence speaks for itself. If a person will with a sincere heart and an open mind make a decision to study out the Bible, they will eventually have "accepted it not as the word of men, but as it actually is, the word of God, which is at work in you who believe" (1 Thessalonians 2:13). Not only that, but if a believer is willing to be intellectually honest enough to question what they believe about the scientific accuracy of the Bible, they will have even greater convictions that will allow their faith to weather the storms of life.

For Today

1. Where does evolution fit into the question of science and the Bible? Does the Bible make specific statements that relate to the evolution of species? What about the evolution of man?[15]

2. Is one's opinion about how to interpret Genesis chapter one—literally as twenty-four hour periods or metaphorically as ages of creation—an important point of Christian doctrine? Why or why not? Galileo asked the question, "Can an opinion be heretical and yet have no concern with the salvation of souls?" How might this relate?

---

15. My book *Is There a God?* deals with these topics in chapter eight. A more detailed treatment can be found in *Nature's Destiny*, by Michael Denton, mentioned above, Michael J. Behe, *Darwin's Black Box*, (Free Press, 1996) and Philip Johnson, *Darwin on Trial*, (InterVarsity Press, 1997).

⊙ Chapter Nine ⊙
The Bible: The Greatest Book Ever Written

*If anyone chooses to do God's will,
he will find out whether my
teaching comes from God or
whether I speak on my own.*

– *Jesus Christ*

Thus far, we have considered what seems like an overwhelming amount of evidence, the sum of which makes belief in the Bible as the inspired word of God almost an intellectual imperative. Believe it or not, despite this fact, we have not yet gotten down to the evidence that ultimately convinces the majority of those who commit their life to Christ. It is the experience of the author that the bottom line cause of faith in the majority derives from one or both of the causes below.

1. Simply reading the Bible. For many, in just reading the Bible, without carefully considering logical, intellectual arguments, the fact of its inspiration by God simply leaps off every page. The ultimate truth of the Bible speaks to the human heart in a way that for most would be difficult to explain in words. In this chapter we will step out on a limb and consider some possible reasons that reading the Bible has this effect.

2. The lives of true disciples. For those fortunate enough to rub elbows with people who have truly devoted themselves to Christ, the lives of such people is a kind of evidence that goes beyond logic and intellect. Despite the confusion created by the great number who take on the name of Christ, but who do not take on the life demanded by Jesus Christ, there is just something about the life of one who has devoted his or herself to following Jesus that speaks volumes to those who are seeking meaning and purpose for their life.

THE BIBLE: THE GREATEST BOOK EVER WRITTEN

Actually, it would be more accurate to say, "The Bible: The Greatest Books Ever Written." The Bible contains sixty-six books. It was written by at least forty different authors over a time span of at least one thousand four hundred years. Despite the daunting task of bringing together the writings of dozens of authors, in three languages, from widely varying cultural, educational and economic backgrounds, the Bible has a unity of theme and message that seems to defy explanation. Despite the fervent efforts of many to find contradictions between the various authors, the Bible holds up very well to all these attacks, when one considers the evidence carefully.

The Bible is an amazingly compact composition. Its writers can get more into one page than most authors can get into five hundred. Although the Bible has one overriding theme throughout, the relationship between God and man, it manages at the same time to be the greatest book the world has yet produced on history, marriage, philosophy...the list could go on seemingly indefinitely. Despite being about eternal truths—about how to get to a better place—the Bible provides the most practical possible advice on how to live a happy and successful life right here on earth.

All these claims taken together may provide at least a partial explanation of the fact that, for many, in simply reading the Bible for itself, a deep conviction is developed that it contains the very words of God. We will consider these claims in some detail.

THE VARIETY OF STYLE, YET THE UNITY OF MESSAGE

Culturally, the authors of the Bible were Mesopotamians, Egyptians, Bedouins and Greeks. Their occupations varied from priest to farmer, soldier and king, tax collector, fisherman, prophet, and prime minister. Some, such as Paul, were extremely well educated. Others were, in the eyes of their contemporaries, "unschooled, ordinary men" (Acts 4:13).

The writing styles of the Bible authors vary all over the map. In the pages of the Bible one can find straightforward historical narrative, along with pithy proverb. Flipping through its pages, the Bible reveals practical moral teaching such as that found in James, along with deep and sometimes even difficult to comprehend theology in Paul. Some Bible authors wax poetical, while others are emotion-laden seers.

Despite all this variety, the Bible, taken as a whole, has an astounding unity of theme and message: the relationship between God and man. Some have claimed that the basic message of the Old and the

New Testament are radically different. This charge does not hold up well to careful study. Although the revelation of the Bible is progressive—certain truths about God are revealed in a fuller way as one progresses from the earlier to the later writings in the Bible, the message and theme is the same throughout. Whether one is reading the book of Deuteronomy or of 1 John one can find such themes as God's love, his grace, and his judgment on those who will not acknowledge his sovereignty. In both books, one can see God's overwhelming desire for a relationship with man, yet the unbending nature of his ultimate justice. The story of the Bible from beginning to end is of God's repeated efforts to create a people who will love him and whom he can love and bless.

Some have said that the God of the Old Testament was a God of judgment, while the God of the New Testament is one of love and grace. The easiest way to refute this claim is to read the Bible. God's love of man and his judgment on the unrepentant are found in Genesis, Joshua, Jonah and John. God's palpable emotional longing for a people, as well as his hatred of sin and rebellion, are found in Exodus, Ezra, Ezekiel and Ephesians. Given the wide variety of its writers in language, culture, and background, how is one to explain the undeniable unity of theme and message throughout the Bible?

> Above all, you must understand that no prophecy of Scripture came about by the prophet's own interpretation. For prophecy never had its origin in the will of man, but men spoke from God as they were carried along by the Holy Spirit (2 Peter 1:20,21).

Is it possible that there is a single underlying author of the entire document? A better question is whether there is any other logical explanation of this unity. The Old and New Testaments fit together like a hand and a glove. From the beginning to the end of the Old Testament, one can clearly see God preparing a people to whom and through whom to send his son, the Messiah. The first Messianic prophecy is found in Genesis 3:15 while the last is found in Malachi 4: 2-5. The Old Testament is the progressive revelation that the Messiah is coming. The New Testament is an emphatic statement that he is here. Through the revelation of the Old Testament, and through the faith of godly men and women such as Abraham and Sarah, God prepared a people special to himself.

The actual historical events in this process of God preparing a people for himself (found in the Old Testament) are prophecies of what is revealed in the New Testament. Captivity and slavery in Egypt is a symbolical (yet at the same time very real) representation of slavery to sin. The success of Moses in freeing the Israelites from slavery is an historical prophecy of Jesus freeing his people from bondage to sin. Even the passing of the people through the waters of the Red Sea is an historical pre-revelation of baptism into Christ (1 Corinthians 10:2). The forty years Israel spent wandering in the wilderness is a prophetic prefigure of the Christian life. Each situation is a process of learning to rely on God, not self.

> He humbled you, causing you to hunger and then feeding you with manna, which neither you nor your fathers had known, to teach you that man does not live on bread alone, but on every word that comes from the mouth of the Lord (Deuteronomy 8:3).

The entry of God's people into the Promised Land under the leadership of Joshua is an obvious prefigure of God's spiritual people entering heaven under the leadership of Jesus (Jeshua or Joshua in Hebrew).

How can the events of history itself be a prophecy? Is there any chance that the correspondence of the New Testament teachings with the actual Old Testament historical events is just a lucky accident that the early preachers picked up on? It stretches the limits of logic and reason to reach any conclusion other than the obvious one. God had a hand in the events and in the recording of those events. Dozens of people and events in the Old Testament besides those already listed could be mentioned as examples of the principle that many things that occurred in the Old Testament are historical prophecies of New Testament teaching.[1]

THE NUMBER OF AUTHORS, YET THE LACK OF CONTRADICTION

Probably the reader has heard statements such as, "The Bible is full of contradictions." Those who have made such charges vary from the casually uninformed to people who have actually studied the Bible fairly carefully. If the Bible has *bona fide* contradictions, then that would be a serious charge against the claim that "all Scripture is inspired by God."[2]

The point of this section is not so much to refute every possible example of supposed contradiction. The point is that to the open-minded

---

[1]. The subject of historical and prophetic prefigures, types and foreshadows of the work of the Messiah in the Old Testament is discussed in great detail in "From Shadow to Reality, by Dr. John M. Oakes (Illumination Publishers, Spring, Texas, 2004).

[2]. 2 Timothy 3:16, *New American Standard Bible,* (Moody Press, Chicago, 1960)

reader, the lack of apparent contradiction—the amazing agreement of all the different Bible writers—is one of the strongest reasons to put faith in the inspiration of the Bible. By the time we are done explaining a few examples of the supposed contradictions of the Bible, one will be able to extrapolate to the conclusion that if there are contradictions in the Bible, they are either very few or very hard to find. In other words, unless one is purposefully reading the Bible to find supposed contradictions, a straightforward reading of the Bible will lead to the conclusion that it is amazingly—one might say miraculously—consistent with itself. Examples of inconsistencies that critics attempt to point out fall into categories such as:

• Claims that the doctrine which is taught in two different passages is contradictory.

• Identical events described by two different authors have details of fact that appear to contradict.

• Numbers of objects, people or years in two different passages do not agree.

It will obviously be impossible in this short section to deal with all the possible examples of supposed contradictions in the Bible, or even to deal with all the major ones that come up repeatedly. What we will do is to consider a set of questions that can be used to sort through apparent contradictions that one might come across. Such a list of helpful questions might include the following:

• Is this a legitimate contradiction? In other words, is there a perfectly reasonable explanation of the supposed contradiction that can be found simply by reading the relevant passages in context?

• Is there any chance that a scribal error could explain the apparent discrepancy? This will be a particularly relevant question if the supposed contradiction involves numbers from the Old Testament text.

• Is it possible that the two passages, rather than contradicting one another, actually complement one another? In other words, is it possible that the two apparently discrepant scriptures, when taken together, actually create a fuller picture of what God is trying to communicate?

To illustrate what is involved, it will be helpful to consider some fairly typical examples of what some have called mistakes or contradictions in the Bible. What will be done is to use examples taken more or less at random directly from various web sites that skeptics have set up to support the claim that the Bible is full of contradictions. Some typical examples of such claimed Bible errors follow.

1. "Genesis 7:17 says that the flood lasted forty days, but Genesis 8:3 tells us that it lasted one hundred and fifty days."

This is an example of a supposed contradiction that is very easily eliminated by simply reading the relevant passages in their context. Genesis 7:17 describe forty days of rain, while Genesis 8:3 states that the duration of the flood was one hundred and fifty days. Apparently after the rain stopped, there was a significant amount of time before the waters receded.

2. "In addition there is a contradiction regarding the question of whether God punishes children for the sins of their parents. In Ezekiel 18:20, the Lord states: 'The son shall not bear the iniquity of the father....' However, in Exodus 20:5, God says: '...I the Lord thy God am a jealous God, visiting the iniquity of the fathers upon the children unto the third and fourth generation of them that hate me.'"

This is a more serious example. The explanation would fall under the third category above. When one reconciles the two quoted passages a more complete understanding is reached. In Ezekiel 18, one finds the clear and consistent Bible teaching that when Judgment Day comes, a person will only be held personally responsible before God for their own actions—not those of their parents or children or of anyone else.[3] The passage in Exodus 20:5 is discussing God's treatment of a nation or a group of people as a whole. It is a consistent teaching in the Bible that although each individual is responsible to God for his or her own actions, God will bring punishment or discipline on a nation that turns their back on him. The punishment anticipated in Exodus 20:5 is of a physical nature, such as warfare or drought. The eternal destiny of individuals is a separate issue. Israel was sent into exile because, as a nation, she turned to idolatry. Despite this fact, some were still faithful to God even during this time and presumably will not be judged for eternity by God individually for the sins of the whole people.

A more personal application of Exodus 20:5 would involve noting that sin has repercussions that proceed in this life from generation to generation. For example if a person has a physically abusive father, he is statistically much more likely to fall into that same sin. Or at the very least his entire life is affected by the sin of his father. Divorce, adultery, sexual sins, even pride or cowardice, can have this effect, proceeding

---

3. And thus, by the way, the doctrine of original sin is not biblical.

sometimes even "unto the third and fourth generation," though each person is judged for their own personal sin. In any case, there is no contradiction between the teaching of Exodus 20:5 and Ezekiel 18.

3. "As to the death of the apostle Judas, Matthew 27:5 states that Judas took the money that he had obtained by betraying Jesus, threw it down in the temple and then 'went and hanged himself.' However, Acts 1:18 reports that Judas used the money to purchase a field and 'falling headlong, he burst asunder in the midst, and all his bowels gushed out.'"

This is an example of a supposed contradiction that is removed by reading the two relevant passages and simply thinking carefully about how they might be resolved. What actually happened is that out of remorse, Judas brought the money given to him to betray Jesus and threw it down at the feet of the elders and chief priests who had put him up to the betrayal. In the context of Matthew 27, it is clearly described how the chief priests "decided to use the money to buy the potter's field as a burial place for foreigners" (Matthew 27:7). After returning the money, it would appear that Judas hanged himself. After only a few hours in a hot climate, hanging from the rope, his body was extremely bloated. That would explain why, when he was cut down, "his body burst open and all his intestines spilled out." In summary, Judas returned the money, it was used to buy a field, he hanged himself, and when his body was cut down it burst open. There is no contradiction.

The passages in Matthew 27 and in Acts 1 are two of many examples that support the claim that the gospel accounts as well as Acts provide independent parallel records of the same events. When one allows for the possibility that the two accounts compliment rather than contradict one another, the meaning is easily worked out. A great number of the supposed contradictions in the Bible come from different eyewitness accounts that include correct but different details of the same event. Rather than providing evidence for mistakes in the Bible, they support the claim that the gospel accounts are separate but reliable records.

4. "David took seven hundred (2 Samuel 8:4) or seven thousand (1 Chronicles 18:4) horsemen from Hadadezer. Which is correct?"

This is an example of a contradiction that was produced by a scribal error. In other words, almost certainly in the original 2 Samuel and 1 Chronicles, the numbers agreed. When numbers are copied in Hebrew, it is extremely easy for an error to occur. Similar to Roman numerals, letters are used to represent numbers in Hebrew. Some of the letters that represent numbers are very similar, making copy errors after several rounds of copying the text very likely. A mistake by a factor of ten (seven hundred versus seven thousand, for example) is even more likely to occur. As stated in chapter six, the reader of the Old Testament should be cautious in assuming the numbers found in our text are identical to the original writing. Bottom line, a copying error is not a Bible contradiction.

5. "In describing Jesus being led to his execution, John 19:17 states that Jesus carried his own cross. In contrast, Mark 15:21-23 says that a man called Simon carried Jesus' cross to the crucifixion site."

This is another example where simply reading the relevant passages and considering how, reasonably, the accounts can be justified will easily solve the supposed error. In Matthew 27:32, one finds "as they were going out," (to Golgotha) "they met a man from Cyrene named Simon." Evidently, Jesus carried the crossbeam part of the way, while Simon carried it the rest of the way, possibly because Jesus was unable to continue under the burden. As with example three above, the complete story is more fully understood when the parallel accounts are compared and justified, supporting the claim that the gospel accounts are independent but reliable accounts.

6. "In Genesis 37:36 it says that Joseph was sold into Egypt by Midianites, while in Genesis 39:1 it says that he was sold by Ishmaelites."

Would it be a contradiction to say that George Bush is a Texan and at the same time that he is an American? The Midianites were an Arabic tribe. A common general name for Arab tribes in ancient times was Ishmaelites, showing that they were descended from Abraham's first son, Ishmael.

7. "Exodus 20:8, 'Remember the Sabbath day by keeping it holy' contradicts Isaiah 1:13 'Your...Sabbaths and convocations—I cannot bear...'"

This is an example of not understanding the meaning of a passage in its context. Of course, God commanded the Jews to observe the Sabbath. In Isaiah, God is telling his people that their going through the motions of worship without renouncing their blatant sin is so hypocritical that their worship disgusts him. To put it in a modern context, it would be like God saying to one of us: "You are in such gross sin—your example is so bad—it would be better for you to stay home than to put on an act and go to church." There is no contradiction here.

8. "'Do not answer a fool according to his folly or you will be like him yourself' (Proverbs 26:4) contradicts the verse, 'Answer a fool according to his folly, or he will be wise in his own eyes.' (Proverbs 26:5)"

At first, this might seem like an obvious contradiction, since the two statements seem to be direct opposites. However, given that the two verses are found consecutively in Proverbs, it is very likely that the original writer was well aware of the dual meaning of the two verses. This would be an example of two scriptures that, when taken together, produce a fuller understanding. Comparing the two verses, one can conclude that it is a mistake to get caught up into playing the games of the fool (v. 4), but it is wise to reveal the emptiness of the thinking of foolish people (v. 5).

This process could go on almost indefinitely, but the point should already be made.[4] Those who claim that the Bible is full of contradictions are simply mistaken. There may be some difficult questions. Even careful study may leave some unanswered apparent contradictions, but in the final analysis, all or virtually all of the supposed errors in the Bible are actually errors of the Bible critic himself who is not doing a good job of analyzing the biblical text.

After carefully considering many dozens of supposed errors in the Bible, and finding all of them so easily explained, it would be tempting to close the subject. However, it would be a bad idea for a Bible believer to pronounce the contradiction issue dead. That would not be intellectually honest. If we are absolutely closed to even considering the possibility that there is a mistake in the Bible, we fall into circular reasoning and a form of intellectual dishonesty that may become obvious to those who ask good, honest questions. However, at some point, after a person has addressed a great number of questions, finding that all or virtually all are easily answered, it is reasonable to begin with the presumption that almost certainly when the question is carefully investigated, it will turn out that there is in fact no error or contradiction at all.

In conclusion, it is not unusual to hear the Bible attacked because of all of its supposed contradictions and errors. The charge is far easier to raise than it is to prove. A careful study in context of the scriptures that are supposed to contradict and an attempt to understand the full meaning of Biblical passages will readily answer virtually all these questions. The Bible is the product of at least forty authors, writing over the

---

4. Good sources for answering some of the more difficult examples of what at first look appear to be Bible contradictions can be found at http://www.douglasjacoby.com; John Haley, *Alleged Discrepancies of the Bible*, (Whitaker Press, 1996); and Norman L. Geisler and Thomas Howe, *When Critics Ask: A Popular Handbook on Bible Difficulties*, (Baker Book House, 1999).

course of well over a thousand years, from widely differing cultures and backgrounds. Yet it remains consistent with itself to such a degree that the honest student of the Bible will find him or herself more convinced than ever that it is inspired by God.

THE BIBLE IS THE GREATEST BOOK OF...
(fill in the blank)

Remember, we are trying to get at understanding of why it is that for many, simply reading the Bible is evidence enough that it is inspired by God. We have considered its unity of message and its consistency with itself. We will now move on to consider the simple fact that the Bible works. The Bible contains a kind of wisdom that is so far superior to any other written or spoken word, that for many who read it, no other proof of the inspiration of the Bible is needed.

The same could be said of Jesus himself. When he spoke, the crowds were immediately struck by the fact that he was in a league all by himself, with all the competing wise men of his age very far in the rear. "When Jesus had finished saying these things, the crowds were amazed at his teaching, because he taught as one who had authority, and not as their teachers of the law" (Matthew 7:28,29). People were as amazed at Jesus' teaching as they were at his miracles. "Coming to his home town, he began teaching the people in their synagogue, and they were amazed. 'Where did this man get this wisdom and these miraculous powers?' they asked" (Matthew 13:54). The crowd had direct experience with both the amazing teaching and the miracles. They were equally impressed at both. It should not surprise us, then, that Bible readers who only have direct experience with the amazing teachings of Jesus (ie. do not personally experience his miracles) are often convinced of the inspiration of the Bible from that alone. Modern readers of the Bible cannot hear the tone of authority in Jesus' voice. We rely on eyewitnesses who marveled and were amazed at his air of authority. Mark 1:27 gives additional insight into this effect. "The people were all so amazed that they asked each other, 'What is this? A new teaching—and with authority!'" For many, the inherent authority of the Bible speaks for itself. Many of his enemies tried to trip up Jesus with trick questions. After one of his beautifully simple yet profound answers to one of these trick questions, "Then Jesus said to them, 'Give to Caesar what is Caesar's and to God what is God's,'" there was a natural and spontaneous response: "And they were amazed at him" (Mark 12:27).

The undeniable wisdom of Jesus is reflected in the Word of God—the Bible. For example, although the Bible is not primarily a book on human relationships, it is by far and away the number one book ever produced by man on both the principles and the practice of great human relationships. Similarly, philosophy is not the chief subject of the Bible, yet, despite the impressive work of Aristotle, Descartes, Spinoza, Hume, Kant and Nietzsche, the Bible is the world's most profound work on philosophy.

Clearly, the claims above are subjective, but this author has found them to stand up to the test of both practice and careful study. The readers, of course, must test the claims for themselves. The list of "bests" for the Bible can continue for some time.

• The Bible was not written in order to impress the Pulitzer committee, yet it is an amazing and profound example of literature. The Psalms can hold their own against Shakespeare. If one of the basic principles of effective writing is to say as much as possible in as little space as possible, the Bible holds the record in that area. It never ceases to amaze how the Bible has such density of meaning on so many levels. What other book can be read multiple times without seeming to even begin to exhaust what is there? It speaks equally to the simple and to the profound intellect.

• We have already spent an entire chapter proving that the Bible, though not principally a history book, is easily the best historical record of the ancient world.

• Hundreds of books on marriage have been written. To the extent that they expound on the Bible's teaching on relationships in general, and on marriage in particular, they are effective.

• Even in the area of economics and business, Proverbs provides the simplest, most down-to-earth and wisest advice of all. Practice complete honesty, treat your employees with respect, beware of get-rich-quick schemes, but seek to build wealth gradually. It is not the wealth you have, but what you do with it that counts. Do not count on wealth for ultimate happiness. All these principles are found in Proverbs, stated in simple yet profound way. They also work.

• If only world leaders would follow Solomon's (as well as Jesus') advice on government.

• It is the personal opinion of the author that in addition to their educational theory classes, every prospective teacher ought to spend a considerable amount of time contemplating Jesus' style of teaching if they want to learn how to teach.

• Psychologists and counselors would do well to spend more time studying the Bible if they want to be as helpful to people as possible. It seems that every time one reads a popular book on psychology and finds a concept that rings true, the same concept can be found in the Bible if one is willing to look for it.

The list could continue. No wonder, then, that so many people, when they read the Bible, accept it "not as the word of men, but as it actually is, the word of God" (1 Thessalonians 2:13).

CHANGED LIVES

This brings us to the other principle cause of faith in Jesus Christ, besides simply reading the Bible. The other principle reason for people to arrive at faith in Jesus is their exposure to the changed lives of true followers of Christ. The author can personally attest to the effectiveness of this sort of testimony. My own personal experiences, as well as my exposure to the laws of nature as a scientist, caused me to believe in a creator. My rather limited exposure to the Bible caused me to accept that it was, at the very least, an amazing book that spoke to my deepest self. However, it was when I was exposed to a fellowship of committed disciples—to their lifestyle and love for one another—that was when the key was turned and the door was opened for me. Being a scientist, I would like to think that it had everything to do with logical, empirical evidence. Absolutely, this was a factor, but the fact is that it was exposure to a deep sort of love for one another amongst true disciples that had the greatest impact in causing me to commit to becoming a follower of Jesus.

Actually, this should not be too surprising. Jesus himself said, "By this all men will know that you are my disciples, by your love for one another" (John 13:35). Jesus himself said that the ultimate evidence for Christian faith is love. If the love of God for us is at times difficult to observe directly, the love of one another is very real indeed.

Unfortunately, this kind of evidence is very difficult to put into a book. It is a case of "you had to be there." It is tempting to produce a list of practical examples from the author's own experience, but listing personal testimonies will be ineffective, as a person needs to experience such anecdotal evidence on their own. All the previous evidence mentioned involves fact and intellectual knowledge. This type of evidence involves personal experience. When Philip found Nathanael and shared his experience with Jesus, he encountered an open-minded skepticism. Philip's response was that Nathanael should "come and see" for himself (John 1:43-51). When he came and saw Jesus, he was convinced.

So perhaps the greatest evidence for Christianity is found in the lives of Christians themselves. How is one to expose oneself to such evidence? Unfortunately, it is not as simple as walking up to a person on the street and asking if she is a Christian. It is a sad fact that only a relatively few of those who take on the name of Christ walk the walk of Jesus. In fact, one of the most common reasons people give for not accepting Christianity is the hypocrisy of supposed Christians. Anyone who makes this comment has clearly not been sufficiently exposed to the real deal.

In searching for the most convincing evidence of all—the lives of true disciples of Jesus—consider three suggestions. First, one should look for a person, or even better, a group of persons who are devoted to following Jesus. Jesus himself described the level of commitment required to be a disciple. "In the same way, any of you who does not give up everything he has, cannot be my disciple" (Luke 14:33). Do not look for perfection, but look for people about whom you can say without hesitation, these people are living for God, twenty-four/seven. Second, look for a kind of unity of spirit and purpose that is seemingly miraculous. Jesus, on the night he was betrayed, prayed to his Father, "May they be brought to complete unity to let the world know that you sent me and have loved them, even as you have loved me" (John 17:23). Jesus said that the unity of his followers would mark them as being his people. Look for a group of old and young, well-off and poor, well-educated and not, black, white and everything in between. Look for an uncommon kind of unity among people who probably would otherwise not even have associated with one another. Look for a kind of unity that Jesus said would let the world know that God sent him.

Last, look for the kind of love Jesus discussed in John 13:34-35:

> "A new commandment I give to you: Love one another. As I have loved you, so you must love one another. All men will know that you are my disciples if you love one another."

Look for a group of people who practice unconditional love for one another in a way that appears unexplainable outside the context of following Jesus. Do not look for perfection, but for the kind of love that Jesus himself said would be the hallmark of discipleship. The search for this, the greatest kind of evidence may require time and patience, but it will be worth the effort.

A FINAL CHALLENGE

There is a common saying that "the proof of the pudding is in the eating." What this means is that one can argue all one wants about the best recipe for pudding, but at some point, it comes time to test the pudding and see how it tastes.

Jesus took pains to help people come to faith in him, but at some point, he called those who had been following him around to make a personal decision. To those who had plenty of evidence but were still unwilling to take the plunge, he gave some advice that I will leave with the reader.

> Jesus answered, "My teaching is not my own. It comes from him who sent me. If anyone chooses to do God's will, he will find out whether my teaching comes from God or whether I speak on my own" (John 7:17).

To paraphrase Jesus, he is saying to anyone willing to accept it, that his teaching is from God. If the miracles are not enough evidence for them, then his hearers should try his teaching for themselves. Ultimately, the proof is in tasting the pudding. To anyone who has been presented with evidence of the most convincing nature, but is nevertheless still hesitant to commit to Jesus and to the teachings of the Bible, Jesus gives this challenge. Check it out for yourself. Do what the Bible says. See if it does not bring about the abundant life he talked about. The challenge to the reader is to step out of the boat and begin doing what Jesus said to do. If you do not have sufficient faith to make a total commitment to the teachings of the Bible, then at least start doing what it says. Jesus was supremely confident that people with sufficient faith to begin living a life in obedience to his teachings would see for themselves that his teaching is from God. Jesus is telling the searcher after truth that it is time to put your money where your mouth is, it is time to fish or cut bait. Jesus said in John 8:31,32:

> "If you hold to my teaching, you are really my disciples. Then you will know the truth, and the truth will set you free."

For Today

1. Are there any seeming contradictions in the Bible that you have not yet worked out for yourself? What can you do to resolve the question?

2. Can you think of any other "bests" for the Bible besides the ones listed in this chapter?

3. If you are still struggling with coming to sufficient faith, what are the outstanding issues? What further research might you need to do? Who might you talk to?

4. What do you have to lose by taking Jesus up on his challenge to begin obeying his commands?

Appendix A
Translations of the Bible

A few very brief comments about modern translations are appropriate at this point, even though they do not directly relate to evidence for Christian faith. Obviously, virtually all Bible readers rely on translations from the Greek and Hebrew texts. These translations are not "inspired" in the sense that the original writings were inspired. Therefore, the Bible reader must rely on the integrity and skill of the translators.

There are three basic categories of Bible translations. First, there are paraphrased versions. These involve the translator reading the Greek or Hebrew text, determining for themselves the meaning, and producing a paraphrase that reflects as accurately as possible that meaning, expressing the meaning using more modern expressions and idioms. This type of translation may be very helpful for a reader to understand the overall meaning of the original writings. However, because the paraphrased translation involves more interpretation than the other types of translations, they are not as accurate or reliable as the others. A paraphrase may be good for simply reading the Bible, but not for detailed study of the meanings of words. There is much more room for the translator, even subconsciously, to insert their own bias in a paraphrased translation. Some common examples would include the *Living Bible*, the *New Living Translation* and the *Philips Translation*.

Another kind of Bible is a phrase-for-phrase translation. In this type, the committee of translators maintains a phrase-for-phrase equivalency between the English and the original Greek or Hebrew. In this case, if one attempts to parallel the Greek text with the English translation, there is a nearly word-for-word correspondence, but the word order is altered significantly to make the text flow more smoothly when read in English. In other words, the phrase-for-phrase translation compromises somewhat on the original word order, preferring the normal English sentence structure in order to make the translation more "readable." The *New International Version* and the *New King James* Bible would be common examples.

The third type of translation is a word-for-word translation. In this type of version, there is a virtual one-for-one correspondence between the English translation and the original Hebrew or Greek. This is the most accurate type of translation, but it tends to be more difficult to read in English, as it uses the original Greek or Hebrew word order, which may be more awkward when read in English. An example is the *New American Standard* and the *English Standard* versions. Another recent word-for-word translation is the Holman Christian Standard Bible which is perhaps the most readable of this type available so far.

A few rules follow for choosing what version of the Bible to read.

• It is a good idea to use more than one type of translation, depending on whether one is trying to simply read to get the overall meaning or whether one is trying to study the text in detail.

• The more recent the translation, the better, as scholars have better data to work from than they did even a couple of generations ago.

• A version produced by a committee drawn from various religious groups is to be preferred to one produced by a group drawn from only one denomination, even if the particular group doing the translating is the one you are part of. This avoids most bias in choosing a particular way to translate controversial passages.

There are a number of excellent translations that fit all three of the criteria above. It is the original, not the translation, which is inspired. However, use of a very good translation is almost as good as reading the original.

Appendix B
The Nature of Faith

A Sunday school teacher asked her students to define the word faith. A precosious sudent answered, "Faith is believing in something you know is not true." The famous humanist and skeptic Ambrose Bierce has defined faith as "Belief without evidence in what is told by one who speaks without knowledge, of things without parallel." At first glance, this definition might seem to be at least a little bit similar to one of the definitions of faith found in the Bible: "Now faith is being sure of what we hope for, and certain of what we do not see" (Hebrews 11:1). Both the writer of Hebrews and Ambrose Bierce are saying that faith involves belief in something that cannot be proven to be true by direct evidence. Both would probably agree that it requires faith to believe Jesus' claim that he will come back to the earth some day. One cannot provide any direct evidence that Jesus will come back. Jesus said that there would be a Judgment Day for all who have lived on the earth. It is impossible to prove directly by any sort of physical evidence that there will be a day of judgment. Christians are unanimous in their belief that there is a home waiting for them in heaven. There is no physical evidence to prove that heaven exists. Belief in heaven is based on faith in the authority of Jesus Christ and the inspired word of God.

So both the skeptic and the Bible agree on this. Faith is a part of Christianity. But here the similarity ends. Bierce would claim that Christian belief has no basis in evidence. To him it requires "blind faith." Either he was unaware of the kinds of evidence already presented in this book, or he was deliberately ignoring the available evidence that supports belief in the Bible. Jesus said that he would be raised on the third day, and he was! What more evidence could one need? What about the fulfilled prophesies? What about the miracles, which even his enemies conceded he worked? One need not be intimidated by such baseless claims as that of Ambrose Bierce.

In his sarcastic definition of faith, Bierce also claimed that Christian belief is based on teachings of "one who speaks without knowledge." Is he willing to claim that Daniel had no knowledge of the future? Is he willing to claim that Jesus did not show evidence of his authority to speak on matters of religion? Even Jesus' enemies who grew up around him could find no sin to accuse him of, yet this religious skeptic would say that Jesus had no authority to speak about God.

The Nature of Faith

Perhaps the most famous skeptic of Christianity was the French writer and philosopher Voltaire. He was the leading figure of the French enlightenment in the eighteenth century. This philosopher, author and playwright made many pointed, but often justified criticisms of the established religion of his day. Voltaire led the attempts to discredit the Bible in eighteenth century Europe. It was Voltaire who said, "The truths of religion are never so well understood as by those who have lost their power of reasoning." Applying this claim of Voltaire to Christianity, he was saying that the only way for an intelligent person to believe in what is taught in the Bible is to read it with an uncritical and unthinking mind.

There is a grain of truth in half of Voltaire's charge. It is true that many believers in the Christian religion base their faith purely on emotion. Many fail to consider rational arguments—fail to apply "their power of reasoning," (quoting Voltaire) to their beliefs about the Bible. While it is obviously good to have an emotional attachment to God, the failure of many to carefully consider reasoned arguments *both for and against* belief in the teachings of the Bible is a common mistake of believers. It was the apostle Peter himself who admonished disciples of Jesus to "always be prepared to give an answer to everyone who asks you to give a reason for the hope that you have" (1 Peter 3:15). Bible readers are admonished to apply reason to their belief and to prepare to communicate the reasons for their faith to others. Peter challenged his readers that there is no excuse for intellectual laziness in the believer.

So there is a grain of truth in Voltaire's challenge to Christian belief. Many believers have not used their God-given powers of reasoning to investigate the evidence both for and against Christian belief. In the words of Jonathan Swift (humanist and author of *Gulliver's Travels*), "It is useless to attempt to reason a man out of what he was never reasoned into." However, the other half of Voltaire's charge is absolutely without merit. For any person who is willing to set emotion and preconceived belief aside—to apply reason to the questions such as whether Jesus was who he said he was and whether the Bible is inspired by God—that person will be forced to accept by the sheer volume of the evidence that biblical Christianity is both true and reasonable.

An interesting side note on Voltaire is that he once wrote that if anyone could prove to him that Isaiah chapter 53 (with its multiple prophecies of the Messiah) was written before the time of Christ, he would be persuaded to believe in the Christian faith. It is too bad that the discovery of the Dead Sea Scrolls occurred after the death of Voltaire, as the Isaiah scroll was transcribed some time around 100 BC. If Voltaire were alive today, he would have to eat his words. This author would speculate that even if Voltaire had been confronted with the clear evidence of the Isaiah scroll, he would have backed off on his statement and continued in his skepticism.

The argument between Voltaire and Christianity is reminiscent of the confrontation between the apostle Paul and King Agrippa. In defending his beliefs to Agrippa, Paul challenged him with these words:

> "I am not insane, most excellent Festus," Paul replied. "What I am saying is true and reasonable. The king is familiar with these things, and I can speak freely to him. I am convinced that none of this has escaped his notice, because it was not done in a corner. King Agrippa, do you believe the prophets? I know you do" (Acts 26:25-27).

Agrippa had accused Paul of being crazy for holding so firmly to faith in Jesus Christ. Paul turned the argument around on the king, saying that Agrippa was well aware that the evidence for Jesus Christ was overwhelming to anyone who considered the facts. In essence he said to Agrippa, "You cannot possibly deny that Jesus Christ is the one foretold by the prophets, so how can you accuse me of being insane?" Paul declared to Agrippa, as he would boldly declare to Voltaire or any other skeptic, no matter their education or background, belief in Jesus is true and reasonable.[1]

Yes, Christian belief involves faith in things that cannot be seen. Yes, there are items of belief that cannot be proven. Prayer is an act of faith. The decision to devote one's life to a carpenter who lived two thousand years ago requires faith, but not blind faith. Skeptics such as Voltaire, Bierce, Swift and others would create the false impression that Christianity offers only false hope—a pipe dream based on fantasy, myth and wishful thinking. This claim simply does not hold up to the evidence. Human reason, carefully applied, based on the evidence, will lead to Christian faith.

---

1. Speaking of "true and reasonable," one of finest books on Christian evidences available is: Douglas Jacoby, *True & Reasonable,* (Illumination Publishers, Spring, Texas, 2004). This book includes theological arguments for the Christian religion as well.

Keep up with the
latest news, articles,
books, and events
from the ministry of
John M. Oakes, PhD.

www.evidenceforchristianity.org

CPSIA information can be obtained
at www.ICGtesting.com
Printed in the USA
JSHW021733220521
15069JS00001B/62